DAIRY FARMING FOR MILK PRODUCTION TECHNOLOGY

DAIRY FARMING FOR MILK PRODUCTION TECHNOLOGY

Written By

EIRI BOARD OF CONSULTANTS & ENGINEERS

ENGINEERS INDIA RESEARCH INSTITUTE

4449, Nai Sarak, Main Road, Delhi - 110006 (India)

Ph: +91-11-23918117, 23916431, 23947058, 45120361

* E-Mail: eiribooks@yahoo.com; eiriprojects@gmail.com

*Website: www.eiriindia.org; www.eiribooksandprojectreports.com

PRINTED & PUBLISHED BY
ENGINEERS INDIA RESEARCH INSTITUTE
4449, Nai Sarak, Main Road, Delhi - 110006 (India)
Ph: +91-11-23918117, 23916431, 23947058, 45120361
* E-Mail: eiribooks@yahoo.com
*Website: www.eiriindia.org,
www.eiribooksandprojectreports.com

Sole Distributors:
EIRI PROJECT CONSULTANTS AND PUBLISHERS
4/54 Roop Nagar, Delhi-110007

ISBN: 9789380772097

Printed in New Delhi (INDIA)

₹ 975/-

Printed & Published by Sudhir Gupta for "Engineers India Research Institute", 4449 Nai Sarak, Main Road, New Delhi -110006

Preface

Milk is as ancient as mankind itself, as it is the substance created to feed the mammalian infant. All species of mammals, from man to whales, produce milk for this purpose. Many centuries ago, perhaps as early as 6000-8000 BC, ancient man learned to domesticate species of animals for the provision of milk to be consumed by them. These included cows (genus *Bos*), buffaloes, sheep, goats, and camels, all of which are still used in various parts of the world for the production of milk for human consumption.

Fermented products such as cheeses were discovered by accident, but their history has also been documented for many centuries, as has the production of concentrated milks, butter, and even ice cream.

India derives nearly 33% of the gross Domestic population from agriculture and has 66% of economically active population, engaged in agriculture. The share of livestock product is estimated at 21% of total agriculture sector. The fact that dairying could play a more constructive role in promoting rural welfare and reducing poverty is increasingly being recognised. Milk production alone involves more than 70 million producers, each raising one or two cows/ buffaloes primarily for milk production. The domesticated water buffalo is one of the gentlest of all farm animals ,hence it can be breeded easily. The dairy sector offers a good opportunity to entrepreneurs in India. India is a land of opportunity for those who are looking for new and expanding markets. Growth prospects in the dairy sector are very bright.

Dairy and beef herds account for about 13.9% of Israel's total agricultural production: 11.4% in milk and dairy products and 2.5% in beef products. The dairy sector supplies the country's total dairy requirements, with production potential greatly exceeding domestic needs. Production is regulated by a planning and quota policy, which is currently undergoing structural changes, with emphasis on environmental aspects. Israel's dairy industry faces the challenge of meeting the demand for milk and milk products in a country whose population increased ten-fold since its establishment in 1948. Modern and well established scientific principles, practices and skills should be used to obtain maximum economic benefits from dairy farming. Some of the major norms and recommendations are: Carefull selection of animals, feeding of animals, milking of animals.

There are two types of dairy sectors:

- 708 registered "Moshavim" (family farms - including some agric-schools), each with between 40 and 50 milking cows producing 43% of the national quota
- 208 registered "Kibbutz" cooperative dairy farms, each with between 300 and 400 milking cows

Constant and intensive R&D and extended "on-farm trials", dealing with dairy cattle feeding, nutrition and management with close collaboration with dairy farmers are carries out. Dairy farming is a good source of income; both for family farms and for communal farms. Additionally, value-added milk products are also a good source for income.

The book contains 24 chapters on various aspects on *Dairy Farming for Milk Production Technology, i.e., Dairy Cattle, The Holstein-Friesian, The Jersey, The Guernsey, The Ayrshire, The Brown Swiss, The Milking Shorthorn, The Red Polled, The Lesser Breeds, Types of Dairy Farming and Breed Selection, Selecting the Individual Cow, Fundamental Considerations of Heredity, Measures of the Genetic Makeup, Known Inherited Characteristics in Dairy Cattle, Systems of Breeding, Selection and Care of the Herd Sire, Growth and Development, Calf Raising, Raising the Heifer from Weaning to Calving Time, Factors Influencing the Quantity and Quality of Milk, Management of Dairy Cows, The Milking Machine and Milking, Efficiency and Cost of Milk Production, Common Feeds: Characteristics and Treatment*

Director

ENGINEERS INDIA RESEARCH INSTITUTE

Nai Sarak, New Delhi (INDIA)

*Website: www.eiriindia.org, www.eiribooksandprojectreports.com

Contents-cum Index

Chapter 4

Chapter 5

Chapter 6

Chapter 11

Chapter 12

Chapter 15

Chapter 24

Common Feeds: Characteristics and Treatment 350-374

1

Dairy Cattle

THE FAMILY AND GENUS

All domesticated cattle belong to the family Bovida, whose members ruminate, have hoofs with an even number of toes, and differ from some other ruminants by possessing permanent horns with a bony core. Members of the family have been found in fossils going back to the Miocene age. Domesticated cattle are descendants of wild species belonging to the genus Bos. This genus has five subgenera or groups. Although cattle are descendants of only the first or taurine group, these groups are listed and briefly described, in order to show the close relationship of the other groups to cattle.

Taurine group

All domesticated cattle belong to this group. Its members roamed over Europe, Asia and Northern Africa from the Miocene period until rather recently. Only those that have escaped from domestication are found in the wild state today. They differ from other groups of the genus by having cylindrical horns which are set wide apart on a ridge on top of the skull, a flat forehead, with the eyes far below the horn, and long nasal bones. The back is straight and the hair short. The spinal processes of the dorsal vertebrae slope toward the posterior and are of moderate height. Subdivisions of this group will be discussed later.

Bibovine group

These are humped forms and are natives of southern India. The forehead is shorter with less width at the base of the horns than that of the taurine group. The banting and gam, which measure nearly six feet in height, belong to this family, as does the gayal.

Leptobovine group

This group is extinct. Fossil remains have been found in France, Italy, and India. The fossil bones indicate that members of this group were rather small. Their horns were cylindrical and curved, but were attached far below the vertex of the skull.

Bisontine group

The American bison, the European bison, and the Yak are members of this group. The Yak still ranges over large parts of Asia in the wild state and is also extensively domesticated. The American bison, often but erroneously called buffalo, has not been domesticated except for crossing with cattle for the hybrid "cattalo."

Budaline group

This groups is represented by the true buffalo of Asia and southeastern Europe, where it is used for milk production, for beef, and as a draft animal.

THE TAURINE GROUP

The taurine group is divided into two species: (1) *Bosaurus typicus*, which includes all domesticated types without humps, and (2) *Bosaurus indicus*, those having humps. The latter is confined to Asia and Africa in the form of the zebu, except for the few that have been imported for crossing with cattle, particularly in southeastern United States. The zebu has a hump over the withers, large drooping ears, and a grunting cry which distinguishes it from

Bos typicus. No wild forms of the zebu have ever been found; its complete domestication is reported to have taken place as early as 2000 B.C. It crosses readily with *Bos typicus*, and some students believe that zebu crosses played a part in the development of some of the European breeds of cattle. *Bos Taurus typicus* includes all the modern breeds of cattle in Europe and America. According to Morse there are four wild forms of this species from which the modern breeds have sprung. They are *Bos primigenius*, *Bos longifrons*, *Bos frontosus*, and *Bos brachycephalus*. This classification is based largely upon skull characteristics and is not agreed to by all students of the problem.

Bos primigenius was a large animal 6 or 7 feet in height at the withers, which roamed over all of Europe, Western Asia, and Northern Africa during the Pleistocene and recent geologic periods. The horns were long and strong, and made a semicircular curve forward; the forehead and face were long and narrow. The whole cranium was flat, presenting a straight lien from a lateral view. There is evidence that wild specimens of primigenius have lived in historic times. Caesar, Tacitus, and Pliny referred to them as urus (Fig. 1.1) Tacitus and Pliny described drinking horns that held as much as two ur (about 12 quarts). Some authorities believe that the wild forms were not exterminated until the seventeenth century. The wild cattle of Chillingham Park, England, are said to closely resemble the wild *Bos primigenius*.

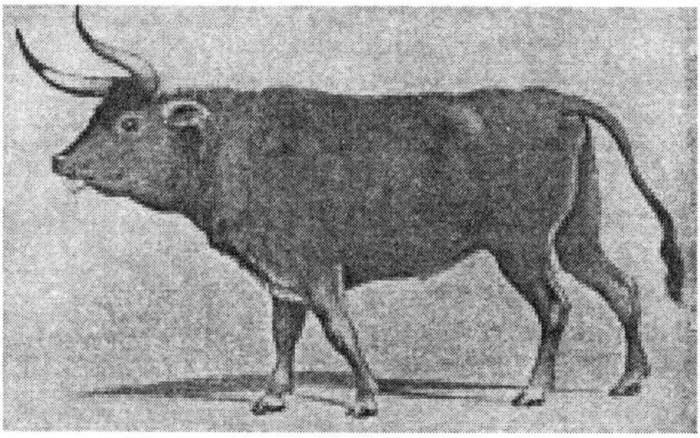

Fig. 1.1 The Urus.

Bos longifrons were much smaller than *Bos primigenius*. The horns of the former were shorter, as was the face, but the forehead was longer and broader than that of *Bos primigenius*, with a ridge in the center of the poll. *Bos longifrons* was of solid colour, a black-brown to gray. Its forehead, too, was deeply dished. The time of origin of *Bos longifrons* is speculative, some claiming its existence in the Pleistocene age, while others claim that it is of a more recent origin. *Bos longifrons* was found all over Europe during the Stone Age and in England during the Roman occupation. It is generally credited as being the ancestor of the Welsh and Highland breeds.

Bos frontosus is found in fossil form in Sweden. Its head, large in comparison to the rest of the body, had an irregular contour with wide forehead. The horns were relatively straight and came out from the top of the skull. Bos frontosus is believed by some to be the ancestor of the mountain cattle of Scandinavia; by others it is said to be the domesticated form of *Bos primigenius*. The Simmenthal breed of Switzerland and some spotted breeds of southern Germany are of the frontosus type, lending support to the contention of some people that its origin was in Germany.

Bos brachycephalus, a short-headed race like Bos frontosus, does not have the support of all authorities as being a distinct type equal with primigenius and longifrons. The skeletons found in the moors of Laibak had heads with foreheads broader than long, and horns attached to a short pedestal.

Whether or not Bos brachycephalus and Bos frontosus are proved types separate and distinct from *Bos primigenius* and *Bos longifrons*, the latter two are unquestionably the most important in the development of the modern breeds.

HISTORY OF CATTLE IN EUROPE

Since all the American and European breeds of cattle originated in European, a brief history of the development of cattle in Europe will be the history of the development of the modern breeds. Exactly when cattle were first domesticated is not known, but that cattle were domesticated at a very early stage of human civilization is certain. Long before man was able to make records, cattle were used by him as beasts of burden and for food. This has been proved by the discovery of the skeletons of cattle in ancient cave dwellings in Switzerland, together with the cave dweller's remains and the crude stone implements which he used.

It is probable that as man changed from savagery to a barbarian stage of civilization, he began to domesticate cattle. With the advent of the Bronze Age, man in all probability began the development and breeding of cattle. The earliest of written records refer frequently to cattle; they are mentioned frequently in the Old Testament of the Bible. The oldest of drawings upon the walls of caves in Switzerland depict cattle as beasts of burden; and from the emphasis given to the udders, it may be assumed that milk production was stressed. The great philosophers of 2,000 years ago, especially Pliny, wrote of cattle breeding as an art. Alexander the Great is said to have imported into Greece more than 2,000 cattle from India. Caesar wrote of the milk and cheese produced in what is now Holland. The Romans brought cattle with them in their invasion of England, and the Celts took cattle with them wherever they went. These are just a few of the many known facts about the early history of cattle in Europe.

Origins of Breeds

How so many breeds have come into existence may readily be understood if one takes into account the fact that cattle were scattered throughout early Europe and that there was little communication between the various peoples, who were banded together in groups for protection against conquest. It is to be expected that each group would select their cattle for certain characters, that these characters would differ from those for which other groups selected their cattle, and that each group would continue to breed for such characters. Sooner or later, then, all the cattle in one locality would become rather pure for such character or characters, and would become a breed. In addition, climatic and food conditions in the different localities had their effect upon the selection of types. The cold of the North necessitated selection for resistance to cold. Scarcity of grazing forced the selection of specimens that were good grazers, while a different, less aggressive type suited the conditions in localities where grasses were luxuriant.

In America there are about 17 breeds of cattle; in Britain there are more than 60 breeds, as listed by McConnell; and in Germany there are about 50 or 60 breeds. The improvement of breeds is discussed in Chapter 15, "Systems of Breeding."

Classification of Cattle

Cattle may be classified according to breed, origin, use, and degree of purity. According to Werner the breeds can be grouped according to the type from which they descended, as follows:

Bos primigenius	*Bos longifrons*
Holstein-Friesian	Brown Swiss
Dutch Belted	Jersey
Shorthorn	Guernsey (crossed with *primigenius*)
Normandy	
Polled Durham	
Red Polled	
West Highland	
Galloway	
Aberdeen Angus	*Bos brachycephalus*
Ayrshire (crossed with *longifrons*)	
	Kerry
	Brittany
Bos frontosus	French Canadian
	Hereford
Simmenthal	Sussex
Breeds of Sweden	Devon

Morse criticizes this classification, stating that the Hereford has about the same origin as the Normandy breed, and that the Ayrshire, West Highland, and Galloway have more longifrons than primigenius. He also believes that the Kerry and Brittany are more longifrons than brachycephalus.

Classification According to Uše

Cattle may be divided into groups according to the use for which they have been specialized. These groups are dairy, beef, dual-purpose, and beast of burden. As oxen belong to an era of the past, no breed in America is bred for this purpose. The American breeds are divided as follows:

Dairy Breeds	Dual-Purpose	Beef Breeds
Holstein-Friesian	Red Polled	Hereford
Jersey	Devon	Shorthorn
Guernsey	Milking Shorthorn	Polled Shorthorn
Ayrshire		Galloway
Brown Swiss		Aberdeen Angus
Dutch Belted		
French-Canadian		
Kerry		

Classification according to degree of purity

Cattle may be divided into four classes according to the degree of purity. The four classes are purebreds, grades, crossbreds, and scrubs.

Purebreds

Purebreds are cattle that trace back through all lines to the foundation cattle of the breed. While they may not necessarily be registered, most purebred cattle are also recorded on the books of their Breed Association office. All "registered" cattle are purebreds. Another term used for purebred is full blood. Thoroughbred is sometimes improperly applied to purebreds.

Grades

There is no universally accepted definition for grades. Some maintain that in order to qualify for the classification of grade, one parent, usually the sire, must be purebred. In common practice, however, any animal not purebred that possesses the major characteristics of a breed is classed as a grade of that breed. When successive purebred sires are used, grades continually approach purebreds in purity, but such animals cannot be registered in America.

Crossbreds

Crossbreds is a term applied to the cross between two breeds; the parents may be purebreds or grades. Crossbreeding is often resorted to when one wants to change from beef production to dairying or vice versa. Some dairymen also resort to crossbreeding when they desire to increase the fat percentage in the milk or the amount of milk to satisfy special market demands.

Scrubs

Animals that do not possess the chief characteristics of any breed or that cannot be classified in any of the above classes are usually referred to as scrubs. The term scrub is also applied to animals of undesirable characteristics even though they may be purebred. Other terms used in designating nondescript animals are mongrel and unimproved.

2

The Holstein-Friesian

Holstein-Friesian is the official name of this breed in America although it is commonly referred to as "Holstein." In Europe and in most other countries, the breed is known as Friesian.

Characteristics

The characteristics of the breed are discussed under the following headings:

Size

The Holstein is one of the largest of the breeds of cattle. The standard is 1,250 pounds for cows and 1,800 pounds for bulls. Several cows have reached a ton or more in weight, the largest recorded being Mantup Pietje Bess Ormsby, who weighted 2,400 pounds. The first prize 3 year old bull at the 1934 Dairy Cattle Congress weighed 2,800 pounds. Researcher reports a purebred Holstein steer weighing 4,365 pounds.

Colour

A Holstein to be eligible for registration must be black and white, varying from nearly all white to nearly all black. The following colours bar registry:

1. Solid black

2. Solid white
3. Black switch
4. Solid black with white on belly only
5. Black on legs, beginning at the feet and extending to the knees and hocks
6. Black on legs beginning at the feet and extending to the knees, with white interspersed
7. Gray, or mixed black and white generally prevailing
8. Patches of colours other than black and white; red, brown, dun, etc.
9. Red and white

The relative amounts of either black or white vary from white with only a small black spot to an almost total black, except for the switch, which must always be white. Red and white is present in the Holstein as a recessive colour and crops out occasionally. In Holland, red and white Holsteins are common; in America, while they do occur, they cannot be registered.

Type

The Holsteins are ruggedly built, with large middles and udders. The head is long and comparatively narrow, with a straight profile. In dairy conformation they vary from extreme clean-cutness to a "rounding" type-rounding over the withers, slightly outcurving thighs, and moderate thickness of flesh throughout. The most desirable type is slightly rounding over the withers and straight in the thighs. The Holstein is frequently criticized for being low at the pinbones and for lack of symmetry of the udder. (Figs. 2.1 and 2.2).

Disposition

The Holstein cow is rather phlegmatic and docile. This characteristic is no doubt due to the environment in which she was developed, where excitable and nervous individuals were not selected for breeding stock. The bulls, however, are frequently vicious. As a grazer the Holstein ranks fair on moderate to poor pastures and excellent on good pastures. Her large size increases

Fig. 2.1: This cow combines high production with good type. She holds the world's record for Holsteins for both milk and butterfat with 38,606.6 pounds of milk and 1,402.0 pounds of butterfat.

Fig. 2.2: An excellent Holstein bull.

her nutrient requirements and handicaps her on poor pastures, since she has to cover much more ground than a smaller cow to secure the needed nutrients.

Reproduction and longevity

Holsteins are not noted for longevity although they average up well with other breeds. Individuals attaining unusual age are not so frequent as in some other breeds. Holsteins are good reproducers. The calves are strong and vigorous, weighing, on an average, about 90 pounds at birth. The birth weight of the calves averages about 7.8 per cent of the body weight of the dam.

Maturity

The Holsteins are late maturing. Heifers are usually not bred until 19 to 21 months of age, producing the first calf at from 28 to 30 months of age. The Holstein attains maximum growth and development at about seven years of age. Only the Brown Swiss among the dairy breeds is later in maturing than the Holstein.

Meat and veal

The Holstein ranks highest among the dairy breeds for meat production. It has the largest carcass of the dairy breeds, is the thickest fleshed, and has the lightest colour of body fat. In some tests Holstein steers have shown up favorably with beef breeds in rapidity of gains and in the quality of beef produced. For veal production the Holstein ranks with the best because of the size of the calf at birth and the light colour of the body. fat.

Character of milk

Averaging 3.5 per cent fat, Holstein milk has the lowest fat content of any of the diary breeds. Some produce milk with less than 2 per cent fat. The low fat content of the milk of some Holsteins has given rise to a serious problem in furnishing market milk. Some milk markets demand a 4 per cent fat milk, and milk producers with Holsteins have found it necessary to introduce cows of the higher testing breeds in order to meet the market requirements. By careful selection of bulls many breeders of Holstein cattle have succeeded in raising the fat percentage of the herd up to as high as 4 per cent.

Holstein milk and butter rank low in colour, although some individuals produce milk that is fairly high in colour. The Holstein apparently converts carotene, which is responsible for the yellow colour of the fat and milk, into colourless vitamin A. With the exception of that of the Ayrshire, the fat globule of Holstein milk is the smallest of all breeds. Because of the small fat globules and low fat content of Holstein milk, claims have been made for its superiority for infant feeding. Such claims, however, are not too well supported by scientific facts.

The small fat globule and the low fat content of Holstein milk adapt it well for cheese making. The small fat particles slow up the rising of the fat, and thus better incorporation of fat into the setting curd is permitted. The fat constitutes 28 per cent of the total solids; this is the best proportion of fat to solids-not-fat for both cheese making and evaporated milk.

The home and origin of the Holstein

The Holstein breed was originally developed in two provinces of Holland, North Holland and West Friesland. The early development is obscure, but it is agreed that these cattle are descendants of the wild species *Bos primigenius*. It is also agreed that they have been bred in Holland for 2,000 years or more. No doubt the conditions in Holland have had a marked influence on the characteristics of the Holsteins of today.

Since the fertile soil and abundant rainfall of the region produce luxuriant pastures, the Holstein-Friesians of Holland have had to live almost entirely upon grass during the summer months. Because of the luxuriance of the pastures, poor grazers were at no disadvantage to good grazers and were, therefore, not eliminated in the development of the breed.

Because winters were cold, it was necessary that the cows be stabled. The stables and homes were frequently under the same roof, necessitating docile animals. The custom of milking the cows out on the pasture also contributed toward the selection of docile animals. This development is reflected in the general character of the members of the breed, as has already been discussed.

The low fat content of Holstein milk can also be explained by environmental factors during the early development of the breed. The chief dairy product of Holland, probably even before the beginning of the Holstein breed, has been cheese, and large quantities of milk are of more importance than high fat content for cheese making. The selection for one of these characters has a tendency to reduce the other. Since the Holsteins were selected for large quantities of milk production without regard to the fat content the characteristics of the breed of today resulted.

Today the Holsteins (or Friesians, as they are called in Holland) are very highly developed in Holland and are described as somewhat more thickly fleshed than the American Holstein. Since the red and white colours have not been objected to in that country, they are quite common.

The Holstein-Friesian has given rise to several other breeds. The Laken-felders or Dutch Belted, the Gronigen of Holland, and the East Friesian and the Oldenberg of Germany, as well as breeds in Russia and Sweden, have all originated from the Holstein-Friesian stock.

Distribution of Holstein-Friesians

The Holstein-Friesians are found in all major countries of the world. In the United States, Canada, Holland, and Japan, Holsteins outrank any other breed from the standpoint of numbers. In Japan 80 per cent of all cattle are Holsteins; and in Canada there are more Holsteins than all other breeds combined. In England the Holstein ranks second to the Dairy Shorthorn in numbers. In Germany a large proportion of the cattle are Holsteins, and several of the German breeds have been developed from original Holstein-Friesian stock. Large numbers of Holsteins are found in Africa, South America, Mexico, Australia, and New Zealand. To the latter four geographic divisions and to the Orient Holsteins have been exported from the United States.

In the United States Holsteins are found in every state. They are the most numerous in the Eastern and North Central states, and in Washington and California in the West. The Holstein is less popular in the South than the smaller breeds. This is largely due to the fact that Holsteins cannot endure heat as well as the smaller breeds can. The five states having the largest number of Holsteins are New York, Wisconsin, Pennsylvania, Ohio, and Michigan.

Families

The Holstein-Friesian breed in America is credited with over 30 families. In the strictest sense, there are no distinct families in the Holstein breed. Rather than saying a Holstein belongs to a certain family, it is more proper to say that it traces back to a certain foundation. De Kol 2nd is the foundation cow of the so-called De Kol family, and appears in the pedigrees of 74 out of the first 75 cows to produce 1000 pouns of butterfat. Johanna, the foundation cow of the family by that name, appears in 54, Inka, in 41 and Aaggie in 72 of the pedigrees of the first 75 cows to produce 1,000 pounds of fat. Other great foundation animals similarly appear in the pedigrees of most of these highest producing cows of the breed this shows that the descendants of great foundation animals have been so interbred as to largely eliminate family lines.

The more noted foundation cows of the breed are De Kol 2nd, Pietertje 2nd, Chlothilde, Aaggie, Johanna, Colantha, Belle Korndyke, Segis, Inka, Lillian Walker, Aaggie Cornucopia Pauline, Pielly, Helena Burke, Aaltje Posch, Springbrook Bess Burke, Pietertje Maid Ormsby, Mooie, Mercedes, and Tritomia. Descendants may or may not carry the names of the foundation animal to which they trace.

Herd books

The records of the Holstein breed are kept by the Holstein-Friesian Association of America, located at Brattleboro, Vermont. This association was organized in 1885 through the union of two associations existing prior to that time. These were the Holstein Breeders' Association of America and the Dutch Friesian Herb Book Association of America. The first herd book was established by the former in 1871, and by the latter in 1877. Animals registered in the former bear the suffix H.H.B. and the latter D.F.

Advanced Registry

One of the important milestones in the Holstein-Friesian history was the establishment of the Advanced Registry. This had its beginning in the Dutch-Friesian Herd Book, started by Solomon Hoxie, who later became the first Superintendent of Advanced Registry for the Holstein-Friesian Association of America. In order to obtain recognition in the Dutch-Friesian Herd Book, a mature female must have produced at least 10,000 pounds of milk in one year; heifers not in milk have to meet certain prescribed development of escutcheons to be eligible; and two to two and one-half year olds must have produced 6,000 pounds of milk.

The first Advanced Registry of the Holstein-Friesian Association of America, established in 1885, required that mature cows produce not less than 15 pounds of butter in seven days, or not less than 10,700 pounds of milk in 365 days, or not less than 589 pounds of milk in ten days. Requirements for younger animals were proportionately lower, calling for 6,500 pounds of milk in one year from a two year old. These records were made by the owner. In addition, the animals had to score 75 per cent in the scale of points, and had to be inspected for "type."

In 1893 the requirements for type were dropped. In 1894 the Babcock test was adopted, and prizes were offered for the best seven day records made under the supervision of the superintendent of the Advanced Registry or representatives of experimental stations. This was the beginning of official testing. Later these tests were extended to seven days, eight months after calving, 30 days, 90 days, and 100 days. In 1908 the semiofficial test for 365 days was adopted, official inspection being made on two days each month. In 1917 the semiofficial test for 305 days was adopted. Since then many changes have been made in the requirements and classification of tests.

Official Tests

The records supervised fall into two classes: Official Testing, and Herd Improvement Test. Both of these are administered by the superintendent of Advanced Registry, located at Brattleboro, Vermont.

Official Testing

Records of 7, 30, 90, and 100 days in length must have supervision for the entire test. These are known as A.R.O. (Advanced Registry Official), as distinguished from the tests for the longer periods, which are known as A.R.S.O. (Advanced Registry Semiofficial). A few long-time tests have had constant supervision and are designated A.R.O. All inspections are done by representatives of the agricultural colleges.

To qualify for a 305 day test, a cow must make 85 per cent of the requirements of the 365 day test and must produce a living calf within 14 months of the previous calving. A 305 day and a 365 day record may be made in the same lactation. These records are again divided into three classes designated by 4X, 3X, and 2X.

"4X" designates a record where the cow was milked four times a day for more than 45 days.

"3X" designates a record where the cow was milked not more than three times daily except for the first 45 days.

"2X" designates a record where the cow was milked not more than two times daily expect for the first 45 days.

To be eligible to enter in the Advanced Registry, the cow must meet the requirements set forth in the following table for age and type of record:

Table 2.1: Requirements in pounds fat

Age	7 Day Record Pounds	305 Day Record Pounds	365 Day Record Pounds
2 years	10	270.3	318
3 years	12	316.2	372
4 years	14	282.1	426
5 years or over	16	360.0	480
For each 1 day	.0055		.148

Bulls are eligible for Advanced Registry when four daughters have qualified for the Advanced Registry.

It is of significance to note that for the past ten years there has been a decided decrease in the percentage of 3X and 4X records. In 1938, 18.4 per cent were 4X, 65.4 per cent were 3X, and 16.2 per cent were 2X. In 1947 the percentages for 4X, 3X, and 2X were 2.5, 47.0, and 49.5 respectively.

Table 2.2 summarizes all yearly records by age groups.

A total of 4,129 cows have exceeded 800 pounds of butterfat in 365 days; 416 have exceeded 1,000 pounds; 88 have exceeded

1,100 pounds; and 21 have exceeded 1,200 pounds up to July 1948.

Table 2.2

	No. Cows	Days	Milk	Per Cent	Fat
Aged Cows	19,188	350	18,794	3.4	648.3
Senior Fours	4,125	351	17,631	3.5	612.0
Junior Fours	4,362	348	17,143	3.5	593.3
Senior Threes	4,961	349	16,311	3.5	566.0
Junior Threes	5,395	348	15,327	3.5	532.2
Senior Twos	7,272	354	14,648	3.5	506.5
Junior Twos	12,694	355	13,994	3.5	485.9
Average for	57,997	351	16,482	3.5	570.4

Table 2.3: Highest record in each type of test on January 1, 1936

Name and Number	Age (Y - Years M - Months D - Days)	Milk	%	Fat
7 days				
Pansje Prilly Abbekcrk 766722	5-0-3	567.1	7.1	40.4
30 days				
Daisy Aaggie Ormsby 3d 571569	7-5-9	3,218.7	4.4	143
305 day.				
Aaltje Sale Hengerveld Segis 823991	9-3-20	28,056.8	3.5	995.9
365 day				
Carnation Ormsby Butter King 1165152	8-5-27	38,606.6	3.6	1,402.0
Lifetime				
Ionia Ormsby Queen 1467685		267,304		8,600.4

Table 2.4: 10 Highest yearly butterfat producers

Name and H.B. No.	Y.M.	Milk	%	Fat
Carnation Ormsby Butter King 1165152	8-5	38607	3.6	1402.0
Carnation Ormsby Madcap Fayne 1639621	8-4	41943	3.3	1392.4
De Kol Plus Segis Dixie 295135	9-1	33465	4.0	1349.3
Carnation Homestead Inka Mutual 1820797	7-8	34681	3.8	1333.8
Carnation Ormsby Nellie 1326284	6-2	35887	3.7	1328.8
Calamity Nig of Elmwood Farms 1560447	8-7	34616	3.8	1327.9
Carnation Ormsby Madcap 1554602	6-3	36851	3.6	1313.0
Carnation Ormsby Segis Beauty 1203395	7-8	31264	4.1	1290.4
Daisy Aaggie Ormsby 3d 571569 (V.G.)	7-5	33140	3.9	1286.2
Carnation Homestead Walker Bessie 1909671	6-6	28222	4.5	1266.0

Table 2.5: 10 Highest yearly milk producers

Name and H.B. No.	Y.M.	Milk	Per Cent	Fat
Carnation Ormsby Madcap Fayne 1639621	8-4	41943	3.3	1392.4
Carnation Ormsby Butter King 1165152	8-5	38607	3.6	1402.0
Segis Pietertje Prospect 221846	6-8	37381	3.1	1159.0
Carnation Prospect Veeman 799610	8-7	36859	2.9	1070.2
Carnation Ormsby Madcap 1554602	6-3	36851	3.6	1313.0
Helm Veeman Woodcrest 486877	4-8	36218	3.6	1003.9
Carnation Ormsby Nellie 1326284	6-2	35887	3.7	1328.8
Lady Pride Pontiac Lieuwkje 849602	8-0	35627	3.3	1186.4
Kolrain Marion Finderne 317396	6-1	35340	2.9	1022.9
Alcartra Ormsby Canary 1135532	8-7	35272	3.1	1105.7

Herd Improvement Test

In 1928, a Herd Improvement Test was established, the results of which are published by the Superintendent of Advanced Registry in what is known as the Red Book. This Test provides that all cows in milk in the herd must be entered, and that the report must be based upon an average production per cow in the herd per year. Any cow whose record is not satisfactory may be omitted from the herd average provided the registration certificate is surrendered and no future offspring are registered. Exceptions also may be made for certain old cows. The following table, giving the summary of the Herd Test by each year, shows a rather steady increase in interest in this division.

Table 2.6: Average production of herd test cows

Year	Herds Tested	Cows	Milk	% Fat	Fat	Herds over 400 Lbs. fat
1929	242	4,834	10,864	3.37	366.4	55
1930	194	4,523	11,045	3.36	371.4	59
1931	229	4,635	10,940	3.35	366.7	64
1932	197	4,379	11,099	3.38	374.6	69
1933	204	4,716	11,256	3.44	386.8	76
1934	225	4,871	10,999	3.45	380.0	76
1935	258	5,328	11,338	3.45	391.2	116
1936	413	8,566	11,044	3.46	381.9	139
1937	493	10,517	11,210	3.45	386.5	187
1938	478	10,660	11,110	3.46	383.9	164
1939	433	10,315	11,354	3.46	393.1	168
1940	412	10,371	11,700	3.46	405.2	210
1941	442	11,285	11,859	3.46	410.0	243
1942	455	11,691	11,642	3.48	404.9	254
1943	477	11,776	11,435	3.49	399.6	233
1944	539	13,118	11,036	3.54	391.1	238
1945	681	16,396	11,071	3.52	389.3	296
1946	874	19,692	11,116	3.53	391.9	403
1947	1,080	23,926	11,119	3.54	393.4	502
Average for	8,326	191,599	11,243	3.48	391.1	3,552

Herd Classification

In 1929 the Holstein-Friesian Association of America adopted a herd classification programme, the first of its kind. Each animal is rated by an official inspector, appointed by the Association, into one of six type-classes as follows:

"Excellent"	range, 90 points or over
"Very good"	range, 85-90 points
"Good Plus"	range, 80-85 points
"Good"	range, 70-80 points
"Fair"	range, 60-70 points
"Poor"	range, below 60 points

Only cows that have freshened and bulls three years old are eligible for herd classification. The registration certificate is cancelled for animals that rate "Poor" and male progeny from females classified "Fair" cannot be registered. Provision is made for reclassification of any individual after a lapse of at least nine months. The following table gives a summary of the classification work for October 1, 1946 to September 30, 1947, with the percent-age found in each class.

	Females	Males	Total	Per Cent
Excellent	170	37	207	1.1
Very Good	2,980	252	3,232	17.2
Good Plus	8,127	291	8,418	44.7
Good	5,488	92	5,580	29.6
Fair	1,350	7	1,357	7.2
Poor	41	0	41	.2
Totals	18,156	679	18,835	100.0

Studies have revealed a fairly good correlation between type classification and milk and butterfat production. An analysis of the type classification of 16,696 cows of which 6,440 had Herd Improvement Records is given in Table 2.7.

Table 2.7: An analysis of the type classification of 16,696 cows

Class Groups	Total Females Class	No. Cows with H.I.R. Records	Per Cent with H.I.R. Records	Average No. Records Per Cow	Average Lbs. Milk	Average Per cent Fat	Average Lbs. Fat
Excellent	511	261	51.1	3.01	17,215	3.49	601.4
Very Good	3,122	1,377	44.1	2.69	15,988	3.47	554.5
Good Plus	5,363	2,213	41.3	2.47	15,754	3.46	544.5
Good	6,283	2,138	34.0	2.27	14,960	3.43	513.6
Fair	1,300	426	32.8	2.17	14,316	3.41	488.1
Poor	117	25	21.4	1.36	12,612	3.41	430.7
Total	16,696	6,440	38.6	2.43	15,492	3.45	534.5

Recognition of Sires

There are three special recognitions of sires provided for by the Holstein-Friesian Association of America. One is based upon the type of his daughters (Silver Medal Type Sire); another is based upon the production of his daughters (Silver Medal Production Sire); and the third is based upon a combination of type and production of his daughters (Gold Medal Proven Sire). The requirements for qualifying for each of these recognitions are:

Silver Medal Type Sire

A bull is entitled to this recognition if 75 per cent or more of his daughters have an average score of at least 81 points. A minimum of ten daughters must be scored. If only 50 to 75 per cent of the daughters are classified, an average score of at least 82 must be gotten. If the classified daughters range from 25 to 50 per cent of the total the score must be 83 or more and for 25 per cent or less a minimum average score of 84 points is required. In all cases a minimum of ten daughters must be classified.

If 50 per cent of his Advanced Registry or Herd Test daughters have qualified with production 50 per cent in excess of A.R. requirements, showing not less than 3.3 per cent butterfat, with a minimum of ten so qualifying, such sire shall be designated a Silver Medal Production Sire and an appropriate certificate shall be issued.

3

The Jersey

Characteristics

Except for the Dexter and the Kerry, The Jersey is the smallest of cattle. The desired weight for mature cows ranges from 900 to 1,100 pounds. The normal weight for mature bulls ranges from 1,300 to 1,600 pounds. Both cows and bulls on the Island of Jersey are, on the average, smaller than in this country. Seldom does a cow on the Island attain 1,000 pounds in weight. In this country a large number of breeders have selected for large size and, as a result, they have developed strains that breed relatively true for this character. Others have bred for the smaller type. Many people refer to the larger type as American and to the smaller and more refined as the Island type. Since many of the smaller and more refined Jerseys have been bred in this country for as many generations as the large so-called American type, these terms are unfortunate.

Type

The Jersey breed has more individuals than has any other breed that approach the classic true dairy type. The good Island type Jersey possesses more dairy character than do individuals from any other breed. The top line is straight, and the level rump is unsurpassed. The true type head possesses what is known as

Fig. 3.1: The Jersey Bull

a double dish; that is, there is a dish between the eyes and another dish presented by a profile view. Jerseys are generally considered as having the best shaped udders and the best udder attachments. They are more angular and more free from excess fleshiness than members of other breeds. The so-called American type, in addition to being larger, is rougher and lacks the pleasing lines of the so-called Island type (Fig. 3.1).

Colour

Of all breeds the Jersey is the most variable in colour. Individuals may be of solid colour or white spotted. Solid coloured animals may be black or any shade of colour from black to a very light fawn. The colour may be a uniform shade over the entire body, or black spots may appear on a lighter coloured background. The degree of white spotting varies greatly, ranging from a few small white spots to spotting so large that most of the body is white. The coloured portion of the spotted animal may possess all the variations in shades that have been described for the solid coloured animals. Some breeders are prejudiced against the black and spotted Jerseys, and select for the solid coloured fawns, usually considered the most typical Jersey colour. However, many black or spotted Jerseys have won the highest awards in the show ring.

The tongue and switch of the Jersey may be either white or black. In applications for registry, the colours of the tongue and switch, usually known as the points, must be stated. The muzzle is black encircled by a light-coloured ring.

Fig. 3.1: The Jersey Cow

Nervous Reactions

The Jersey probably has the most highly developed nervous system of all the dairy breeds. Jerseys are very sensitive and react quickly to stimuli. This characteristic may be either advantageous or disadvantageous. When they are treated well, they are quick to respond favorably; but if they are mistreated, they are equally quick to respond unfavorably. The Jersey bull is more likely to be vicious than are bulls from other breeds.

Grazing ability

The Jerseys rank high as grazers. On moderate pastures the Jerseys have often been observed to do better than members of other breeds. This may be accounted for in two ways. The Jersey, because of her small size, needs less nutrients than do larger cows, and therefore will secure her requirements from smaller areas; and she is inherently active.

Reproduction and Longevity

Jerseys rank high as reproducers and for long productive lives. The calves, however, are small at birth and considered rather hard to raise. The female calf averages about 55 pounds at birth, or less than 6 per cent of the weight of the dam. Bull calves average about 60 pounds at birth. The Jersey calf is not only the smallest of all calves at birth, but also represents a smaller per cent of the weight of the dam.

Maturity

Jerseys are the earliest of all breeds to mature. Heifers are usually sufficiently mature to calve when 24 to 26 months of age. Many come into milk much earlier, but this is not advisable, since there is insufficient development for milk production.

Meat and veal

The Jersey is the poorest of all breeds for both meat and veal. The body fat of the Jersey is yellow in colour, an objectionable feature in meat. The small size, poor fleshing, and poor distribution of the fat also contribute to make the Jersey the poorest of all breeds for either meat or veal production.

Milk

The Jersey is noted for the quality of her milk rather than for the quantity. Jersey milk is superior to all other milk in both its fat and total solids content. The butterfat in Jersey milk varies from 4 to 8.0 per cent, with an average for the breed of 5.3 per cent. The total solids control averages 14.9 per cent. The butterfat constitutes 35.5 per cent of the total solids, as contrasted to 28 per cent for the Holsteins. Because butterfat constitutes such a high percentage of the total solids, the Jersey produces butterfat at a lower cost than other breeds.

Because of the high quality, Jersey milk is more expensive to produce and must sell for a higher price. The American Jersey Cattle Club has copyrighted the term "Jersey Cream Line" to be used on Jersey milk and lends assistance in developing special milk markets where Jersey milk sells at from two to five cents more per quart than ordinary market milk. "Jersey Cream Line" milk is marketed in all large cities.

In addition to the high fat and total solids content, Jersey milk has other distinctive features. The butterfat is high in carotene, which gives the fat a yellow colour. The fat globules are the largest of any, averaging 25 per cent greater in diameter than those of the Holstein. Because of the large fat globules, the cream rises faster and churns more rapidly than does cream from other milk. The ease with which the cream churns sometimes causes difficulty in shipping milk, since the agitation is frequently sufficient to cause partial churning of the fat in the milk.

The milk from Jerseys is especially adapted for special milk markets and for butter or cream production. The fat-to-solids ratio is too high for cheese making or for producing evaporated milk.

The Jersey also ranks first in persistency.

Origin and Native Home

The exact origin of the Jersey is a subject of conjecture. That they are descendants from the wild species *Bos longifrons* is generally agreed upon, but as to whether they are descendants of the cattle of Brittany and Normandy, which resembled the Jersey, is a subject of controversy. They have been developed on the Island of Jersey, one of the four British Islands in the English Channel off the coast of France. The other three islands in this group are Guernsey, the home of the Guernsey cow; Sark; and Alderney. A consideration of what is a known about the environment and the development of the Jersey in its homeland will help in understanding many of the Jersey characteristics.

The Island of Jersey is ten miles from east to west, with an average width of six and one-fourth miles. It slopes from north to south, and has a maximum elevation of 500 feet. Its mean temperature is 40.1°F. for January and 63°F. for August, with an average rainfall of 34.2 inches. Frost lasts for short periods only, and snow seldom more than two or three days. The climate, therefore, is mild, although a chilly, moisture-laden wind is not uncommon.

In 1931 a population of 50,455 was living on the 61.9 square miles, or an average of more than 800 people per square mile. In 1934 there were 1,764 farms, totaling 21,000 acres. Although 30 per cent of these farms contained less than 4.5 acres, 25,657 acres of crops were reported in 1934, a greater area than the total farm area. This was possible because two and even three crops may be raised annually. Early potatoes for the British market are one of the chief crops of the Island. Tomatoes rank second in importance, with greenhouse products next. Since 1867 from 10,000 to 12,000 Jersey cattle have been kept. In 1934 there were about a thousand breeders having 10,682 head, of which all but 123 were registered.

The chief feed is pasture, the grasses of which grow very luxuriantly. The cows are usually tethered in a line across the field and move back and forth as the grass is eaten off. Most cows of the Island are never fed concentrates.

According to Gow, the earliest references to the cattle on the Island were made in 1734, when they were described as being "superior to the French Cattle." In 1885 the U.S. Consulate in Liverpool declared that the Jersey had been purebred for 500 years. While there is no proof of this statement, the Islanders have traditionally had pride in their cattle and confidence in their superiority over other cattle, and, therefore, have kept them purebred for a long time. In 1789 a law was passed forbidding transportation of cattle to the Island except for immediate slaughter.

The smallness of the Island and the long time during which they have been bred pure have done must to establish the Jersey characteristics. The Islander first selected for rich milk. The closeness with which cows were associated with humans (barns and houses being together) made it imperative that the animals be docile, and brought about their being responsive to good care. Because roughage has been the chief diet, if not the sole one, they had to be good roughage eaters.

On the Island the Jerseys are very uniform as to type. This is attributable to the system of registration, which requires inspection of all animals by a committee before registration. At stated periods a committee of judges will respect cattle at a given point. The owners desiring registration take the animals before the judges, where they are given a rating on the basis of type. If they meet with the approval of the judges, they are classified as commended, and a "C" is placed after the registration number. If superior, they are given a rating of highly commended, or H.C. Bulls must be accompanied by their dams at inspection. As all animals on the Island are eligible to registration whether or not now registered, an unregistered animal is given the suffix F.S. (Foundation Stock) after its registration number. All those with registered ancestry carry the suffix P.S. (Pedigreed Stock). Parish shows have been another important factor in bringing about breed uniformity and improvement. Since 1834, when the first Parish show was held, these shows have been extended to every one of the 12 Parishes. At these shows valuable money prizes are offered for bulls, and those for which money awards are received must be held for public service for one year. Bulls classed as undesirable at these shows are slaughtered.

On the Island the keeping of official records of production has never been extensive. A system similar to the American Register of Merit testing has been adopted, but it has been used comparatively little. The Jersey breeder on the Island has been more interested in type, in the belief that the right type makes for high production.

Importation and Distribution

In England

According to Gow, Jerseys were known in England as early as 1771. The most significant importations were those made by Phillip Dauncey, who began importations in 1821. Dauncey selected the largest and most rugged Jerseys he could find on the Island and continued to breed for these characteristics in England. By inbreeding, he fixed large size, ruggedness, and high production. W.G. Duncan bred for the same objective, and also imported stock from the Island. Many importations of stock from these herds were made to America, where the inbreeding practices of these two English breeders were continued; these herds, then, were the sources of the so-called American type. The English Jersey Cattle Society Herd Book was started in 1879. At present, there are about 900 members. The British Royal Family have been breeders of Jerseys for three generations.

Quite a number of Jerseys were imported from England before the Jersey Cattle Club in 1875 stopped such importations. In 1900 this rule was rescinded by the membership, and since then a few Jerseys have been imported; but the disease situation in England has interrupted this trade. The foundation animals of the St. Lambert family were imported from England, coming from the W.G. Duncan herd there.

Jerseys are found in every state of the Union. In numbers of Jerseys, the leading states rank as follows: Ohio, Texas, New York, Pennsylvania, Missouri, Kentucky, and Tennessee. In general, Jerseys are most numerous in the South and East and in Oregon on the Pacific Coast. In the early '80's a Jersey cow sold for $25,000. This gave a great impetus to the Jersey breed, as did the winning of the dairy tests in the World's Fair in Chicago in 1893, and again in St. Louis in 1904. During the boom following World War I, the prices for Jerseys did not advance as much as for some other breeds, nor did they drop as much in the depression period.

Jerseys are found in practically every country in the world, but they are the most numerous in the United States in England.

Families

No other breed has as well-defined families as the Jersey. While there have been intercrossing of families, the Jersey breeders have practiced line-breeding and inbreeding to a greater extent than is found in any other dairy breed. Most of the Jersey families trace back to a bull for the foundation animal, whereas the foundation animal of a Holstein family, for example, is usually a cow. There are so many families and subfamilies in the Jersey breed that space forbids mention of all of them.

Of the American type the St. Lambert, Sophie Tormentor, Golden Glows, and the St. Mawes are the most prominent families. Another prominent family is the Golden Ferns, of which Golden Fern's Lad is the foundation sire. He is said to have had a greater influence upon the breed than any other bull. The Golden Jolly, Flying Foxes, Eminent, Noble, Raleigh, Majesty, Sybil, Fauvic Prince, and Golden Glow families trace back to Golden Fern's Lad or his grandsire, Golden Lad. The Owl-Interest Blonde, Volunteer, and Design Families are also very prominent.

Registration

All records of Jerseys are kept by the American Jersey Cattle Club, with offices in Columbus, Ohio. This club, organized in 1868, publishes the herd book known as the Herd Register of the American Jersey Cattle club. Until 1882 registering Jersey cattle and publishing the herd book were the only functions of the American Jersey Cattle Club. Since that time, the organization has taken over the supervision of official testing and breed promotion work. At the present time the American Jersey Cattle Club employs several field men for promoting the interests of the breed.

In order to be eligible to register in the herd books of the American Jersey Cattle Club, Club, animals must have registered parents, or when imported, be registered or eligible to registry in the Island, Canadian, or English herd books. Before an application for registry can be made, the animal must be tattooed with a suitable mark in the ear.

Testing

The administration and recording of official production records is a very important function of the American Jersey Cattle Club. The system is known as the Register of Merit. The American Jersey Cattle Club began the supervision of tests in 1884 when they authorized 7 day butter tests to be made under the supervision of the Club. Prior to that, records made privately have been published, the first of which was made in 1853 when the cow, Flora, was credited with 511 pounds and 2 ounces of butter in 350 days.

The first authenticated tests were published in 1889. In order to qualify for entrance to the list, a cow must produce 14 pounds of butter in seven days. All of these early records were made privately and reported under oath to the Cattle Club. In 1891 the tests were extended to include records of any length above seven days, thus making the system absurd, since owners reported on all possible lengths of test periods. In 1902 the Club voted to accept seven day tests authenticated by colleges, and in 1903 it established the Register of Merit system, which has undergone many changes down to this date; but it required from the beginning authentication by experiment stations for acceptance. Private tests were accepted up to 1911; and in 1919 short-time tests were dropped.

There are now two types of records accepted – the Register of Merit Tests, and the Herd Tests. Both of these tests are conducted under the supervision of the Superintendent of Official Testing of the various states.

Register of Merit

The Register of Merit has three classes, with requirements as follows:

Class A: to be eligible to Class A, a cow must produce 290.5 pounds of fat as a two year old, or 400 pounds of fat when mature.

Class AA: To be eligible to this class a cow must meet the production requirements for 365 days and, in addition, give birth to a living calf carried not less than 155 days during the test.

Class AAA: To be eligible to this class a cow must produce in 305 days at least 250.5 pounds of fat as a two year old and 360 pounds of fat as a mature cow, and give birth to a living calf within 13 months from the previous calving.

Discarding all short-time records, 76,862 production records have been accepted by the Club up to March 31, 1948. These records are divided as follows:

Kind of Test	No. of Tests	Average Milk Pounds	Average Fat Pounds	Average Fat Per Cent
305 days	35,743	8,203	438.2	5.34
365 days	41,119	9,037	485.3	5.37

In 1942, there was established an awards known as Lifetime Butterfat Champion, to be given each year. Three cows have won that award up to and including 1947, as follows:

Table 3.1

Year Awarded	Name of Cow	Milk (lbs)	Fat (lbs)
Initial	Radiant Romance Storrs 587210	154,327	7,706
1942	Daisy Gray Fern 868266	114,101	6,251
1943	Silken Lady's Ruby of F. 919141	122,280	6,654
1944	Silken Lady's Ruby of F. 919141	133,180	7,242
1945	Silken Lady's Ruby of F. 919141	146,236	7,975
1946	Silken Lady's Ruby of F. 919141	155,988	8,550
1947	Silken Lady's Ruby of F. 919141	166,020	9,165

Silken Lady's Ruby of F. still producing at 18 years of age has the highest lifetime butterfat production record of all breeds at any time.

The butterfat champions for each of the recognized age groups in both the 305 and the 365 day divisions as of July 1, 1948 are presented in Tables 3.2 and 3.3.

The Herd Test

In 1928 rules were adopted for Herd Improvement Registry. This test may be conducted in conjunction with Register of Merit testing. All tests are under the supervision of the State Superintendent of Official Testing. The test covers 365 days, and the butterfat periods without preliminary milkings, or bimonthly 24 hour official test periods with preliminary milking. All registered cows in milk in the herd must be tested. The latter feature is one which prevents selecting the good cows for test and leaving out the poor ones. A certificate is issued by the Club giving the number of cows tested, and the average milk and butterfat production with the average fat percentage. Individual lactation certificates may also be had. Up to April 1948, this test had been elected for 5,433 herds with a total of 145,659 cows. These averaged 375.9 pounds of fat, 7,036 pounds of milk, and a fat percentage of 534.

Awards

In addition to a Register of Merit Certificate, cows that meet certain specifications are awarded medals or special certificates. Only one of each medal can be awarded a breeder. For subsequent animals that qualify, appropriate certificates are furnished.

A Medal of Merit is issued for each cow producing 740 or more pounds of fat in Class AAA, or 850 or more pounds of fat in Class AA. Bulls having three or more Medal of Merit daughters out of different dams qualify as Medal of Merit bulls. A Gold Medal is issued for cows producing between 610 and 730 pounds of fat in Class AAA and between 700 and 849 pounds of fat in Class AA. A bull having three Gold Medal daughters out of different dams qualifies as a Gold Medal bull.

Table 3.2: National 365 day butterfat champions

Class	Name and H.R. Number	Class	Milk	% Fat	Fat	Age
Yr.	St. Mawes Lad's Lady 451568	A	11,756	7.05	829.08	1-11
Jr. 2	Raleigh's Toron'os Meme 544207	A	16,085	5.61	902.15	2-5
Sr. 2	Viola's Rinda Fancy 716673	A	12,738	7.38	939.96	2-10
Jr. 3	Poppy's Dortha 378520	A	17,804	5.58	994.25	3-4
Sr. 3	Welcome Volunteer Tiff 1316589	AA	19,416	5.55	1,076.80	3-11
Jr. 4	Darling's Jolly Lassie 435948	AA	16,425	6.95	1,141.28	4-0
Sr. 4	Vive La France 319616	AA	14,926	6.91	1,031.64	4-7
Over 5	Stockwell's April Pogis of H.P. 694544	AA	17,880	6.81	1,218.48	8-3
Over 12	Silken Vive Glow Dinah 905153	A	17,336	5.88	1,018.77	12-2

Table 3.3: National 305 Day Butterfat Champions

Class	Name and H.R. Number	Class	Milk	% Fat	Fat	Age
Yr.	The Lion's Lilac 671092	AAA	10,752	6.91	742.44	1-9
Jr. 2	Tristram Basil Cleo 1465209	A	13,482	5.32	717.87	2-3
Sr. 2	Sybil Tessie Lorna 996685	AAA	15,357	5.63	865.07	2-10
Jr. 3	Volunteer Bell Rosalie 1178965	A	14,177	6.07	861.16	3-5
Sr. 3	The Loin's Lilac 671090	AAA	13,844	6.69	926.55	3-11
Jr. 4	Dairylike Maid Cleo 1131609	AAA	15,303	6.36	972.69	4-5
Sr. 4	Fon Sayda 704373	A	13,020	6.53	850.56	4-6
Over 5	Missionary Noble Alice 1199012	AAA	19,390	5.35	1,038.03	8-5
Over 12	Gilsland B. Foxy Poetess 991549	A	13,757	6.02	827.60	12-3

Silver Medals are awarded to cows under five years of age producing 410 pounds of fat in Class AAA and 500 pounds of fat in Class AA at two years of age, with increased requirements of .2 pounds of butterfat for each day older than two years. A bull having three or more Silver Medal daughters qualifies as a Silver Medal bull.

Bulls are given a Superior Sire award when the following requirements are met:

1. At least ten daughters have completed lactation periods of 270 days either in Register of Merit or Herd Improvement Registry.
2. More than 50 per cent of all registered daughters four years old or over are tested.
3. The average butterfat production exceeds 600 pounds of fat on a mature basis.
4. At least ten daughters have been classified, and the average score for all daughters classified is 82 or more.

Ton of Gold Certificate

Any cow producing 2,000 pounds of butterfat or more in four consecutive 365 day herd test periods is entitled to a certificate known as the Ton of Gold Certificate.

Gold Star Herd Award

This award is a recognition for continuous meritorious production. To qualify, herds in Herd Improvement Registry must average annually for four consecutive years not less than the following for herds of different sizes:

Size of Herd	Minimum Annual Av. Butterfat Pounds
5 to 10 cows	475
11 to 50 cows	450
Over 50 cows	425

Tested Sire

Any bull having ten or more daughters having completed records in either Register of Merit or Herd Improvement Registry is known as a tested sire.

Constructive Breeder's Certificate

This award is regarded as the highest recognition of the America Jersey Cattle Club. To qualify for this awards the following requirements must be met:

(1) The herd must be re-entered on H.I.R. and have completed an average of 400 pounds fat if 10 cows, and 340 if 40 cows or more.

(2) A total of 50 per cent of animals in the herd that ever calved must have been bred by the owner; 65 per cent must have been bred or owned at least four years at the date of qualification.

(3) At least 60 per cent of all animals in the herd must have been officially classified with a minimum average of 82.00 per cent at the date of qualification.

(4) The herd shall be federally T.B. Certified.

(5) The herd shall be Bang's-free or certified by the state veterinarian to be in process of Bang's eradication.

(6) The breeder must show evidence of membership in his state or local club.

Star Bull Award

This scheme is an attempt to evaluate bulls before they are proven by rating the performance of the ancestors. One star will be awarded for each five credits provided that not over two-thirds of the credits can come from either the top or the bottom half of the pedigree. A bull may obtain as many as seven stars but to qualify for four or more stars at least three credits must come from classification. The following table shows how credits are obtained.

Table listing credits for stars

Sire

Having 10 or more tested daughters averaging:

360 lbs. fat merits 1 credit

390 lbs. fat merits 2 credits

420 lbs. fat merits 3 credits

450 lbs. fat merits 4 credits

480 lbs. fat merits 5 credits

510 lbs. fat merits 6 credits

540 lbs. fat merits 7 credits

Having 10 or more officially classified daughters averaging:

81 per cent merits 2 credits

82 per cent merits 3 credits

84 per cent merits 4 credits

(Transmitted Credits)

A 2 Star Bull may transmit 2 credits.

A 3 Star Bull may transmit 4 credits.

A 4 or more Star Bull may transmit 5 credits.

Paternal Grandsire

Having 10 or more tested daughters averaging:

420 lbs. fat merits 1 credit

450 lbs. fat merits 2 credits

Having 10 or more officially classified daughters averaging:

81 per cent merits 1 credit

82 per cent merits 2 credits

Paternal Grandam

Having 3 or more tested progeny averaging:

420 lbs. fat merits 1 credit

450 lbs. fat merits 2 credits

Dam

Having a 2 x 305 M-E production record of:

390 lbs. fat merits 2 credits

450 lbs. fat merits 3 credits

510 lbs. fat merits 4 credits

"Ton of Gold" or Owner's

Notice of its equivalent,
Merits 5 credits (in place of
individual lactation record)

Having an official classification of:

"Good Plus" merits 2 credits
"Very Good" merits 3 credits
"Excellent" merits 4 credits

Having 3 or more tested progeny averaging on the 2x305 M-E basis:

360 lbs. fat merits 1 credit
390 lbs. fat merits 2 credits
420 lbs. fat merits 3 credits
450 lbs. fat merits 4 credits
480 lbs. fat merits 5 credits
510 lbs. fat merits 6 credits

Maternal Grandsire

Having 10 or more tested daughters averaging:

420 lbs. fat merits 1 credit
450 lbs. fat merits 2 credits

Having 10 or more officially classified daughters averaging:

81 per cent merits 1 credit
82 per cent merits 2 credits

Maternal Grandam

Having 3 or more tested progeny averaging:

420 lbs. fat merits 1 credit
450 lbs. fat merits 2 credits

Herd classification

With the objective of improving the type of the Jersey, the American Jersey Cattle Club in 1932 adopted a plan for classifying animals in a herd on the basis of type. The classification is made by judges approved by the American Jersey Cattle Club. Animals are to be classified into six groups according to conformation on the basis of score as follows: excellent, if scored 90 or more points according to the official Scale of Points; very good, if scored

85 to 90; good plus, if scored 80 to 85; good, if scored 75 to 80; fair, if scored 70 to 75; and poor, if scored under 70.

Certificates giving the classification of each animal are furnished the owners. In making application for Herd Classification the applicant must agree to surrender for cancellation the certificates of all animals classifying "Poor," and the registration of future progeny of such an individual is prohibited. He must further agree not to register any male calves from cows rating "fair."

Up to April 1948, 91,848 Jerseys had been classified with the following distribution in each of the classes.

Class	Number
Excellent	2,431
Very Good	25,364
Good Plus	42,981
Good	18,418
Fair	2,594
Poor	60
Total	91,848

The average butterfat production calculated to a 305 mature equivalent base is given for each class as well as the numbers as follows:

Class	Number	Average Fat Pounds
Excellent	801	483
Very Good	4,213	460
Good Plus	6,060	448
Good	2,700	434
Fair.	369	420
Poor	4	425

It is of special interest to note the significant decrease in average fat production with each drop in classification grade except for the "Poor" in which the number is too small to be significant.

4

The Guernsey

Characteristics

Guernsey cows very in weight from, 800 to 1,400 pounds, with 1,100 pounds as the preferred weight. Bulls vary from 1,200 to 2,200 pounds, with 1,700 pounds as the preferred weight. The Guernsey cow, being a near relative of the Jersey, resembles her in many respects. The Guernsey, however, in addition to being larger than the Jersey, is somewhat coarser and does not possess quite the straight lines and symmetry. The udders of Guernseys are good but a little less symmetrical than those of the Jersey. The head is double dished but to a less degree than on the Jersey. Some of the more serious criticisms of the Guernsey are its weakness over the loin, roughness over the rump, and lack of symmetry of the udder. (Fig. 4.1)

Colour

The Guernsey varies in colour from an almost red to a every light fawn, with various sizes of white markings always present. The white markings are usually found on the face, legs, flank, and switch; the rest of the body is predominantly coloured. The white spotting, however, may be found on any part of the body. The preferred colour of the nose is a cream or buff colour. A black or smoky colour of the nose is frequently found due to a factor

Fig. 4.1: A Guernsey bull

for skin pigment that is present in the breed extensively. The skin of the Guernsey is generally highly pigmented with the yellow carotene. This is noticed particularly inside the ears, on the udder, and at the end of the tail.

Nervous reactions

The Guernsey has excellent nervous development. She is alive and alert, yet not so easily excited as the Jersey.

Grazing

The Guernsey is not so good a grazer as the Jersey, particularly on poorer pastures. This, no doubt, is due to the larger size of the Guernsey and the correspondingly greater feed requirements.

Maturity and reproduction

On the average the Guernsey matures about two months later than the Jersey. Heifers come into milk when 26 to 28 months of age. In longevity the Guernsey ranks average, although individuals have reached as high as 20 years of age. As reproducers they also rank average. The calves average about 75 pounds at birth, or approximately 7 per cent of the dam's weight. The calves are, as a rule, not strong when born, and are usually regarded as somewhat difficult to raise.

Meat and veal

For either beef or veal, the Guernsey ranks low. The body fat is extremely yellow in colour; this is highly objectionable for beef and veal. The Guernsey also lacks the desired scale and thickness of fleshing that is essential for good beef.

Milk

One of the outstanding characteristics of Guernsey milk is its high yellow colour. The Guernsey possesses the ability to secrete a large proportion of the carotene pigment of the feed she consumes into the milk. The American Guernsey Cattle Club has taken advantage of this character and has copyrighted the trademark "Golden Guernsey" for Guernsey milk. By advertising, the Association has created a sizable demand for this milk, and many Guernsey breeders have secured a fine market for their product at a premium price.

With a fat content of 4.98 per cent, Guernsey milk ranks next to that of the Jersey. The average total solids are 14.49 per cent, sugar 4.98 per cent, and protein 3.84 per cent. The fat, particularly when the cows are on grass, is so highly coloured with the carotene pigment that it is objectionable for the butter market. The fat particles, like those of the Jersey, are large and churn easily when the milk is in transit. With the fat constituting 33.3 per cent of the total solids, the milk is not adapted for cheese making or condensed milk. Because of this, however, they rank with the Jerseys as producers of low cost butterfat.

Home and origin

Being descendants of *Bos longifrons*, the Guernsey is of the same original stock as the Jersey. Foundation stocks are supposed to have been brought over to the Island of Guernsey from Brittany and Normandy, although there is no proof that such is the case. Researcher says he has evidence that both Jerseys and Guernseys were taken to the Island of Alderney and that cattle were brought

Fig. 4.2: A Guernsey cow with calf.

from Alderney back to the Island of Jersey and possibly Guernsey. The home of the Guernsey is the Island of Guernsey, a sister island to the Island of Jersey. It is 22 miles northwest of Jersey and 15 miles from the coast of France. Its greatest length is nine miles and its greatest width is five miles. It has an area of only 24 square miles, or approximately 16,000 acres, 25 per cent of which is not tillable. The condition on the Island of Guernsey are practically the same as those on the Island of Jersey except that the climate is slightly colder, since the slope is toward the north. The population is about 50,000, or more than 2,000 per square mile. The chief crops are flowers and garden truck, much of which is grown under glass.

There are only about 8,000 cattle on the Island. They are found mostly in small herds of from two to seven cows. The cows are tethered as they are on the Island of Jersey; and, also as on Jersey, they are fed largely upon roughage. While gardening is the chief occupation of the inhabitants of the Island, the cattle have been highly valued for a long time. In 1824 laws were passed forbidding the importation of cattle except for immediate slaughter. In 1830 a "Scale of Points" was adopted, and from that time on great improvement in uniformity of the breed has been noted. In 1879 the first Herd Book, to which all cattle on the Island were eligible for registry, was established. In 1911 the Royal Guernsey Agricultural and Horticultural Society set up an Advanced Registry system patterned after the system of the American Guernsey Cattle Club. In 1881 the first local show on the Island was held. From that time to 1912, foundation cows admitted to the Herd Book carried the connotation C. (Commended), H.C. (Highly Commended), or V.H.C. (Very Highly Commended). After 1912 all cows were admitted and marked "Qualified at a local show."

According to Hill many Alderney-bred cattle were brought to Guernsey and entered in the Herd Book there. This author also states that many cattle brought to America and England from Guernsey came originally from Alderney. Now all Alderney cattle are eligible to registry in the "Herd Book of the Bailiwick of Guernsey." The cattle from Sark and Hern are also registered in the Guernsey Herd Book. No bull on the Island can be stood for service until he is 15 months old and has been taken to a local show with his dam and approved by the Herd Book committee.

Importation and distribution

Just when the first Guernseys were brought to America is not known. In 1818 cattle called Alderneys were brought to Pennsylvania. At that time, however, no distinction was made between Guernseys and Jerseys; therefore it is not known whether these were Guernseys. According to Hill, the first importations that were kept pure were made by a Mr. Price of Massachusetts in 1830 or 1831. Descendants from these have been registered by the American Guernsey Cattle Club. Another importation was made in 1840 by a Mr. Biddle of Pennsylvania. Heavy importations began during the '80's and still continue, since Guernsey Island is free of diseases against which the United States government has established quarantines. To date there has been imported a total of approximately 113,000 head.

The Guernsey outside its Island home is found mainly in England and the United States. In England they have been owned and developed mainly by the nobility. In the United States they are found mostly in the East and in the North. The leading states, listed according to the number of Guernseys, are Wisconsin, Pennsylvania, New York, Ohio, Michigan, and Minnesota.

Since 1877 the importations by decades are as follows:

1877 to 1887	921
1887 to 1897	318
1897 to 1907	813
1907 to 1917	6,250
1917 to 1927	3,852
1927 to 1937	639

No importations were made from 1937 to 1948.

The Guernsey has increased continuously in popularity in this country. During the depression the Guernsey prices were maintained much better than those of any other breed. The demand comes from butter-producing and market-milk areas. The demand that has been built up for the yellow coloured milk has been a large factor in Guernsey development around large population centers.

Families

The Guernsey has no definite families, although many outstanding foundation animals have been credited with founding families. With the exception of May Rose 2nd, who may be considered the founder of the May Rose family, none of the blood of the great foundation animals has been concentrated enough to be classified as a family.

Registration

The records of Guernseys are kept by the American Guernsey Cattle Club, with offices at Peterborough, New Hampshire. The Club was organized in 1877 and therefore is younger than either the Holstein or the Jersey organizations. At first the American Guernsey Cattle Club was concerned only with the registration and transferring of Guernsey Cattle and the publishing of the Herd Books. In 1903 the Association inaugurated supervision over Official Testing; following this they gradually developed educational and promotional work until today the work done for the promotion and development of a breed and its product by the American Guernsey Cattle Club is unexcelled.

There are 3,560 active members and more than 38,000 breeders registering cattle with the American Guernsey Cattle Club in 1948. Over 428,000 males and 1,000,000 females have been registered since the beginning of the organization. During the depression years the decline in the numbers of Guernseys registered was less than for other breeds. Since then the numbers registered have increased each year.

Testing

While comparatively little testing was done by the earlier breeders of Guernsey cattle, remarkable development has taken place in this work until there are more yearly official records on Guernseys than on any other breed. The first private record of an Alderney cow was made in 1818. This was a seven day test of 14 pounds of butter. A second private record of 14 pounds and five ounces of butter in seven days was reported in 1860. Following 1860 to 1898, a total of 160 private weekly butter tests was published by the American Guernsey Cattle Club. This is but a small number when compared with the tests reported for Jerseys and Holsteins, but the people in whose hands the Guernseys were at this time were not interested in production records.

In 1898 churn tests for yearly records were adopted. In 1901 the Advanced Register was adopted, accepting both seven day and yearly records. Both minimum fat and milk production requirements were specified as qualifications for entry in the Advanced Register. A two year old must produce 250.5 pounds of fat and 6,000 pounds of milk to qualify. Additional production was required with age increments; the minimum requirements for a five year old were 360 pounds of fat and 10,000 pounds of milk. Both the seven day tests and the milk requirement for long-time tests were soon dropped, and all efforts were then concentrated on long-time testing.

The American Guernsey Cattle Club was the first breed association to adopt long-time tests only. For many years this association had a unique system for designating the age and class of record.

The first seven letters of the alphabet were used to designate the age at which the record was made. A indicated the age of

5 years or over; B, 4½ to 5 years; C, 4 to 4½ years; D, 3½ to 4 years; E, 3 to 3½ years; F, 2½ to 3 years; and G, 2 to 2½ years.

Single letters designated a record made in 365 days without any calving requirement.

Double letters- AA, BB, etc. – designated 365 day records in which the cow carried a calf for 200 days.

Triple letters – AAA, BBB, etc.- designated records of 305 days in length, that the cow carried calf for 175 days or more, and that she was milked not more than twice daily. When milked three times daily four letters were used.

A fourth class of records is open to Guernsey breeders in the Herd Improvement Test. This test is similar to the Herd Test of the Holstein and Jersey breeds.

Designation of Kind of Record

Beginning January 1, 1947 the American Guernsey Cattle Club adopted a new method of designating the Advanced Registry Records. The new system gives the year in which the record was started, age of the cow including whether a junior or senior, the division in which the record is entered, the total number of milkings, the milk record, and the fat record. If the age is preceded by Jr., the record was begun before the cow was six months over the year indicated and if preceded by Sr. that she was six months or more over the indicated years. In the Division whether the record 365 days or 305 days is indicated. If the requirements are met this is followed by a C to indicate that a cow has carried a calf for at least 175 days in the 305-day division and 200 days in the 365-day division.

The rate with which testing has increased is illustrated by Table 4.1 giving the total number of these tests made by ten year periods.

A total of 112,358 records were made up to 1948. It will also be noted that there has been a consistent improvement of the production records from an average of 443.9 pounds of fat in the period up to 1917 to 519.6 pounds of fat for the 10 year period ending in 1937. The average production for the last 10 year period is not available.

Table 4.1

Period	Number of Records	Average Butterfat Pounds
1901-1917	5,776	443.9
1917-1927	17,747	497.6
1927-1937	23,231	519.6
1937-1947	65,604	-

Table 4.2 presents the number of records and the average milk, butterfat, and fat percentage for each of the four divisions as of June 1, 1948:

The highest milk and butterfat producers for each of the four divisions are as follows:

365-day, no calving requirement.

Milk record: Murne Cowan; 8 yrs.' 15. 24,008 pounds milk and 1,098 pounds fat.

Butterfat record: Cathedral Rosalie; 5 yrs.' 37. 23,714 pounds milk and 1,213 pounds fat.

365-day, carrying calf 200 days.

Milk and butterfat record is held by Flying Horse Royal Rose 5 yrs.' 47. 22,558 pounds milk and 1,154 pounds fat.

305-day, carrying calf 175 days, 3X milking.

Milk record: Guernsey Goodwill, 6 yrs.' 47. 19,634 pounds milk and 861 pounds fat.

Butterfat record: Sister Sue of Green Acres, 5 yrs.' 48. 16,077 pounds milk and 900 pounds fat.

305-day, carrying calf 175 days, 2X milking.

Milk and butterfat record is held by Elm's Barbara Rose, 6 yrs.' 48. 17,844 pounds milk and 869 pounds fat.

The lifetime production record is held by Caumsett Ida with 194,280.9 pounds milk and 8,513.5 pounds fat.

Table 4.2: The number of records and the average milk, butterfat, and fat percentage for each of the four divisions as of June 1, 1948

Length of Record (Days)	Carried Calf (Days)	Times Milked	Number of Records	Milk Pounds	Butterfat	
					Pounds	Per Cent
365	200	-	29,302	10,716	532	4.9
365	-	-	57,860	10,560	522	4.9
305	175	2X	26,135	8,080	396	4.9
305	175	3X	1,754	9,834	475	4.8

5

The Ayrshire

Characteristics

The Ayrshire is a little larger than the Guernsey. Cows should weight between 1,100 and 1,400 pounds, and bulls between 1,700 and 2,300 pounds. The Ayrshire is noted for its beauty of form. No breed excels it in general style, straightness of top line, levelness of the rump, and symmetry of the udder. Great emphasis has always been laid upon the shape of the udder, and as a result, the Ayrshire is unexcelled in this respect. In recent years the phrase "Vessel Type Ayrshire" has been used to designate cows with this specially desired characteristic.

The Ayrshire is noted for its long, especially curved horns that added materially to the appearance of the animal. The typical hours must possess the right curves, usually attained through special training by use of appropriate apparatus. In dairy conformation the Ayrshire varies from individuals of extreme refinement to others that are quite beefy. The average Ayrshire is more thickly fleshed than either the Jersey or the Guernsey (Fig. 5.1 and 5.2).

Colour

The typical Ayrshrie is red with white spotting. The red varies from light red through brown to a colour almost black which is

Fig. 5.1: The Ayrshire Bull

Fig. 5.2: The Ayrshire Cow

usually referred to as mahogany. The darker colour usually predominates about the head and forequarters, fading into lighter shades toward the rear, although some animals may be of uniform dark colour throughout. The black is dominant in the male and the lighter red is dominant in the female; this accounts for a much large proportion of mahogany coloured males than females.

The extent of white varies greatly. Some individuals are almost entirely white, while others are almost entirely pigmented. The predominating red colour is preferred by most breeders.

Disposition

The Ayrshire is more active than any other breed. The cows are quite nervous and are sometimes hard to manage. On account of their nervous disposition and well-developed horns, considerable damage may be done to members of the herd from horn injuries. The bulls are frequently vicious. These cattle are unexcelled as grazers. Their unusual stamina and activity enables them to obtain adequate nutrients from pastures where some other breeds would starve.

Maturity and longevity

The Ayrshire is somewhat slower in maturing than the Guernsey and earlier than the Holstein. Under normal conditions Ayrshire heifers are sufficiently developed to come into milk when 26 to 28 months of age. Maximum weight and production are attained at from six to seven years of age. Claims are made, although adequate figures to sustain them are not available, that are Ayrshire is the longest lived of any of the breeds. There are as many cows producing and reproducing at 20 or more years of age as are found in any breed, if not more.

Reproduction, veal, and meat

As a reproducer the Ayrshire ranks high. The calves weigh from 70 to 80 pounds at birth and are strong, vigorous, and easy to raise. Ayrshire calves make veal of high quality; but due to a smaller birth weight they are not so desirable for this purpose as are the Holstein and Brown Swiss calves. The Ayrshire ranks high among the dairy breeds for beef. Dry cows, as well as steers and heifers, fatten readily. The fat of the Ayrshire does not possess the high yellow colour of the fat that detracts from the beef value of the Jersey and the Guernsey.

Milk

Judging from the leading records of the breed, the Ayrshire does not reach the high production of either butterfat or milk that some other breeds do. A number of Ayrshires lack somewhat in persistency, although some are excellent in this respect. The milk of the Ayrshire; on an average, contains 4.0 per cent fat, 3.34 per cent protein, and 12.72 per cent total solids. The milk is especially well adapted for market milk and cheese making. Because the fat particles are the smallest found in milk of any breed, claims are made of the superiority of Ayrshire milk for infant and invalid feeding. Claims are also made that the curd of Ayrshire milk is softer than that of milk from other breeds.

Home and Origin

The Ayrshire is the youngest of the dairy breeds. The chief development of the breed took place following 1750, when the other dairy breeds were well established. The Ayrshires were developed in the County of Ayr (Ayrshire), located in southwestern Scotland. There is nothing definitely known about the stock from which the Ayrshire was developed, but it is generally supposed that cattle from Holland (Holstein), the Channel Islands (Guernseys and Jerseys), and Teeswater cattle were used to produce the Ayrshire. The Ayrshire, therefore, has its origin in both the longifrons and the primigenius types.

The climate of Ayr is not favourable to livestock raising because it is cold and damp a great part of the year. In the early development of the breed the forage was scant, as the soil of this part of Scotland is not fertile. The extreme hardiness and rustling ability of the animal undoubtedly is attributable to the character of the country in which she was developed, as only those individuals with unusual ruggedness could have survived to reproduce their kind. Originally the Ayrshires went by the name of Dunlap; later they were known as the Cunningham breed; and not until 1803 were they generally known as Ayrshire.

Importation and distribution

The first importation of Ayrshires was made in 1822. None of these was kept pure. The first Scotch settlers of Canada brought cattle from Ayr with them; but like the first importation into the United States, they were not kept pure. From 1830 to 1860 there were frequent importations of Ayrshires into the United States. Commencing about 1860, Ayrshire importations declined in favour of importations of Holsteins and the Channel Island breeds. Importations are still made from Scotland and Canada.

In the United States Ayrshires are not numerous in New York, the New England states, Pennsylvania, and Ohio. The Ayrshire is the leading dairy breed in Scotland and is numerous in Finland, England, New Zealand, Australia, and eastern Canada.

From 1929 to 1947, 38,968 Ayrshires were imported from Canada. Of these, only 31.3 per cent were registered in the herd books of the Ayrshire Breeders Association even though all importations were purebreds. Since purebreds come in free while commercial cattle are subject to importation duty, it is obvious that most of these cattle were purchased for commercial dairy purposes. In 1947, the total importations from Canada was 3,762 head, of which 1,864 were registered.

Registration

All records are kept by the American Ayrshire Breeders Association, with offices in Brandon, Vermont. This association was organized in 1875. The American Ayrshire Breeders Association, like the other dairy breed organizations, not only keeps the Herd Book records, but also has supervision of the Advanced Registry and engages in promotional work for the breed. To date, the Ayrshire Association has not employed field men for promotional work but has relied upon literature for this purpose. A total of 91,185 males and 361,521 females have been registered by the Association up to 1948. During the depression years, Ayrshire registration held up very well. In 1934, 17,436 males and females were registered; this was the highest number to be registered in one year up to that time.

The increase in annual registrations has been great. In 1947, a total of 30,046 animals were registered by an estimated 10,000 breeders. In 1947, approximately 4,000 breeders were members of the Ayrshire Breeders Association.

Special provisions are made for the registration of polled Ayrshires, by which the symbol X precedes the registration number. In 1947, 103 polled Ayrshires brought the total up to 427.

Testing

The Ayrshire Breeders Association adopted an Advanced Register system in 1902. At that time and for many years thereafter the regulations permitted of four time daily milking and provisions were made for 305- and 365-day records with or without calving requirements. Minimum requirements in milk and butterfat were set up for each of the customary age groups for qualifications for entry in the Advanced Register. With the adoption of the Herd Test plan in 1925, the emphasis was shifted from Advanced Registry until today all testing of Ayrshires is virtually on the Ayrshire Herd Test plan. This breed was the first to adopt such a test plan.

Under the Herd Test, all cows in the herd must be entered on test. Certificates are issued for the herd and each individual cow regardless of the production level. No record of production exceeds 305 days that must be consecutive but may include portions of two lactation periods.

Meritorious Certificates for Individual Cows

Meritorious Certificates are issued for individuals that drop living claves within 14 months from their previous freshening and that on twice daily milking equivalent, produce not less than the following milk and butterfat in 305 consecutive days with average butterfat test of at least 3.9 per cent. The 305 days may be in one or in portions of two lactations.

Age	Milk Pounds	Fat Pounds
Mature	10,000	400
Sr. 4	9,400	376
Jr. 4	8,800	352
Sr. 3	8,200	328
Jr. 3	7,600	304
Sr. 2	7,000	280
Jr. 2	6,400	256

Bulls are admitted to the Advanced Registry when four daughters from four different dams have qualified for entry. Meritorious Herd Tests are accepted on the same basis as the Advanced Register records in qualifying a bull for Advanced Registry.

A total of 66,554 production records have been made that average 9,016 pounds milk and 367.8 pounds butterfat with an average of 4.08 per cent butterfat. In 1947, 12,054 cows were on test which represents a larger proportion of Ayrshires on test than any other breed.

Garclough May Mischief holds the American record for high milk production with 25,329 pounds of milk and 894.9 pounds of fat. The butterfat record is held by Lily of Willowmoor with 955.6 pounds of fat and 22,596 pounds of milk.

The highest producing Ayrshire in Scotland is Nether Graig Janet, who has a record of 30,910 pounds of milk and 1,171.4 pounds of fat.

Approved sire

This is a term applied to Ayrshire bulls that have ten or more tested daughters out of tested dams that met the following requirements:

1. The average of all tested daughters shall be not less than 9,000 pounds milk and 360 pounds fat with a test of not less than 3.9 per cent.
2. The equal parent index of an Approved Sire shall be note less than 8,500 pounds milk and 340 pounds fat with a test of at least 3.9 per cent.
3. At least 60 per cent of the tested daughters shall each have 9,000 or more pounds milk or 360 pounds fat.
4. A least 50 per cent of all registered three year old daughters must be tested. All such daughter in a herd that is on test must be included.

Provisions are made for approving bulls that have daughters in herds not testing in which event 15 daughters will be used as a minimum. All records are computed to mature equivalent twice daily milking basis of not more than 305 days and the first lactation records shall be used except by breeder request when averages of all records of each tested daughter are used in the computation.

Herd Test, Advanced Registry, and Roll of Honor records shall be used. Dairy Herd Improvement Association records may also be used provided the record books are sent in to the Ayrshire Breeders Association for checking and approval.

Approved Dams

To qualify as an Approved Dam an Ayrshire cow must have three or more daughters that are tested and all such meet the following requirements:

1. The average shall be not less than 9,000 pounds milk and 360 pounds fat with at least 3.9 per cent test or at least 10,000 pounds milk and 400 pounds fat if testing less than 3.9 per cent.
2. Not less than 60 per cent of all tested daughters must each produce not less than 8,500 pounds milk and 340 pounds fat.

The types of records used and the method of computation of these records are similar to those specified under Approved Sires. Once either a cow or a bull has become Approved they will retain such designation even though subsequent tested progeny may reduce the requirements below that required for qualification.

Type Classification

In 1942, Type Classification was adopted for cows and in 1947, the system was opened for bulls. A total of 16,297 cows and 312 bulls had been classified to the end of 1947. The breakdown of the numbers and per cent for the various classes are shown in Table 5.1.

Selective registration of bulls

In 1945, the Ayrshire Breeders Association adopted a plan for selective registration of bull claves in which bulls are grouped into three classes:

(1) Standard,

(2) Selected, and

(3) Preferred pedigrees.

Table 5.1: Type Classification

Class	Number	Per cent
Excellent	645	4.0
Very Good	4,588	28.2
Good Plus	6,943	42.6
Good	3,546	21.8
Fair	557	3.4
Total	16,297	100.0

The objective of this programme is to encourage matings which have a better chance of improving production.

Standard pedigree

Any bull whose parents are registered will be registered upon proper application. Such a registration is classed as Standard.

Selected pedigree

A bull upon registration will be given a Selected pedigree when none of the six nearest ancestors (parents and grandparents) show any evidence of low production and where at least satisfactory production is evidenced for at least one parent or two grandparents or satisfactory progeny performance for at least one parent or two grandparents. At least 8,500 pounds milk and 340 pounds butterfat in 305 days on two times daily milking as a mature equivalent is required for a satisfactory rating. Females in the pedigree will be rated satisfactory for the Selected pedigree with this or greater production. Bulls must have five or more daughters that average at least this amount of milk and butterfat. All individuals in the first two generations must meet the minimum set forth above if tested.

Preferred Pedigree

To qualify for the preferred pedigree rating one of four combinations of approved breeding must be met. These four combinations are:

(1) Approved Sire and Approved Dam,

(2) Approved Sire and Approved Maternal Grand Sire and the dam having produced at least 9,000 pounds milk and 360 pounds butterfat in 305 days on twice daily milking and mature equivalent basis,

(3) Approved Sire and the dam producing not less than 9,000 pounds milk and 360 pounds butterfat in 305 days on twice daily milking and mature equivalent basis, and

(4) Approved Dam and sire with at least 5 daughters averaging not less than 9,000 pounds milk and 360 pounds butterfat in 305 days on twice daily milking and mature equivalent basis.

6

The Brown Swiss

Characteristics

The Brown Swiss is the largest and most rugged of the dairy breeds. Cows under normal conditions weigh 1,300 to 1,400 pounds, and bulls weigh 1,800 to 2,500 pounds. Originally the Brown Swiss was regarded as a triple-purpose cow and is still used as such; in her native home, in addition to producing milk, she is used as a beast of burden and is the source of practically all meat used. In America the Brown Swiss is strictly a dairy breed. The head is large and somewhat dished. The bones are heavy and the skin is thick and loose, usually forming heavy folds about the throat and brisket. On an average the Brown Swiss is rougher than the other dairy breeds. However, no breed has made as rapid improvement as the Brown Swiss. Animals shown at the leading shows are as good a type as any other breed. The udders are usually well formed and well attached (Figs. 6.1 and 6.2).

Colour

The colour varies from a light fawn to an almost black, with a mouse colour predominating. The muzzle is encircled by a mealy shaded band and the lips are light in colour. Along the backbone is a stripe of lighter colour which gradually blends with the darker colours of the side. The nose, tongue, switch, and horn

Fig. 6.1: The Brown Swiss Cow

Fig. 6.2: The Brown Swiss Bull

tips are always black. White is absent except on the inguinal region and on the udder. The calves are light in colour when born and become darker as they grow older.

Disposition

The Brown Swiss are docile and not easily excited. They are easy to manage in the everyday routine about the dairy. Frequently, however, Brown Swiss are stubborn and refuse to respond when attempts are made to alter the regular routine, such as changing them to another stall or training them for showing. When once they learn that such things are expected of them, they comply and become co-operative.

While the Brown Swiss are phlegmatic, they are excellent rustlers. In spite of their large size and consequently great nutrient requirements they do well on ordinary pasture. Their general ruggedness enables them to withstand adverse conditions, such as rough treatment and cold, better than members of other dairy breeds.

Maturity and Longevity

The Brown Swiss is the slowest of the dairy breeds to mature. normally, heifers are not sufficiently developed to come into milk until they are 30 to 36 months of age. Cows are not considered mature for official test purposes until they are six years of age, while for all other breeds cows are considered mature for this purpose when they are five years of age.

To compensate for the lateness in maturing, the Brown Swiss live and produce and reproduce longer than individuals of other breeds. Brown Swiss authorities claim a higher proportion of old cows for their breed than is found in other dairy breeds. A 13 year old Brown Swiss cow has produced over 1,000 pounds of butterfat in 365 days.

Reproduction

The Brown Swiss rank high as reproducers. Relatively litter sterility is reported for the breed. The calves are large, strong, and rugged when born and are easy to raise. The average birth weight of the calves ranges from 90 to 95 pounds. It is not uncommon for Brown Swiss calves to weight as much as 120 pounds at birth.

Meat and veal

Because of the large birth weight and white fat, Brown Swiss calves rank among the best for veal production. Among the dairy breeds the Brown Swiss cattle also rank high for beef production.

When they are not milking, they fatten readily to produce beef of fair quality.

Milk

The milk from the Brown Swiss is adapted to a variety of uses. It contains, on the average, 4 per cent fat; this makes it particularly well adapted for market milk, cheese production, and condensed milk, as well as for butter making. The milk is described as white. The fat particles are small and low in yellow colouring matter.

Home and origin

The Brown Swiss is probably the oldest of dairy cattle breeds. They are descendants of *Bos longifrons*, and were developed in the mountain territory in the northeastern part of Switzerland in the Cantons of Zurich, St. Galen, Lucerne, and Schwyz. From the literature it is apparent that the cattle of Switzerland at the time of Caesar answered the description of the present Brown Swiss. The bones found in the ruins of the Swiss Lake dwellers date back to probably 4000 B.C. and resemble closely the skeleton of the modern Brown Swiss.

Conditions in Switzerland

The home of the Brown Swiss is the most rugged country in which agriculture is practiced. The cattle are usually pastured on the mountain slopes, beginning at the foot in the spring and going up the mountainside as the snow recedes. In the fall they are brought down the mountainside and housed in barns located in the valleys. Their feed during the spring and summer months is limited entirely to the grasses on the mountain slopes. In the winter time, they are fed mainly on meadow hay grown in the valleys. Occasionally roots and oil cake are added to the winter's ration.

Today, as for many centuries past, the Swiss are famous for their cheese production; these cheeses are made from the milk produced by the cattle pastured on the mountain slopes. Since only hardy animals, able to withstand frequent exposure to storms and to endure the ruggedness of the country in which they have been developed, could have survived to reproduce, it is easy to understand that the Brown Swiss have the strongest constitution of any of the dairy breeds.

Importation and Distribution

A total of 25 bulls and 160 females has been imported into the United States. The first importation was made in 1869 by H.M. Clark of Massachusetts, and the most recent importation was made in 1931 when four bulls and one heifer were imported. From 1916 to 1931 no importations were made because of the difficulty of getting animals out of Switzerland without going through territory infected with foot and mouth disease.

From the 185 imported animals over 100,000 Brown Swiss have been recorded. Brown Swiss are found in all the states, but they are most numerous in Wisconsin, Illinois, New York, and Michigan. The breed has never experienced a boom, but it has enjoyed a steady growth in which the demand for cattle has exceeded the supply. As a result, the prices paid for Brown Swiss declined but little during the depression years. The Brown Swiss has also experienced a greater percentage increase in registered stock than any other breed.

Record Keeping

All records pertaining to the breed are kept by the Brown Swiss Breeders Association, with headquarters at Beloit, Wisconsin. The organization was formed in 1880, but it did not publish the first Herd Book until 1908. It is the youngest of the major dairy breed associations. The Brown Swiss Association sponsors the monthly publication, The Brown Swiss Bulletin, for the breed. It has also published promotional literature and assisted with prize money at fairs. In 1948 there were about 2,400 members of the Association and about 10,000 active breeders of Brown Swiss cattle. A total of 185,415 females and 89,880 males had been registered to July, 1948. In 1947 alone, 22,469 animals were registered.

Advanced Registry

In 1911 the Brown Swiss Breeders Association adopted a

system of Advanced Registry known as the Register of Production. In 1932 a Herd Improvement Test, a test similar to the herd test plans of the other breed associations, was adopted.

Four classes of records are recognized by the Register of Production. These are the yearly test, the ten months' (305 days) test, the 365 day farmers' class, and the 305 day farmers' class. In order to qualify for entry in the Register of Production in the 365 day test, the individual must produce at least 250.5 pounds of fat when 30 months of age (the youngest age provided for) and an additional 1 pound of fat for each day older than 30 months up to five years and six months, when the requirement is 360 pounds of fat. To qualify for entry in the 10 months' division, a minimum butterfat production is required which is 30 pounds less than the requirements for the corresponding ages in the 365 day test. In addition, a living calf must be dropped within 14 months from the date of the last calving.

The requirements for entry into the Farmers' division, 365 and 305 day tests, are the same respectively as those listed in the preceding paragraph. For the Farmers' class, cows may not be milked more than twice daily except for the first 15 days, when they may be milked three times daily. For the other Register of Production Classes the limitations as to the number of milkings daily is four.

Up to October 1947, there were a total of 1,815 Register of Production records of all classes. In recent years Herd Improvement Records have been stressed resulting in a great increase in the numbers tested on this plan.

Tables 6.1 and 6.2 present the numbers tested in each age class with the average milk, fat and fat percentage for 2 X milkings.

A total of 18 cows have completed yearly records above 1,000 pounds butterfat, the ten high of which shown in table 6.3.

A total of 63 cows have produced more than 4,000 pounds of fat in a lifetime up to 1948. Twenty of this group were added during the fiscal year ending September 30, 1947. The highest lifetime record is held by Swiss Betty I, 19935, with 171,336.4 pounds milk and 7,464.59 pounds butterfat in 4,140 days.

Table 6.1: Herd improvement records production averages 305-day 2 X lactation records

No. Cows	Pounds Milk	Ave. Per Cent	Pounds Fat
Mature			
3,538	10,331.5	3.91	404.47
5 Year			
1,347	9,878.3	3.99	394.31
Sr. 4 Year 605	9,691.6	4.00	387.46
Jr. 4 Year 1,042	9,314.2	3.89	362.56
Sr. 3 Year 1,105	9,022.2	4.01	361.69
Jr. 3 Year 901	8,630.0	3.80	327.85
Sr. 2 Year 1,079	7,867.8	4.06	319.33
Jr. 2 Year 1,291	7,526.0	4.06	305.91
12 Years and Over 263	9,446.3	3.87	365.43

Table 6.2: Herd improvement records production averages 305-day 3 X lactation records

No. Cows	Pounds Milk	Average Per Cent	Pounds Fat
Mature			
285	13,137.1	4.00	524.83
5 Year			
102	12,808.1	3.93	503.32
Sr. 4 Year 69	12,462.2	4.01	499.92
Jr. 4 Year 71	11,846.9	4.00	473.87
Sr. 3 Year 68	11,820.0	4.01	474.36
Jr. 3 Year 63	11,03‾ 7	3.97	438.50
Sr. 2 Year 71	9,574.1	4.15	397.65
Jr. 2 Year 71	9,086.0	3.95	359.30
12 Years and Over 11	11,778.2	3.82	449.51

Table 6.3: Brown Swiss cows having produced 1,000 pounds butterfat

Name of Cow	Age	Pounds Milk	Pounds Fat
Illini Nellie 26578	8-4-2	29,569.5	1,200.41
Mary's Nell 36395	6-11-17	29,487.2	1, 109.71
Swiss Valley Girl 10th 7887	12-4-15	27,513.6	1,106.33
Jane of Vernon 29496	4-7-18	23,569.0	1,075.58
Illini Nellie 26578	9-10-5	27,897.6	1,062.80
June's College Girl 11427	5-11-25	24,571.6	1,062.30
Royal's Dominie of Lee's Hill 66540	7-7-4	24,978.4	1,056.54
Royal's Dominie of Lee's Hill 66540	9-2-7	25,437.2	1,047.93
June's College Girl 11427	10-7-12	24,167.4	1,043.02
Jane of Vernon 29496	10-11-12	21,880.2	1,039.08

Type Classification

In 1942 the Brown Swiss Cattle Breeders Association, adopted a type classification programme. Since that time up to the end of the fiscal year 1946-1947, a total of 8,674 cows were classified. Bulls are not classified, and cows that have received ratings of Excellent and Very Good are reclassified on reclassification of the herd. In rating Brown Swiss cows, the classifying judge must ascribe a classification value to each of the following: general appearance, with subratings for: legs and feet, rump, dairy character, and body capacity; and mammary system, with subratings for fore udder and rear udder.

The percentage distribution of the 8,674 cows classified for each of the six classes is given in Table 6.4.

Table 6.4: Percentage Distribution of the 8,674 Cows

Class	Classification Rating	General Appearance	Mammary System
Excellent	1.2	1.8	1.7
Very Good	22.9	24.5	18.5

Class	Classification Rating	General Appearance	Mammary System
Good Plus	47.9	38.8	46.1
Good	25.4	23.4	29.1
Fair	2.7	1.7	4.5
Poor	.0	.0	.6

The Brown Swiss Cattle Breeders Association have adopted the standard score card.

7

The Milking Shorthorn

Characteristics

The Milking Shorthorn ranks with the Holstein and the Brown Swiss in size. Normal mature cows weigh from 1,400 to 1,600 pounds, with individuals weighing over a ton. Bulls weigh 2,200 pounds and upward. Either polled or horned Shorthorns may be Milking Shorthorns. Up to 1935 no distinction was made in registration between milking and beef types. Beginning in 1935, the breeder who wishes to have his cattle recognized as Milking Shorthorns declares them to be of the milking type, and the registry certificate issued bears the words "Milking Shorthorn" on the face.

The Milking Shorthorn may be white, red and white, or roan in colour. The red varies from a moderately light shade to a fairly dark shade. When individuals are red and white, the red usually predominates, and the legs are red.

Type

There is no sharp line of demarcation between the beef Shorthorn and the dairy Shorthorn. Much variation is found in the type of the Milking Shorthorn, from extreme beef to extreme dairy types. Many of the highest producing Shorthorns resemble the Holstein except for colour. The standards for the breed, however, call for a true dual-purpose individual. (Fig. 7.1 and 7.2)

Fig. 7.1: The Milking Shorthorn Cow

Fig. 7.2: The Milking Shorthorn Bull

Dairy Characteristics

For reasons just mentioned, the Milking Shorthorn is the most variable of the breeds for milk and butterfat production. Many breeders have developed herds with extreme dairy conformation and high production. Others change the designation from dairy to beef and *vice versa* periodically, depending upon market conditions; these breeders frequently alternate in using bulls of the milking and beef types. While the Milking Shorthorn people aim to breed cows that are intermediate between beef and dairy types, they point with pride to the fact that an Australian Shorthorn cow, Melba 15th of Darbalara, for many years held the world's record over all breeds for butterfat production, with 1,614.1 pounds. The avowed aim of the breeders of Milking Shorthorns is to breed cows that will produce 8,000 to 10,000 pounds of milk testing 4 per cent fat annually when the cows are mature. Under average farm conditions 6,000 pounds of milk and 240 pounds of fat would be considered good.

The milk resembles that of the Ayrshire. The fat content averages 4 per cent; the fat particles are small; and the colour is rather low. The milk is particularly adapted for market milk, condensed milk, and cheese production.

Because there is a great variation in the inheritance of beef and dairy tendencies the breeders of Milking Shorthorns have a difficult problem in maintaining the dual-purpose type. The tendencies are for individuals to revert either to strictly beef or to extreme dairy types. Milking Shorthorns are not so persistent as the more highly specialized dairy breeds.

Beef Characteristics

The Milking Shorthorn cows excel all other milking breeds for beef. They usually lose flesh when in full milk, but they fatten rapidly when dry. The steers grow rapidly and make beef of the highest quality.

Calves and Reproduction

The weight of the calves at birth normally varies from 75 to 80 pounds. This is about 6 per cent of the mature weight, or the smallest value for any breed. Because the birth weight of the Shorthorn calves is small, they are not so well adapted for veal production as the Holstein or the Brown Swiss calves. The Shorthorn ranks only average as reproducers. The calves, however, are vigorous and quite easily raised. In maturity they rank with the Holsteins. Heifers of normal growth and development come into milk at 28 to 30 months of age.

Adaptation

The Shorthorn is particularly well adapted to large farms where both milk and beef production is desired. On such farms a number of the superior milk producers may be selected for milking and the rest used for strictly beef production. By careful selection and use of the proper bulls, a high producing herd may be established under such conditions.

Origin and Development

As for some of the other breeds, the origin of the Shorthorn is obscure. Its native home is in northeastern England in the Counties of Durham, Northumberland, and York. In the past they were also known as Durhams. It is generally believed that the early invaders of England, particularly the Romans and the Normans, brought cattle from the Continent, and that these cattle had a large part in the development of the Shorthorn. Later Flemish cattle were brought over from Holland and crossed with the native cattle, and possibly other cattle were also used.

At the beginning of the eighteenth century the cattle from which the Shorthorns have been developed were mediocre and lacked uniformity. It was through the efforts of great breeders that the superior breed of cattle now known as the Shorthorn was developed. The accomplishments of the breeders who developed the Shorthorn breed are classic; and as a result the names and work of Charles and Robert Colling, Amos Cruickshank, Thomas Booth and his sons John and Richard, and Thomas Bates have become historic in the livestock field. Of these the work of Thomas Bates is of particular interest to those interested in dairying.

Thomas Bates selected and bred for high milk production, while the rest of the great breeders selected mainly for superior beef qualities. Although not all the Milking Shorthorns trace back to the breeding of Bates, most of them do, and the principles he followed in establishing a high producing strain of Shorthorns are still sound and practiced by the best breeders. Bates began his breeding operations about 1790, or about ten years after the beginning of Shorthorn improvement, which was started with the work of the Colling brothers.

Bates selected and bred Shorthorns for a combination of dairy and beef qualities. Only those animals that met with his standard were selected for breeding purposes, and inbreeding was extensively practiced. He developed about six families, of which the Duchess family was the most noted. As a result of the intensive inbreeding, considerable loss in fertility was experienced. After the death of Bates in 1849, the herd was dispersed, and no great breeder carried on the programme developed by him. His results, however, were so outstanding and the influence so great that most of the Milking Shorthorns of today trace back to his cattle.

Importation and Distribution

The first Shorthorns were brought to America in 1783 by Gough and Miller of Virginia. The first pedigreed Shorthorns were imported in 1817 by S.M. Hopkins of New York. Since that time thousands of Shorthorns have been imported. Until recently no distinction was made between dairy and beef types, and therefore there is no way of knowing what proportion of the importations were Milking Shorthorns.

In England the Milking Shorthorn is a major dairy breed. In the United States the majority of Shorthorns are of the beef type. Not until 1935 was any attempt made to ascertain the relative numbers of dairy and beef Shorthorns. Since then about 30 per cent of all Shorthorns registered have been designated Milking Shorthorn. A total of 25,072 such animals were registered from April 1, 1935, to August 20, 1937. Milking Shorthorns are moist numerous in Minnesota, Iowa, Illinois, Wisconsin, Kansas, and Michigan.

Breed organization

The records of the Milking Shorthorns up to 1948 were kept by the American Shorthorn Breeders' Association, with headquarters at Chicago. The Milking Shorthorns were registered in the same herd book as the beef types. The Milking Shorthorn breeders are represented upon the board of directors of the American Shorthorn Breeders' Association in proportion to the number of milking type cattle registered. In 1948, the Milking Shorthorn people set up their own herd books and formed a society known as the American Milking Shorthorn Association, with offices in Chicago. All animals registered as Milking Shorthorns in the American Shorthorn Herd Books and their offspring are eligible to be registered in the new Herd Book.

Advanced Registry

In 1912 an Advanced Registry system was adopted by the American Milking Shorthorn Club. This is known as the Record of Merit; and in order to be eligible for admittance thereto, a cow must produce 5,250 pounds of milk and 210 pounds of fat in 365 days at the age of 30 months. The requirement increases until the cow is five years of age, when she must produce 8,000 pounds of milk and 300 pounds of fat.

If a living calf is produced within 14 months from the previous calving, entrance to the Record of Merit may be attained from a production of 90 per cent of the 365 day requirements in 305 days. This is also known as the double letter record.

Four classes of records are accepted, each of which is designated by a letter. Class A records are supervised by the State Agricultural College and are also known as official tests. Class B are supervised by the tester of a cow testing association and are known as semiofficial tests. Class C are privately kept records. All three of these classes of records require that daily milk weights be kept by the owner and forwarded monthly to the association. A fourth class, CT, also known as the Dairy Herd Improvement Association Records, does not require daily milk records, but a monthly report of the testers' findings is necessary (See Table 7.1).

Table 7.1: Ten highest milking shorthorn fat records

Name	Pounds of Milk	Pounds of Fat	Class
Ruth B 568209	21,641.0	956.70	B
Mountain Princess 1635668	21,023.2	853.51	A
White Molly 1415398	18,346.3	806.88	A
Lady Ury 1506672	17,723.0	800.48	C
Bonvue Rose Meade 1284449	20,429.9	785.55	A
Trixie 3d 1329412	16,119.8	770.21	B
Allington Kirklevington 1542774	20,543.1	754.78	A
Trixie 3d 1329412	16,543.6	745.93	B
Queenston Belle 764413	15,203.4	744.90	C
Glenside Pearl Clay 921066	18,005.6	719.61	B

Up to June 1947 a total of 17,205 cows have both milk and fat records averaging 324.7 pounds of fat, and 7,835 cows have milk records averaging 8,188 pounds of milk.

Grading up Plan

The Milking Shorthorn Society has adopted a plan making it possibly successive use of purebred sires to develop animals that are eligible for registry. This plan is similar to plans adopted by most British breed societies. The stages of improvement and registry are as follows:

Class A	Foundation cows that have freshened once or more, duly inspected and approved as being of suitable Milking Shorthorn type and conformation and rating Good Plus or better under regular classification requirements. Such cows must also have completed a record of production equal to the standard Record of Merit for the breed according to the age of the animal.
Class B	Females only, the progeny of Class A cows and sired by a Registered Milking Shorthorn Bull.
Class C	Females only, the progeny of Class B cows and sired by Registered Milking Shorthorn Bull.
Class D	Females only, the progeny of Class C cows and sired by Registered Milking Shorthorn Bull.
Class E	Females only, the progeny of Class D cows and sired by Registered Milking Shorthorn Bull- are eligible for registry in the official herd book of the American Milking Shorthorn Society and must be entered therein for future registry of progeny as purebreds. Both males and females from Class E dams are eligible for registry.

Scale of points for Milking Shorthorn Cows

Head: Feminine in character, finely cut, not too short; horns flat and well set on without coarseness at base (if polled, head tapering from a line drawn across it, just above the eyes, to a rounded protuberance on top, as if an orange were under the skin at that

point, ears held normally); forehead broad; eyes large and of gentle expression; nostrils wide and expansive; nose clean; throat clearly defined	10
Neck: Lean but not weak	4
Withers: Not too wide	4
Shoulders: Flat and sloping	4
Chest: Broad and deep, not running wide at the girth	4
Barrel: Hooped, well ribbed up, and of good depth	10
Back: Broad over the loins, the top line being straight from withers to the tail	5
Hips: Wide apart but not too prominent	4
Rump: Long, broad, and level, with tail fine and neatly set in	6
Hindquarters: Wide, the legs when viewed from behind being straight and without nearness when walking	6
Udder: Well carried, thin skinned with pronounced milk veins, large in capacity (not fleshy or split up between the quarters), extending high up at the back, hanging almost perpendicularly, and running well forward in line with the belly; tests of good and even size, squarely placed and wide apart; milk veins about the abdomen tortuous and highly developed	15
Eacutcheon: Even and well defined (there being an absence coarse hair between its upward growth and the downward growth of the ordinary coat), high and wide horizontal markings in addition to vertical being of especial importance	2
Skin: Mellow, flexible to the touch, fairly thin, carrying a good coat of hair. Patchy and faded colours are to be avoided	8
Flesh: Level, with an entire absence of unevenness or cushions	8
Carriage and Action in Walking: Gay and agile	5
General Appearance: Symmetrical, combining size and scope	5
	100

Scale of points for Milking Shorthorn Bulls

Head: Masculine in character, finely cut, not too short, horns flat and well set on without coarseness at base (if polled, head tapering from a line drawn across it, just above the eyes, to a rounded protuberance on top, as if an orange were under the skin at that point, ears held normally); forehead broad; eyes prominent and lively; nostrils wide and expansive; nose clean; throat clearly defined	10

Neck: Long, arched, muscular, not heavy	10
Withers: Strong but not too wide	4
Shoulders: Flat and sloping, indicating style and liberty	4
Chest: Broad and deep, not running wide at the girth	4
Barrel: Hooped, well ribbed up, and of good length	10
Back: Broad over the loins, the top line being straight from withers to the tail	10
Hips: Wide apart, but not too prominent	4
Rump: Long, broad, and level, with tail neatly set in	6
Hindquarters: Wide, the legs when viewed from behind being straight and without nearness when walking	6
Rudimentary Teats: Well developed, set horizontally, wide apart and away from the scrotum	8
Escutcheon: Even and well defined, the horizontal marking high up, the more pronouncedly vertical the better	2
Skin: Mellow, flexible to the touch, fairly thin, carrying a good coat of hair. Patchy and faded colours are to be avoided	8
Flesh: Level, with an entire absence of unevenness or cushions	10
Carriage and Action in Walking: Gay and vigorous	5
General Appearance: Symmetrical, combining size and scope	5
	100

8

The Red Polled

Characteristics

The Red Polled are smaller than the shorthorn and larger than most of the dairy breeds. The desired weight for mature cows is from 1,300 to 1,500 pounds. Mature bulls should weigh from 1,800 to 2,000 pounds, and individuals sometimes weigh as much as 2,500 pounds. As is indicated by the name, they are hornless. Any sign of horns or scurs disqualifies an animal for registry.

Colour

The colour may be any shade of red, a cherry red being preferred. Light or very dark shades are not uncommon, but they are not considered desirable by the breeders. No white is tolerated except for the switch of the tail, the udder, and the inguinal region. While dark or cloudy noses are found in the breed, they are considered objectionable. The nose should be a clear flesh colour.

Type

The Red Polled is a true dual-purpose breed (Fig. 8.1 and 8.2). The most desired type in the breed is intermediate between the angular dairy type and the blocky beef type. These cattle are rounded over the withers, have somewhat outcurving thighs, and are generally fairly well covered with flesh. One of the real problems

Fig. 8.1: The Red Polled Cow

Fig. 8.2: The Red Polled Bull

in breeding Red Polled cattle is to keep them midway between the dairy and beef types, as the tendency is to go to either the extreme beef or the dairy type.

The Red Polled have rather straight lines, and on the average deviate from the true type no more than older established breeds. The udders, however, frequently lack in symmetry, having a tendency to quarter and divide between the halves. The teats are sometimes irregular in shape and not squarely placed upon the udder.

Temperament

The Red Polled are active yet easily handled, and are not easily excited or disturbed; these are points in favour of the breed for ordinary farm conditions. They are generally considered excellent grazers.

Maturity and reproduction

Red Polled are average from the standpoint of maturity. Heifers of normal growth and development come into milk between 27 to 30 months of age. No reliable data are available as to how the Red Polled rank as reproducers.

Meat and veal production

The Red Polled rank high among milking cattle for beef production. The steers are usually blocky and dress out high. Red Polled steers are recorded as having won first place in national carcass contests. when they are through milking, the cows fatten rapidly to produce satisfactory beef. The calves are not so large at birth as are the calves of the Holstein and Brown Swiss breeds, and therefore are not so desirable for veal production, although they rank high in this respect.

Milk

The Red Polled rank lower than any of the strictly dairy breeds for butterfat production. In milk production they exceed only the Jersey and Guernsey breeds. A good average yearly milk production under average farm conditions is from, 5,000 to 6,000 pounds of milk and from 200 to 250 pounds of butterfat.

The milk averages 4.3 per cent of fat; this makes it ideal for market milk, cheese production, or condensed milk. The milk is moderate in colour, ranking with the Ayrshire in this respect.

Origin and development

The Red Polled originated and developed in Norfolk and Suffolk counties in eastern England. The foundation stock from which they were developed is unknown. Some claim that the breed has been developed from cattle brought over by the Danes in the fifth century, while others claim that they have been developed mainly from the Galloway breed.

The modern Red Polled is the result of crossing the cattle of Norfolk and Suffolk. Up until 1862 the cattle from these two counties went under separate names- Norfolk Polled and Suffolk

Polled. In 1862 they were recognized as one breed and called the Norfolk and Suffolk Polled cattle. In 1882 the name was shortened to the Red Polled.

According to the history of the breed, the cattle in Norfolk were developed along different lines than were those of Norfolk until the beginning of the nineteenth century. From the beginning of the nineteenth century, by intercrossing, the cattle in the two counties became identical. The earliest records show that the Suffolk cattle were exceptional milkers, with the milk having rather low fat content, and that they were polled. They are also reputed to have been of rather extreme dairy conformation.

The early Norfolk cattle, on the other hand, were more rugged and more beefy in character. As late as 1800 the cattle in Norfolk were partly polled and partly horned. They are also reputed to have produced higher testing milk than the Suffolk cattle, although not so much. The crossing of the cattle from the two counties resulted in the breed now known as the Red Polled, the main characteristics of which are intermediate between the dairy and beef breeds.

Importation and Distribution

While cattle from both Norfolk and Suffolk were brought over to this country by the earliest settlers, none of them were kept pure. According to Eckles, the early importations of these cattle were responsible for the polled cattle in New England in the early days. The first importation into this country that was kept pure was made in 1873 by G.F. Tabor of New York. Several other importations were made up to 1890 from which the Red Polled in America have been developed.

Excluding their native home, the Red Polled are confined to Australia, New Zealand, and America. In the United States they are confined largely to the Midwest and the Southwest. The states leading in the number of Red Polls are Minnesota, Illinois, Iowa, Michigan, Texas, Kansas, Indiana, Nebraska, North Dakota, and Ohio.

Registration

The records of the breed are kept by the Red Polled Cattle

Club of America, which was organized in 1883. The association has no permanent office, the headquarters changing with each change of secretary. Up to August, 1937, a total of 141,298 head had been registered, of which 83,120 were females and 58,178 were males.

Advanced Registry

In 1908 the Red Polled Cattle Club adopted an Advanced Registry plan. In order to be eligible for entry in the Advanced Register, a mature cow must produce 300 pounds of fat and 6,000 pounds of milk. To date 1,197 cows have qualified. These average 8,827 pounds of milk and 381.2 pounds of fat (See Table 8.1).

Table 8.1: Ten highest producing red polled cows

Name	Pounds of Milk	Pounds of Fat
Jean Duluth Beauty 31725	20,280.6	891.58
R.L. Josephine 52620	15,310.2	772.14
R.L. Lilly Ella 52624	17,045.7	723.67
R.L. Dorcas 58725	15,313.1	707.36
Jean Duluth Pear 28991	16,598.4	707.24
R.L. Dewie 72432	13,512.2	703.10
R.L. Paulina 62208	14,123.5	700.14
Lula 63235	14,883.5	688.04
Golden Plutie 47408	11,733.9	677.85
R.L. Peggy 72438	16,335.10	631.01

Score Cards

The Scale of Points for the Red Polled differ rather fundamentally from the Scale of Points of the strictly dairy breeds in the desired qualifications of many parts. The Red Polled Scale of Points calls for more fleshing, and a rounding of parts that should be angular for the strictly dairy breeds. The red Polled should be rounding over the shoulders and hind quarters, with good covering of flesh over the hips and back. The Red Polled Scale of Points also lays slightly less stress on mammary development.

9

The Lesser Breeds

While the breeds previously discussed make up nearly all of the strictly dairy cattle in the United States, several other breeds have representatives that are strictly dairy in character. The most important of the minor dairy breeds is the Dutch Belted, followed by the Red Danes, French Canadian, and the Dexter and Kerry breeds.

THE DUTCH BELTED

Characteristics

The chief distinguishing characteristic of the Dutch Belted breed is the silvery white belt around the middle of an otherwise cola black animal. No black is tolerated on this belt, which begins immediately back of the shoulder and sometimes extends back to the hook bones. The only other white on these cattle is the small amount sometimes found on the feet. The belt may be of varying widths, but of the animal to be eligible for registry, is must be at least 6 inches wide at its narrowest point.

The Dutch Belted is a little smaller in size than the Holstein, which they otherwise resemble to a considerable degree. Mature cows weigh from 1,100 to 1,400 pounds, and bulls from 1,600 to

2,200 pounds. As a rule the Dutch Belted is finer boned than the Holstein and not quite so deep of middle (Figs 9.1 and 9.2). The calves weigh from 65 to 90 pounds at birth and are vigorous and easy to raise. The body fat is said to be white, making presentable veal and beef carcasses from that standpoint.

The milk, containing 4.0 per cent of fat with low colour, resembles that of the Ayrshire. The fat particles are small.

Origin and History

The exact origin of the Dutch Belted is obscure. It is generally believed that they sprang from the black and white cattle of Holland. Some authorities claim that they were in existence as early as the sixteenth century. Until recently they have been entirely in the hands of the nobility in Holland. While so confined, the main objective in breeding was to fix the belted character. In Holland they are known as the Lakenwield breed.

The first importation into the United States was made in 1838. In 1840 the most important importation was made when P.T. Barnum brought over a number of head to be used for show purposes. A total of 69 animals have been imported.

Dutch Belted cattle are found in most states but the numbers are few New York, New Jersey, and Florida have the largest numbers.

Record Keeping

Registration, transfer, and recording of Official Test records is done by the Dutch Belted Cattle Association. This association, organized in 1886, has its offices at Buchanan, Michigan.

In 1920 the Association adopted an Advanced Registry system. Up to January, 1935, 99 cows had been admitted. These average 10,570 pounds of milk, 417 pounds of fat, and a 3.94 fat percentage. The highest record cow of the breed is Loraine of Brunswick, with 816.5 pounds of fat and 18,211 pounds of milk.

Scale of points for Dutch Belted cows

Points		Count
1	Body colour black, with a clearly defined continuous white belt. The belt to be of medium width, beginning behind the shoulder and extending nearly to the hips	8
2	Head comparatively long and somewhat dishing; broad between the eyes. Poll, prominent; muzzle, fine; dark tongue	6
3	Eyes black, full, and mild. Horns long compared with their diameter	4
4	Neck fine and moderately thin, and should harmonize in symmetry with the head and shoulders	6
5	Shoulders fine at the top, becoming deep and broad as they extend backward and downward, with a low chest	4
6	Barrel large and deep with well-developed abdomen; ribs well rounded and free from fat	10
7	Hips broad and chine level, with full loin	10
8	Rump high, long, and broad	6
9	Hindquarters long and deep, rear line incurving. Tail long, slim, tapering to a full switch	8
10	Legs short, clean, standing well apart	3
11	Udder large, well-developed front and rear. Teats of convenient size and wide apart; mammary veins large, long, and crooked, entering large orifices	20
12	Escutcheon	2
13	Hair fine and soft; skin of moderate thickness, of a rich dark or yellow colour	3
14	Quiet disposition and free from excessive fat	4
15	General condition and apparent constitution	6
	Perfection	**100**

Scale of points for Dutch Belted Bulls

The scale of points for males shall be the same as those given for females, except that No. 11 shall be omitted and the bull credited 10 points for size and wide spread and placing of rudimentary teats, and 10 additional points for perfection of belt.

Fig. 9.1: A typical Dutch Belted Bull

Fig. 9.2: A typical Dutch Belted Cow

FRENCH-CANADIAN

While there are but few French-Canadian cattle in the United States,. this breed merits consideration because it is the only breed of diary cattle developed in America. The French-Canadian breed has been developed around Quebec from importations of cattle from France made by the early French settlers at Quebec. The breed originates from the Normandy and Brittany cattle of France and is, therefore, closely related to both the Guernsey and Jersey breeds.

French-Canadian cattle are of the same size and general body conformation as the Jersey. They are, however, somewhat rougher, and the udders lack the symmetry of the Jerseys. They are very hardy and excellent grazers. The milk averages 4.5 per cent fat. In colour they are mostly solid black, although some individuals have a light band around the muzzle and a light strip along the back.

In certain parts of the Province of Quebec, French-Canadian is the predominating breed. A few are found in the northeastern part of the United States. There is no registry association in the United States. In Canada the affairs of the breed are looked after by the French-Canadian Herd Book Association, with headquarters in Quebec. An Advanced Register was established in Canada in 1907. No large records have as yet been reported.

THE DEXTER AND THE KERRY

The Dexter and the Kerry deserve mention because at one time there was a registry association for these two breeds of cattle in the United States. The association has been disbanded for several years because of lack of interest in these breeds.

The Kerry originated in Kerry County, Ireland, where it is favoured by small farmers. It is somewhat smaller than the Jersey, averaging about 900 pounds and is clean cut and of strictly dairy conformation. These cattle are solid black, except for occasional white spots in the inguinal region and on the udder. They produced a moderate amount of milk averaging about 4 per cent fat.

The Dexter is an offshoot of the Kerry and differs from it in that the legs are much shorter and the total size somewhat smaller. The mating of Dexter to Dexter produces on an average one Kerry, two Dexters, and one so-called "Bulldog" calf which is born prematurely and dead. A recessive gene when present in the homozygous conditions responsible for the Bulldog calf. When in the heterozygous condition this gene is responsible for the short-legged condition that is characteristic of the Dexter cattle.

THE RED DANES

The dominant breed of dairy cattle in Denmark is the Red Dane. This breed was developed in Denmark to suit the special conditions of that country. The Red Dane is solid red and horned.

Because of long selection and breeding the Red Danes in their native country are uniform in size, type, and in the characteristics of their milk. The fat percentage of the milk is 4 per cent. The more highly developed dairy breeds will have members that exceed the best of the Red Danes in production capacity but it is alleged that there are fewer poor producers among the Red Danes (Figs. 9.3 and 9.4).

Fig. 9.3: A typical Red Dane bull.

Fig. 9.4: A typical Red Dane cow.

10

Types of Dairy Farming and Breed Selection

Before discussing the choice of a breed for dairy purposes, it is well to consider the different types of dairy farming, as the choice of a breed is influenced to a certain extent by the type of dairying that is to be practiced. Dairy farming varies widely with different conditions. Although not all dairy farms can be put definitely into any one of the different classes, in general dairy farms may be classified on at least three bases: the intensity with which dairying is practiced, the kind of cattle used, and the product marketed.

DAIRY FARMS

On the basis of intensity

On the basis of intensity dairy farms may be divided into three groups. These groups are specialized dairy farms, diversified farms, and farms where dairying is but a side line.

The specialized dairy farms are those on which the major or sole income is derived from the dairy. This type of farm is common around large cities, to which it supplies milk, in the dairy regions where cheese and condensed milk are made, and in many sections where butter is produced. Some of the specialized dairies produce no feed. These dairies are usually located close to large cities with good markets, where the land is too expensive to use for producing feed for cattle. The increased cost of production incurred by having to purchase all the feed used is offset by favourable location to the market. Another group of specialized farms grows only the roughage needed for the dairy and purchases most or all of the concentrate feeds. These farms, too, are usually located near large cities where the acreage is limited. A third group produces all the feed needed for the dairy. The specialized dairy farms in the Midwest fall largely into this group. On farms of this type the size of the herd is determined by the amount of feed that can be grown on the land. It is on this type of dairy farm that the most economical production of milk is possible.

Diversified dairy farms are those on which dairying is not the sole source of income but constitutes one of the important sources of revenue. This type of farm is very common in the corn belt. In addition to income from the dairy, such other farm enterprises as growing hogs, poultry, horses, sheep, and cash crops are important sources of income.

The third type of dairy farm is than on which the income from the sale of dairy products is merely incidental. It may come from surpluses of a few cows kept mainly to supply the household with milk and cream. Farms producing beef cattle may milk a few of the higher producing cows and sell the cream. Frequently such farms milk cows only when the butterfat prices are high or when other sources of income from the farm have failed. Others practice milking a few cows year in and year out regardless of the price condition. This type of dairy farm, found chiefly in the Western and Southwestern states, constitutes an important source of butter.

On the basis of kind of cattle kept

Dairy farms may be classified on the basis of whether the cows are raised on the farm or are purchased for the herd. Farms on which dairy cattle are raised fall into three classes, depending upon whether purebreds, grades, or nondescripts are raised.

Purebreds comprise 4.7 per cent of all dairy cattle, according to government estimates. They are important not because of numbers, but because grade herds, which produce a large part of the dairy products of the country, are dependent upon purebred bulls for existence. There are several types of purebred herds.

With some herds the sale of milk or cream is the main source of income, and the sale of surplus cattle is more or less incidental. With others the emphasis is placed upon the sale of breeding stock, and the income from the sale of milk and cream becomes more incidental. Some are kept as a fancier's hobby, elaborate setups being maintained for the production of show cattle as the chief objective. Those fanciers who carry on a sound breeding programme for breed improvement do so often at great expense in costs of herd bulls and testing expense, but they do render outstanding service to the dairy cattle enterprise.

Grades comprise from 80 to 85 per cent of all dairy cattle in this country and are the source of a larger proportion of the total milk and cream supply. The majority of specialized dairy farms are stocked with grades of the special dairy breeds; these grades comprise about two-thirds of all grade dairy cattle. The other third of the grade population consists of members of the dual-purpose types.

Non-descripts are cattle lacking sufficient of the characteristics of any breed to be classified as belonging to a breed. This group comprises about 11 per cent of the total dairy cattle population of the United States. In this group are found the lowest producers and in general the most undesirable of dairy cattle. While members of this group are found everywhere, they are the most common on the non-specialized dairy farms.

On the type of dairy farm on which no calves are raised, all milking cows are purchased either as springers or as fresh cows. When the milk production of any cow drops below the point of being profitable, the cow is sold for slaughter, and a fresh cow is purchased for replacement. This type of dairying is limited to the production of market milk.

On the Basis of the Type of Market

All dairy farms can be classified as selling either milk or cream. A few sell both.

Whole milk is sold from the farm for market milk, cheese manufacture, condensed milk, casein, and dried milk. Approximately one-half of the milk produced for sale is sold off the farm as whole milk. Farms where all the milk is sold as whole milk are located chiefly around large cities and in cheese-producing and condensed-milk areas. In some butter-producing areas the cream is sold for butterfat, and part or all of the skim milk is sold for the manufacture of dried skim milk and casein.

About one-half of the milk produced for sale is used for butter making; it is sold either as cream to butter factories or in the form of butter made on the farm. Where this is practiced, the skim milk is available on the farm for feeding purposes. Farms in this class usually keep poultry or hogs to utilize the skim milk.

CHOOSING THE DAIRY BREED

The most important consideration in establishing a high producing herd of dairy cattle is the individual animal. The variation between individual within any one breed is infinitely greater than variations between breeds. There are, however, a number of factors of considerable importance to be taken into account when selecting a dairy breed. The important considerations, as well as of some of the claims for superiority that cannot be substantiated, made by some breed organizations, are given under the following headings:

1. Personal preference
2. Breed predominating in the community
3. Type of market
4. Climate
5. Grazing
6. Demand for surplus stock
7. Efficiency of digestion
8. Maintenance requirements
9. Utilization of roughage
10. Vigor of calves
11. Early maturity
12. Beef value of cows
13. Dual-purpose cows

Personal preference

One is likely to become enthusiastic over a breed for which he has a personal preference, and enthusiasm may be the deciding factor in carrying the enterprise through to success. Most people who like livestock are capable of transferring their personal preferences from one breed to another. However, some people are so prejudiced in favour of one breed, because of early contacts with that breed, that it is difficult for them to do anything but criticize the other breeds.

Breed Predominating in the Community

Anyone starting dairy farming would do well to select the predominating breed in the community. Breeders of one breed of cattle naturally fall into a fraternity because of the many common interests, and there are many advantages in being a member of such a fraternity. Again, the breed most prevalent in the community has considerable advantage when surplus cattle are to be marketed. Buyers are more likely to come to a community where there are large numbers of the breed of cattle in which they are interested. To name the communities in the United States that have become famous for their cattle would require a volume. In Wisconsin, for instance, Ft. Atkinson, Fond du Lac, and Barron County are known all over the United States for the numbers and quality of their cattle. In the case of these communities, where dairying is by far the major farm enterprise, both Guernseys and Holsteins are found. In Minnesota the Northfield community has confined its efforts to the Holsteins. Because of concentration on this one breed, it has become nationally famous; cattle from this community have been sold to practically every state in the Union and to several foreign countries.

Type of Market

That some dairy breeds are better adapted for certain markets than others cannot be questioned. For butter production there is no particular advantage of one breed over another. It is true that the higher testing breeds produce butterfat at a lower cost per pound than do the lower testing breeds; but to compensate for this, the lower testing breeds produce more skim milk, which has additional feed value on the farm. For cheese production the higher testing breeds are not so well adapted, as it becomes necessary to remove part of the fat in order to have the correct proportion of fat to solids-not-fat. Breeds testing 4 per cent or less are the best fitted for cheese production. The proportion of fat to solids-not-fat in condensed milk is the same as for cheese; therefore, the breeds best adapted for cheese production are likewise best adapted for the production of condensed milk.

For market-milk production there are conditions under which any one of the breeds may be best adapted. Where the fat standard is 3.5 per cent and where a small differential is allowed for the excess fat in the milk, the lower testing breeds have a decided advantage. In milk markets where the differential for increased fat content is sufficiently large to adequately compensate for the additional cost of high testing milk, the low testing breeds have no advantage over the high testing breeds.

Around many population centers there are opportunities to develop markets for special milks at good prices. Different breed associations through advertising campaigns have developed special demands for the milk from their particular breed. The Guernsey and Jersey breed associations have respectively copyrighted "Golden Guernsey" and "Cream Line" as trade names of the two milks. Anyone located near a market where sales for either one of these have been developed would do well to investigate the possibilities before making the choice of a breed.

Recently some breed associations have made claims that their breed produces milk with a lower curd tension than that of other milk, and that it is, therefore, more easily digested. Although it has been demonstrated that there are marked variations in the curd tension of the milk as between individual cows, there are too few data available at the present time to say that one breed is superior to another in this respect.

Climate

While adaptation to climate is not a major consideration in the selection of a breed, there are differences in the abilities of breeds to withstand different climates. For hot climates the small breeds are distinctly superior; they have a larger body surface per unit of weight than larger breeds, and therefore are more efficient in getting rid of surplus heat. The breeds of black colour absorb more heat from the sun than the lighter coloured breeds, and consequently suffer more from heat. The larger animals are able to stand cold better than the smaller ones, since their body surface is proportionately smaller and they lose heat less rapidly. However, with the modern housing conditions the larger breeds have no particular advantage over the smaller ones in this respect. Some of the most successful Jersey farms are found in the northern part of Canada, where the winters are extremely cold.

Grazing

Considerable differences have been noted in the abilities of breeds in grazing. All the reasons for this are not clear. The larger animal has greater feed needs and consequently must cover more ground to satisfy its nutrient requirements; therefore it would not be expected to do as well on pasture as the smaller animal. However, the Brown Swiss, one of the largest of the breeds, is regarded as one of the best of grazers.

The Ayrshires, medium in size, would possibly rank first. This can be accounted for by the fact that they have been developed in a country of scant pasture, and that only those having superior grazing abilities would be selected for breeding purposes. However, the Jersey, an excellent animal as a grazer, has been brought up under ideal grazing conditions. The Guernsey, brought up under similar conditions and of approximately the same size, is not as good a grazer as the Jersey. Where pastures are luxuriant, there is no difference in breeds in regard to grazing. Where pastures are scant the differences in grazing ability are sufficient to merit serious consideration in the selection of a breed.

Demand for Surplus Stock

For the breeder of purebred cattle the demand for his surplus stock is a most important consideration, as a good share of the revenue from a purebred establishment may come from the sale of stock for breeding purposes. The demand for surplus stock is inversely proportional to the supply. During the depression years, it was observed that the Guernsey and the Brown Swiss breeds experienced the least decline in prices, chiefly because the numbers of these two breeds are much smaller than for Holsteins and Jerseys.

Efficiency of Digestion

While different breed associations have made claims for superior powers of digestion for their particular breed of cattle, the evidence clearly shows that there are no breed differences in the ability to digest food.

Maintenance Requirements

Food for maintenance is in direct proportion to the size of the animal, and the requirements for maintenance are definitely known. According to the revised Haecker feeding standard, 7,000 pounds of total digestible nutrients are needed daily for the maintenance of 1,000 pounds live weight. The larger breeds, therefore need more food for maintenance than do the smaller ones. The Holsteins require from 20 to 30 per cent more feed for this purpose than do the Jerseys, and must produce proportionately more in order to be as economical converters of feed nutrients into milk nutrients.

Utilization of Roughage

In the utilization of roughage, different breed associations have claimed superiority for their breed. Adequate data to prove or disprove this are lacking. However, it is questionable that any breed is superior to another breed in its ability to consume and utilize roughage. In 1912 Woll, studying the relative amount of grain and roughage used by different breeds on farms in Wisconsin, found that 47.6 per cent of the digestive nutrients came from roughage for the Holsteins, 53.1 per cent for the Guernseys, and 59.8 per cent for the Jerseys. These figures are subject to criticism because the Holsteins had much higher yearly production than did either the Jersey or Guernsey and, therefore, had been fed concentrates more liberally. Savage found that Holsteins obtained 52.8 per cent and Jerseys 51 per cent of their nutrient from roughage. The latter figures too, are subject to criticism, in that they did not measure the maximum roughage-consuming abilities of the breed. At the Minnesota Station when cows were allowed roughage only, great individual variation was found; but there were no differences that could be attributed especially to breed differences. In the main, the larger animal is able to consume more roughage than the smaller one, but the true criterion of utilization of roughage is the amount consumed per hundred pounds of live weight. At the Minnesota Station the Holstein and the Jersey were found to be alike in this respect.

Vigour of calves

From the standpoint of the average farmer the strength and vigour of calves at birth and the ease of raising are very important considerations. The losses of calves are as a rule high on farms. The Brown Swiss are outstanding in the strength and vigour of the calves; the Holsteins and the Ayrshires are next; and the Jersey and the Guernsey follow with the weakest calves.

Factors involved in veal production are discussed under another heading. However, for some conditions the production of veal may be an important economic item. Only the larger breeds are to be considered for veal production. The calves of small birth weight require too long a time and too much milk to bring them to marketable weights for veal.

Early Maturity

Early maturity is a consideration not often given attention; nevertheless it is important from an economical standpoint. The cost of growing an animal into production age is a very important item. The longer it takes to grow an animal, the grater the cost; and since as the animal increases in age there is a constant increase in cost of maintenance, the last two months may cost more than the three preceding months. Because the larger breeds mature later than the smaller ones, there is considerably more invested in them at production age. In addition to this, the larger breeds cost more for the same age. Henderson, Bowling, and Hermann studied the cost of raising heifers to 24 months of age and found that Holsteins cost $103.17 and Jerseys $94.61. Since Jerseys come into milk at this age, the figure represents the cost of raising to milk producing age, an added cost is incurred, bringing the total to $130.00. Part of the increased cost of growing the larger animal will be recovered in the increased sales value when the animal is through producing; therefore not all the differences in cost of raising can be charged as net increases.

Beef value of cows

Some, when selecting a breed for dairy purposes, lay undue emphasis upon the value the cow will have as beef when it is disposed of. That such beef is produced uneconomically becomes apparent when one considers all the facts. The average productive life of a dairy cow is five years; therefore cows are disposed of at an average age of seven years. The feed required for maintaining a pound of beef for this period costs far more than will be realized from the sale even on a favourable market. The producers of beef cattle realize the high feed costs for maintenance, and therefore grow their beef animals into marketable size as rapidly as possible.

Another objection to selecting dairy cows with beef tendencies is that such animals are seldom as good milk producers as are those of strictly dairy conformation. Feed cannot be used for both beef and milk production at the same time. Animals with beef tendencies are naturally inclined to divide to use of the feed between beef production and milk production, resulting in less economical use for either one.

Dual-purpose cows

A dual-purpose cow or breed is one that is intermediate for both beef and milk production, between strictly beef and milk animals or breeds. As has been shown, these cows are neither so economical as producers of beef as are strictly beef cows, nor so economical as producers of milk as are strictly dairy cows. The champions of dual-purpose cattle claim special adaptability of this type to general farms. The claims of superiority of dual-purpose in addition to the greater beef value of the cows are:

1. Dual-purpose cows are more rugged and require less attention than the specialized dairy cows.
2. The calves are more easily raised.
3. The calves are grown into more valuable beef animals.
4. Dual-purpose animals permit a shift from dairy to beef or vice versa.
5. Dual-purpose cattle make greater use of roughage.

On the large farms where the facilities for dairying are limited and it is advisable to have a large herd of cattle, these claims are valid. Lower producing cows do not require the attention in feeding and care that high producing cows do. Neither do they require as good housing. The dual-purpose breed can make a higher proportion of the total production on roughage that can the high producing specialized dairy breeds.

While the calves from dual-purpose cattle may not be easier to raise, they have greater meat values than calves from the specialized dairy breeds. This is of particular value on large farms where a large portion of the calves raised are to be used for beef production.

11

Selecting the Individual Cow

The first essential in establishing and maintaining a profitable and desirable dairy herd is intelligent selection of the individual animals. Whether cows are to be purchased or raised on the farm, the problem of selecting the cows for the milking herd is always present, and to a large extent the success of the dairy enterprise depends on the judgement used in the selection. Cows may be selected on one or more of the following three bases: on production of milk and butterfat as indicated by records, on pedigree or the records of the parents, and on appearance or type.

BASIS OF SELECTION

Production records

Records of production offer the most reliable means for selecting profitable cows. An experienced judge of dairy cattle is able to select very poor cows from good ones by their appearances. In the average dairy herd, however, the problem is to select the better cows from more mediocre ones, and this cannot be done from appearance even by the most skilled judges. The relationship between the level of production and profit and the factors influencing milk production will be discussed in other parts of this book. At this point it will suffice to state that, other things being equal, the more milk and butterfat a cow produces, the more profitable she will be.

In evaluating production records of a cow, care should be taken to ascertain the conditions under which the records were made. Good cows may have low production records because they were improperly fed and cared for, and poor cows may have comparatively better records because they were unusually well fed and cared for. Cows with records of 600 or more pounds of fat per year made on three or four times daily milking and heavy grain feeding may not produce over 300 to 400 pounds of fat on twice a day milking and ordinary good care. Sickness and other adverse conditions may also contribute to lowering the production record of a cow. Such records are not representative of the producing abilities of cows, and should be given careful consideration in selecting or eliminating cows.

Pedigree

Dairy animals, bulls in particular, are often selected on the basis of pedigree. This is done with the belief that "like begets like" and offspring, therefore, possess the good qualities of their parents. The pedigree may be a valuable and fairly reliable guide in the selection of individuals, but more often than not it falls short

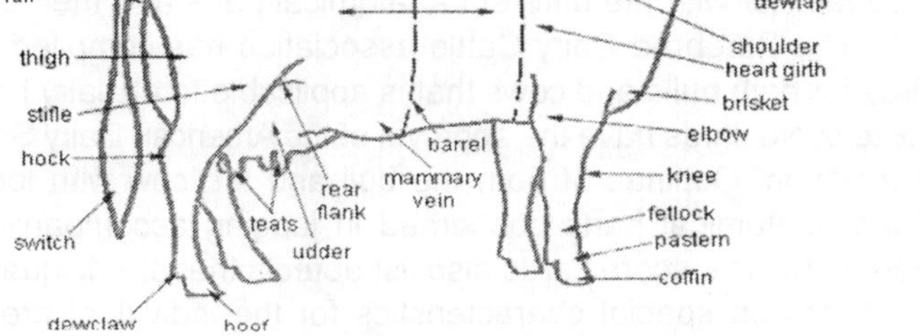

Parts of a dairy cow

Fig. 11.1: Parts of the cow referred to in the score card are shown here

of having any real value in evaluating the producing capacity of the individual concerned. For the breeder of purebred cattle, consideration of the pedigree is essential for a number of reasons that are discussed in other parts of this book.

Appearance

Dairy cows are brought and sold on the market mainly on the basis of appearance. While experts are able to select large numbers that will average high production, this method is not reliable for individual selections except for certain types that are certain to be poor producers. Animals of the type illustrated in Fig. 11.1 are certain to be poor and unprofitable producers. Cows of good dairy conformation may not be high producers.

A knowledge of what constitutes good dairy conformation and type, however, is essential to the student of dairying and the breeder of dairy cattle - not because such knowledge enables one to select high producing from low producing cows, as is usually claimed, but because it is desirable to recognize and breed dairy cattle of the approved type. Over a period of time certain standards have been set as to the approved type of the various dairy breeds. The approved type is to be admired more from an esthetic standpoint than as an indication of producing ability. The approved dairy type, therefore, while not in conflict with what is required for high production, is not necessarily an assurance of high production but something to be valued for the sake of beauty.

MAJOR CONSIDERATIONS OF DAIRY TYPE

In order to properly evaluate the type of an animal it is necessary to be familiar with the different anatomical parts and their correct form. The Purebred Dairy Cattle association has compiled score cards for both bulls and cows that is applicable to all dairy breeds. These score cards have the approval of the American Dairy Science Association. Outlines of both the bull and the cow with location of the anatomical parts concerned in judging accompanies the score card. The score cards also list defects that are disqualifying and notes on special characteristics for the individual breeds.

EVALUATION OF DEFECTS

In a show ring, disqualification means that the animal is not eligible to win a prize. Any disqualified animal is not eligible to be shown in the group classes. In slight to serious discrimination, the degree of seriousness shall be determined by the judge.

Eyes

1. Total blindness: Disqualification.
2. Blindness in one eye: Slight discrimination.

Wry face

Serious discrimination.

Parrot jaw

Slight to serious discrimination.

Shoulders

Winged: Slight to serious discrimination.

Capped hip

Slight discrimination.

Tail setting

Wry tail or other abnormal tail settings: slight to serious discrimination.

Legs and feed

1. Lameness- apparently permanent and interfering with normal function: Disqualification.
   - Apparently temporary and not affecting normal function: Slight discrimination.
2. Bucked knees, blemished hocks, crooked hind legs, weak pasterns: Serious discrimination.

3. Evidence of arthritis, crampy hind leg: Serious discrimination.
4. Enlarged knees: Slight discrimination.

Absence of horns

No discrimination.

Lack of size

Slight to serious discrimination.

Udder

1. One or more blind quarters: Disqualification.
2. Abnormal milk (bloody, clotted, watery): Possibly disqualification. A slight to serious defect.
3. Udder definitely broken away in attachment: Serious discrimination.
4. A weak udder attachment: Slight to serious discrimination.
5. One or more light quarters, hard spots in udder, side leak or obstruction in teat (spider): Slight to serious discrimination.

Dry cows

In case of cows of apparently equal merit: Give preference to cows in milk.

Overconditioned

Serious discrimination.

Temporary or minor injuries

Blemishes or injuries of a temporary character not affecting animal's usefulness: Slight discrimination.

Evidence of sharp practice

1. Animals showing signs of having been operated upon or tampered with for the purpose of concealing faults in conformation, or with intent to deceive relative to the animal's soundness: Disqualification.
2. Heifer calves showing evidence of having been milked, in an attempt to deceive regarding natural form of udder: Serious discrimination.

Ayrshire characteristics

Colour - Red of any shade, mahog-any brown or these with white, or white, each colour clearly defined. Distinctive red and white markings preferable; black or brindle markings strongly objectionable.

Size - A mature cow in milk should weighs, about 1,150 pounds.

Horns - Inclining upward, small at base, refined, medium length, and tapering toward tips.

Brown swiss characteristics

Strong and vigorous. Size and ruggedness with quality desired. Extreme refinement undesirable.

Colour - A shade of brown varying from a sliver to a dark brown. Hair inside ears is a lighter colour than body. Nose and tongue black, with a light coloured band stretching around nose. Colour markings which bar registry are: white switch, white on sides, top, head or neck, and legs above knees or hocks. White on belly or lower legs objectionable.

Size - A mature cow in milk should weigh about 1,400 pounds.

Horns - Inclining forward and slightly up. Moderately small at base, medium length, tapering toward black tips.

Guernsey characteristics

Colour - A shade of fawn with white markings clearly defined, black or brindle markings objectionable. Skin should show

DAIRY COW SCORE CARD

Ideals of type and breed characteristics must be considered in the application of the terminology of this score card

Based on order of observation	Perfect score	Cow under observation	Official score
1. GENERAL APPEARANCE	30		
Attractive individuality, revealing vigour, femininity with a harmonious blending, and correlation of parts. Impressive style and attractive carriage with a graceful walk 12			
Breed characteristics (see below) 12			
Head: medium in length, clean-cut; broad muzzle with large open nostrils; lean, strong jaw; full, bright eyes; forehead broad between the eyes and moderately dished; bridge of nose straight; ears medium size and alertly carried. —			
Shoulder blades set smoothly against chest wall and withers, forming meat junction with the body.			
Back strong and appearing straight with vertebrae well defined.			
Loin broad, strong, and nearly level.			
Rump long, wide; top-line level from loin to and including tail head. 10			
Hips wide, approximately level laterally with back, free from excess tissue.			

Thurls wide apart.			
Pinbones wide apart and slightly lower than hips, well defined.			
Tail head slightly above and neatly set between pinbones.			
Tail long and tapering with nicely balanced switch.-			
Legs wide apart, squarely set, clean-cut, and strong with forelegs straight. **Hind legs** nearly perpendicular from hock to pastern. When viewed from behind, legs wide apart and nearly straight. Bone, flat and flinty, tendons well defined. Pasterns, of medium length, strong and springy. Hocks cleanly moulded.	8		
Feet short and well rounded, with deep heel and level sole.	-		
2. DAIRY CHARACTER		20	
Animation, angularity, general openness, and freedom from excess tissue, giving due regard in period of lactation.Neck long and lean, blending smoothly into shoulders and brisket; clean-cut throat and dewlap.Withers well defined and wedge-shaped with the dorsal processes of the vertebrae rising slightly above the shoulder blades.	20		
Ribs wide apart. Rib bone wide, flat and long.Plank deep, arched and refined.Thighs incurving to flat from the side; wide apart when viewed from the rear, providing sufficient room for the udder and its attachment.Skin of medium thickness, loose, and pliable. Hair fine.	-		
3. BODY CAPACITY			
Relatively large in proportion to size of animal, providing ample digestive capacity, strength, and vigour.	12		
Barrel deep, strongly supported,			

Based on order of observation		Perfect score	Cow under observation	Official score
ribs wide apart and well sprung; depth and width rending to increase toward rear of barrel.	–			
Heartgirth large, resulting from long, well sprung foreribs, wide chest floor between front legs, and fullness at the point of elbow.	8			
3. MAMMARY SYSTEM		30		
A capacious, strongly attached, well carried udder of good quality, indicating heavy production and a long period of usefulness.				
Udder – Capacity and shape, long, wide, and of moderate depth. Extending well forward, strongly attached, reasonably level floor. Rear attachment, high and wide. Quarters evenly balanced and symmetrical.	25			
Texture soft, pliable, and elastic. Well collapsed after milking.Teats uniform, of convenient length and size, cylindrical in shape, free from obstructions, well apart and squarely placed, plumb.	–			
Mammary veins long, tortuous, prominent and branching, with numerous large wells. Veins on udder numerous and clearly defined.	5			
Total	100			

golden yellow pigmentation. When other points are equal, a clear buff muzzle will be favoured over a smoky or black muzzle.

Size - A mature cow in milk should weigh about 1,100 pounds.

Horns - Inclining forward, small and yellow at base, refined, medium in length, and tapering toward tips.

Holstein characteristics

Colour - Black and white markings clearly defined. Colour markings which bar registry are: solid black, solid white, black in switch, black belly, black encircling leg touching hoof, black from hoof to knee or hock, black and white intermixed to give colour other than distinct black and white.

Size - A mature cow in milk should weigh about 1,500 pounds.

Horns - Inclining forward, incurving, small at base, refined, medium length, and tapering toward tips.

Jersey characteristics

Colour - A shade of fawn, with or without white markings.

Fig. 11.2: Poor dairy type. A cow of non-descript breeding lacking in all the essentials for economic production. Cows of this type may be safely eliminated without testing.

Size - A mature cow in milk should weigh about 1,000 pounds.

Horns - Inclining forward, incurving, small at base, refined, medium length and tapering toward tips.

Dairy conformation

The term dairy conformation signifies that appearance which indicates a tendency to produce milk rather than to produce beef. It is generally characterized by angularity leading to the presentation of three wedges when viewed from the side, front, and top.

The top and bottom lines, if extended, will meet in front of the head to form a wedge. When viewed from the front, the two lines over the shoulders form a wedge, with the apex at the withers. The third wedge is formed by the lines drawn from the hook bones to the withers, with the apex at the withers. For the ideal beef animal, these lines are parallel. (Fig. 11.3) The difference in the conformation of dairy and beef types is due to differences in fleshing, as the skeletons of the two are essentially the same (Fig. 11.4)

In addition to the three wedges, all parts should be clean-cut and free from excess fleshing. The head and face should be clean-cut and feminine in appearance; the neck should be long, slender, and neatly joined with both head and shoulders. The shoulders should be free from coarseness. The back, hook bones, and pinbones should be prominent yet free from coarseness. The legs likewise should be clean-cut and free from coarseness, with clean-

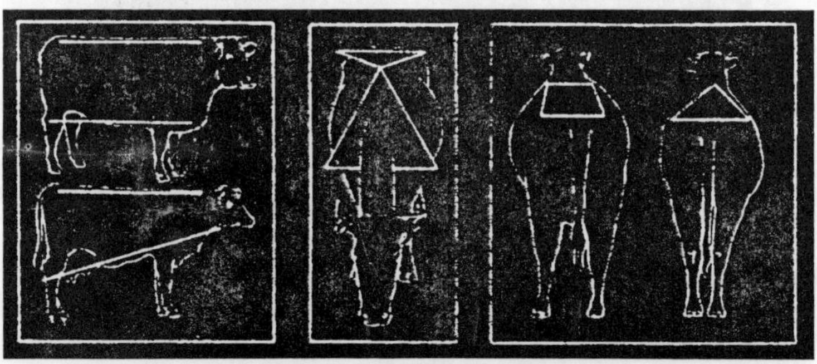

Fig. 11.3: The top and bottom lines, the side lines, and the lines over the withers tend to form wedges on the dairy type, while the some lines are parallel on the beef types.

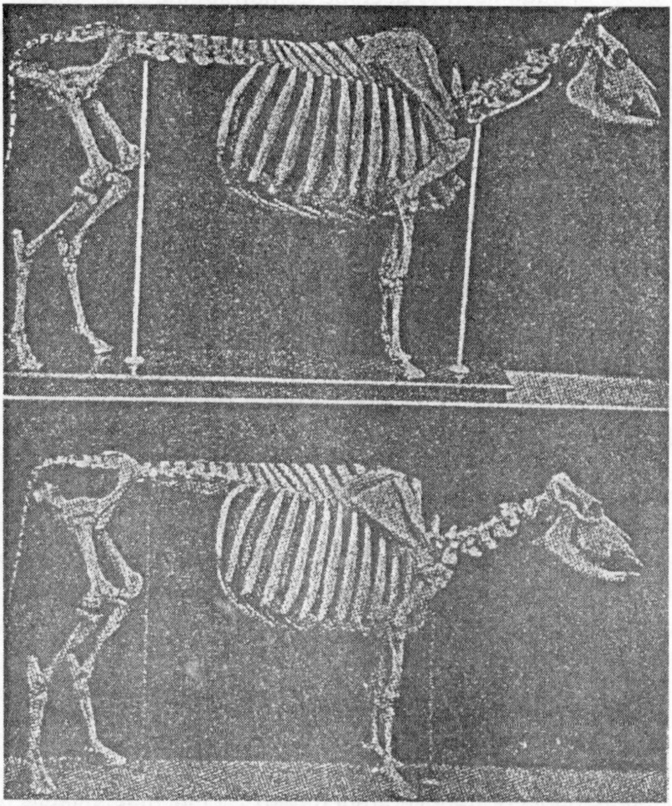

Fig. 11.4: Showing the similarities between the skeletons of beef and dairy types. The upper is that of Sophie 19th of Hood Farm, a highly specialized dairy cow of the Jersey breed, while the lower is that of Blackbird of Dallas, a purebred Angus and highly specialized beef cow.

cut and preferably incurving thighs.

The cow should also be active in disposition, indicating capacity for work. Sluggish animals are seldom good feeders. Too nervous and easily excitable animals are undesirable because of difficulty in handling them and also because a large amount of energy is wasted in unnecessary excitement.

Well fed dry cows frequently acquire sufficient flesh to assume more of the lines of the beef cow. Undernourished beef cows may also lose enough flesh to assume somewhat the angularity of the typical dairy type. In these cases there are other characteristics that must be watched for. The size and shape of the udder and the difference in spring of ribs help differentiate between diary and beef types. The ribs come out at more nearly right angles from the vertebrae on the beef animal than on the dairy animal.

Constitution and Vigour

The high producing dairy cow performs an enormous amount of work in the mastication and metabolism of the large amount of feed that she must consume for the needs of milk production and body maintenance. It is, therefore, essential that she posses a strong constitution and much vigour. Strong constitution and vigour are indicated by the general healthy appearance of the animal and to some extent by certain anatomical features. The clean, alert eye, large nostrils, and large chest are the most significant. Size of chest - and, therefore, increased room for heart and lungs - is secured by depth, width of the chest floor, and spring of the foreribs. A long body also increases chest capacity.

Feed Capacity

Cows vary greatly in the capacity for feed consumption. To some extent the ability to handle feed is indicated by body conformation. Animals with very shallow and narrow barrels are seldom capable of handling much feed. Sometimes animals with deep, wide, and long barrels do not posses the ability to consume large quantities of feed, but as a rule they are superior to those of smaller proportions.

In addition to large middles, large capacity for feed is indicated by a large muzzle and a soft, loose skin.

Mammary Development

The extent of the mammary development is the most significant anatomical feature in predicting the producing capacity of a cow. More weight is given to this than to any other major feature listed on the score card. While the mammary development is the most reliable indication of the milk-producing ability of a cow, it is not infallible. Many cows with excellent udder development have been known to be poor producers; they are undoubtedly lacking in the inheritance of the hormones that stimulate the glands into continued activity.

The mammary development includes the udder, teats, and milk veins. The size, quality, and shape of the udder are important considerations. The udder must be large enough to make and hold the milk that is produced; cows with small udders cannot be high producers. Next to size, the quality of the udder is important. The udder consists of glandular secreting tissue, ducts, storage reservoirs, and connective tissue. The connective tissue tends to give the udder a hard texture, while the ducts and reservoirs produce a soft texture. Large udders consisting largely of connective tissue are hard to the touch and of poor quality. Such udders are not capable of producing large amounts of milk. Good quality udders "collapse" following milking, while poor quality udders change but little either in shape or texture following the removal of milk. Udders or parts of udders that have been severely infected with mastitis develop large lumps. This is due to the secretory tissue being replaced by hard connective tissue.

The shape of the udder is important for three reasons. The correctly shaped udder has greater capacity than many of the poorly shaped types. A properly shaped and attached udder is not so subject to injury from various causes as a pendulous type, and the correctly shaped udder adds greatly to the beauty of the animal.

The desirably shaped udder is long and wide, and has a level udder floor. When both the fore and rear attachments are strong, thus type of udder will have the greatest capacity and refrain from breaking down to become pendulous.

For convenience in milking, the teats should be of convenient size and placed squarely on the udder. Large tortuous milk veins extending far forward and entering the chest cavity through large milk wells are considered indications of good producing ability. Nearly all high producing cows possess these qualities, but not all cows with the desirable veining are capable of high production.

Defects in shapes of udders

There are many types of defects in the shapes of udders. The more common of these defects are illustrated in Fig. 11.5.

An udder that is lacking in size and quality, regardless of shape, is to be avoided, notwithstanding what other qualities the animal may possess; for it is impossible to obtain much milk from a small udder lacking in quality.

The pendulous udder should also be avoided, since such udders are subject to injuries. A pendulous udder may receive bruises from objects over which the cow may pass, from striking the legs in walking or running, from being stepped on in arising, and in various other ways. These injuries not only result in inconvenience

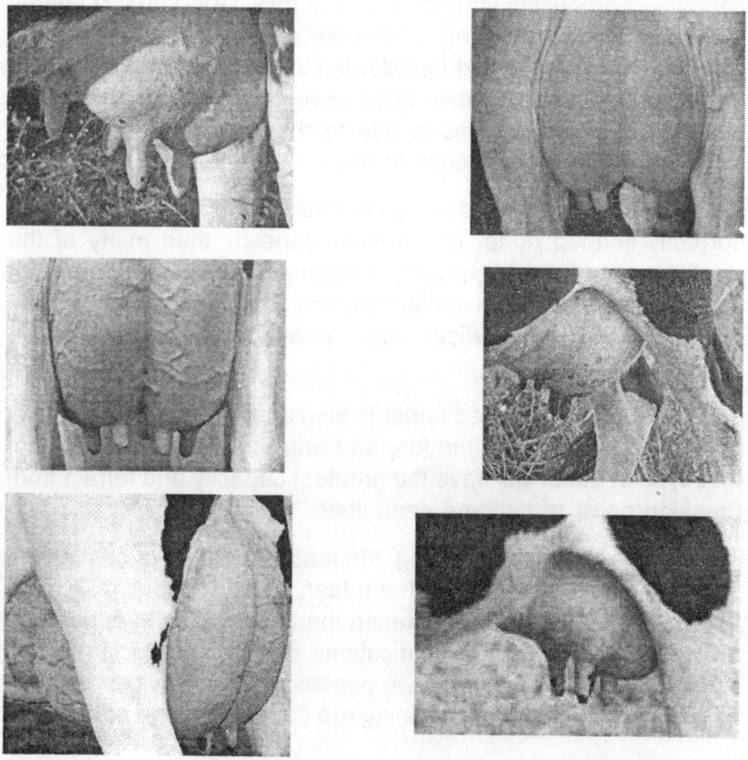

Fig. 11.5: Poor types of udders.

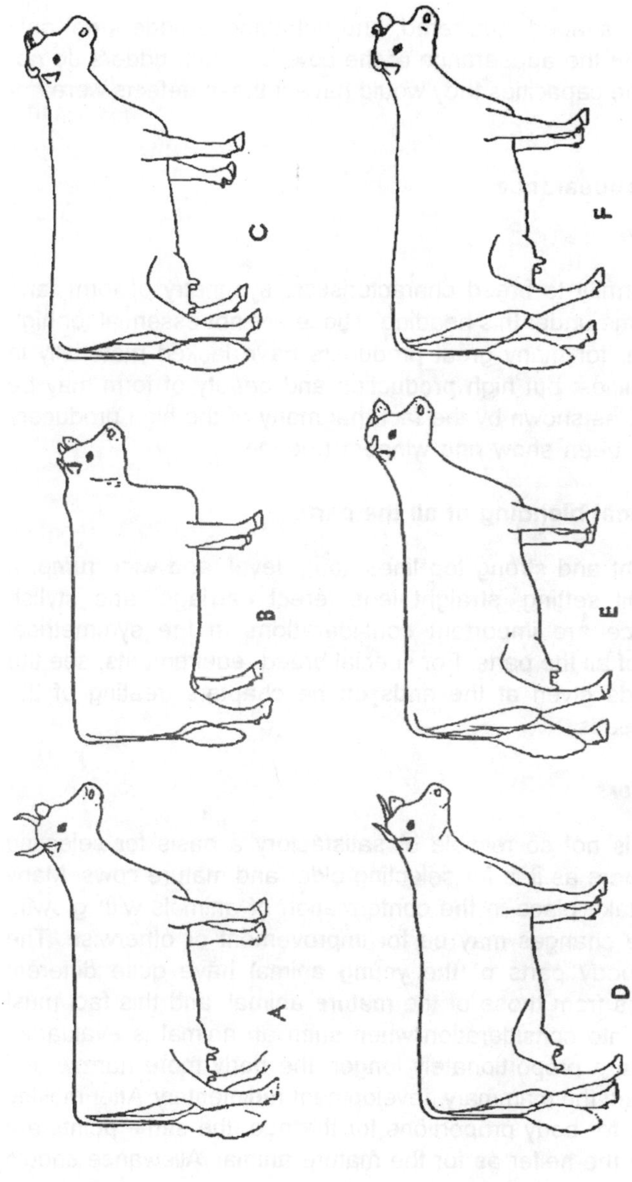

Fig. 11.6: Outline of the true type of each of the five dairy breeds compared with that of a beef cow. Note the similarity of outline of the different breeds. A, Ayrshire; B, Beef Shorthorn; C, Guernsey; D, Brown Swiss; E, Holstein; F, Jersey.

in milking but may also be the predisposing factor for mastitis, a disease that causes great financial loss to dairymen.

Funnel shaped, quartered, and unbalanced udders not only detract from the appearance of the cow, but such udders do not possess the capacities they would have if these defects were not present.

General appearance

Breed type

Conformity to breed characteristics, symmetry of form, and beauty come under this heading. These are not essential for high production, for many great producers have lacked materially in these qualities; but high production and beauty of form may be combined, as shown by the fact that many of the high producers have also been show ring winners (Fig. 11.6).

Symmetrical blending of all the parts

Straight and strong top lines, long, level, and wide rump, a square tail setting, straight legs, erect carriage, and stylish appearance are important considerations in the symmetrical blending of all the parts. For special breed requirements, see the score cards given at the ends of the chapters treating of the various breeds.

Dairy heifers

Type is not so reliable or satisfactory a basis for selecting young heifers as it is for selecting older and mature cows. Many changes take place in the conformation of animals with growth, and these changes may be for improvement or otherwise. The different body parts of the young animal have quite different proportions from those of the mature animal, and this fact must be taken into consideration when such an animal is evaluated. The legs are proportionately longer, the body more narrow and shallow, and the mammary development rudimentary. After making allowance for body proportions for the age, the same points are desired in the heifer as for the mature animal. Allowance should also be made for more fleshing in young stock than is tolerated in mature milking cows.

Many people believe there is good correlation between the degree of mammary development of the heifer and milk production when mature. It is also commonly believed that the placement of teats and the shape of the udder on the heifer are good indications of the shape of the udder when mature. While there is little experimental evidence available pertaining to these points, the validity of either one is to be questioned. The udder of the heifer consists almost entirely of fatty and connective tissues into which the glandular tissue develops. The shape of the developed udder is dependent upon the direction the growth of the ducts and glandular tissue takes.

The extent of the glandular development in each of the four quarters in the growing heifers probably is a fair criterion of the size the udder will ultimately attain, but not of its shape. The glandular tissue can be palpated as more or less solid masses extending upward from each teat.

12

Fundamental Considerations of Heredity

IMPORTANCE OF HEREDITY

The amount of milk and fat a cow produces is dependent upon two groups of factors: (1) inherited capacity for production, and (2) the environmental factors, such as feed and care. While a good cow may be fed and cared for in such a way that she will produce poorly, no amount of feed or care will make a high producer out of a cow which lacks the proper hereditary factors for a high production.

All the known hereditary factors behave according to definite laws. The science which deals with these laws and heredity in general is known as genetics. To properly understand the inheritance of any character or group of characters one must become familiar with certain fundamental considerations, which may be divided into two groups: namely, those which deal with the physical basis of inheritance, and those which deal with the laws governing inheritance. A knowledge of these fundamental considerations will help materially in understanding the problems encountered in the breeding of dairy cattle.

PHYSICAL BASIS

The body cell

The cell is the structural unit of all body tissues. It is microscopic in size, and differs in shape and composition in the various tissues of the body. The structure is complicated, but only one of the component parts, the nucleus, will be discussed here.

Since the nucleus contains all the factors involved in inheritance, a knowledge of the structure of the nucleus and its component parts is pertinent to this discussion. All cells capable of reproducing themselves are alike in that each possesses a nucleus that in turn governs the reproduction of cells. (Unnucleated cells, like the red blood cells and certain white blood cells, originate from nucleated cells.)

The nucleus of the cell in the bovine is exceedingly small, yet it is made up of a number of complicated structures. The structures that we are concerned with from the standpoint of inheritance are known as chromosomes. These carry all the hereditary factors. In all body cells the chromosomes are found in pairs. For a cow it is now believed that there are 30 pairs of chromosomes, one of each pair originating from the sire and the other from the dam. Each chromosome is further divided into parts known as genes. The gene is the unit of heredity; each gene is responsible for a character or part of one or more characters (Fig. 12.1).

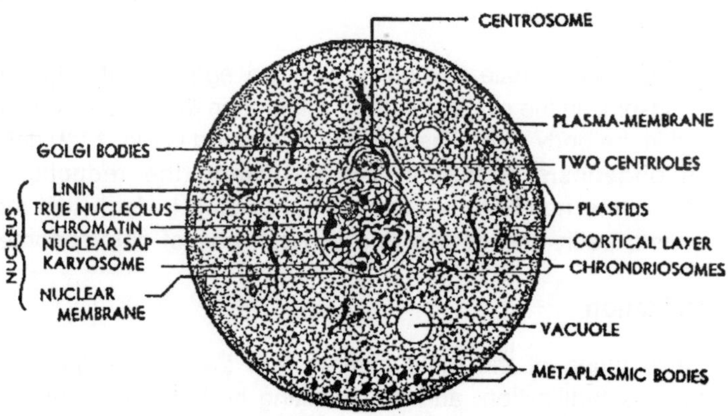

Fig. 12.1; A schematic representation of the body cell. Attention is called to its complexity and the fact that the factors for heredity are located in the nucleus.

Sex cells

Early in the embryological development certain cells are differentiated from the rest of the body for reproduction. For the male they come to be located in the testes, and for the female in the ovaries. These cells are like other body cells in that they are nucleated and have chromosomes in pairs. In the process of maturing, however, two important physiological changes take place in the development of the sex cells. One is an increase in the number of the reproductive cells, and the other is a process of reducing the number of chromosomes from the paired condition to the single condition in which they are found in the mature sex cell or gamete, as it is commonly referred to in genetics. The process in the female is known as oogenesis, and in the male as spermatogenesis.

Oogenesis

Oogenesis is illustrated by diagram in Fig. 12.2. An important point in this process is the reduction in the chromosome numbers, effected by casting off half of the chromosome in what is known as a polar body. In the casting off of these chromosomes the chances are even as to which one of a pair of chromosomes will be retained and which will be cast off.

Spermatogenesis

The mature male gamete is like the egg in that it has the chromosome in the single condition rather than the double condition found in the body cells. The process, illustrated in Fig. 12.2, differs from oogenesis in that in the last stage the reduction of chromosome numbers is effected by dividing to form two male gametes, each one getting one of each pair of chromosomes.

Fertilization

The union of the male gamete and the female gamete is known as fertilization, and the resulting body from the union is known as a zygote. The zygote differs from either one of the gametes by having the chromosomes in pairs, one of each pair coming from the female, and once from the male. Neither of the

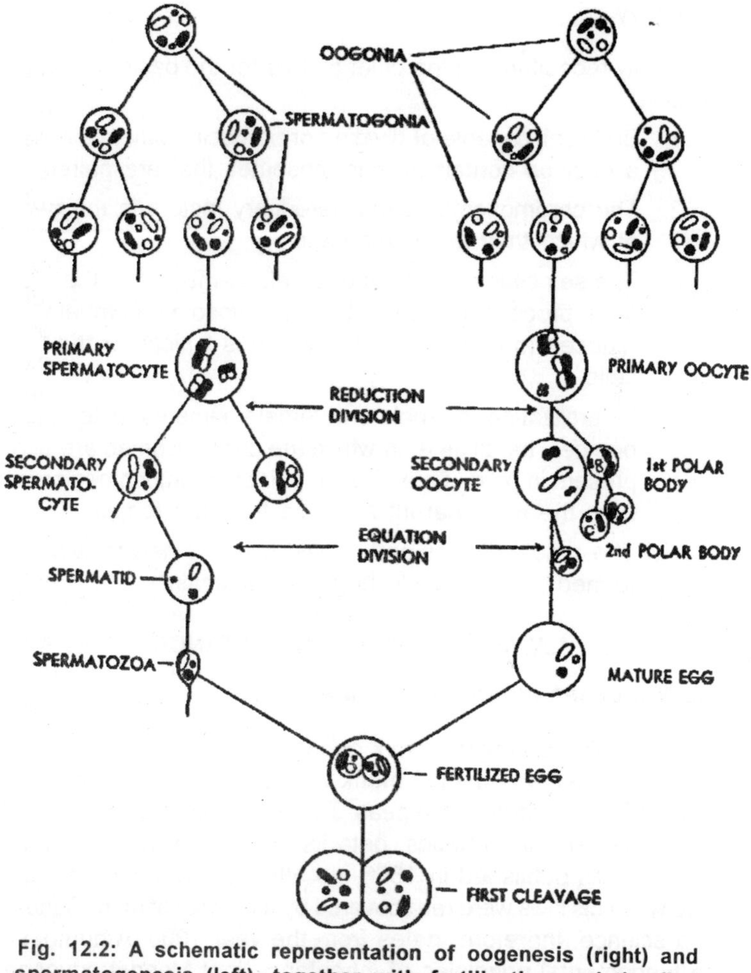

Fig. 12.2: A schematic representation of oogenesis (right) and spermatogenesis (left), together with fertilization and the first cleavage.

gametes has the power of multiplying, but the zygote has this power, and cell multiplication goes on rapidly when it is implanted in the endometrium of the uterus. The zygote first divides to form two cells; these divide in two for the four cell stage, the four cells for the eight cell, the eight cells for the sixteen, and so on. In each division the chromosomes divide first, so that all new cells have the same chromosome numbers as the parent cell.

Summary

Briefly recapitulating the chief factors for the basis of heredity we have:

1. Body cell capable of dividing or producing other cells have a nucleus containing chromosomes that are paired.
2. The chromosomes carry hereditary factors in the genes of which they are composed.
3. The sex cells or male and female gametes are the result of a process in which the chromosome numbers are reduced to one-half of that which is typical for the body cells.
4. In fertilization the male and female gametes unite to form one cell, the zygote, in which the chromosomes are again present in pairs. One of each pair of chromosomes comes from the male parent and one from the female.
5. The zygote divides and redivides until a new individual is formed and the cycle begins over again.

LAWS GOVERNING INHERITANCE

The Mendelian Inheritance or Mendelism

The first experimental work on inheritance was conducted by Gregor Mendel, as Austrian monk who studied the inheritance of seven different characters in peas. The term Mendelian Inheritance, commonly used in genetics, gets its name from Mendel. While his work was published in 1866, no attention was paid to it until 1900 when his laws were rediscovered by a number of men. Genetics as a science, therefore, dates from the year 1900. A number of the fundamental principles of inheritance that Mendel advanced still hold. Some have been modified as new discoveries have been made. To understand the nature of inheritance one must become familiar with these fundamental principles, a discussion of which is given in the following paragraphs.

Dominance, recessiveness, and epistasis

When a gene expresses itself and completely prevents the expression of its allelomorph, it is said to be dominant, and the gene that it is dominant to is said to be recessive. If a gene expresses itself completely over another gene located in a different position in the chromosome or in some other chromosome it is said to be epistatic. The difference between epistasis and dominance is not always recognized. Black is usually said to be dominant to red when more probably it is epistatic to red.

While Mendel claimed that all characters behave as dominant and recessive, there may be partial dominance or intermediate inheritance or even cumulative inheritance. There is no positive intermediate inheritance in cattle. In plants, however, this type of inheritance is quite common. A red snapdragon crossed with an ivory snapdragon produces F_1s (the first filial generation) that has pink flowers. Cumulative or blending inheritance is that type of inheritance in which each of the allelomorphic genes contribute a portion toward the expression of a character. Some people believe that this type of inheritance is important in milk production.

Unit Character

Mendel believed that each character was the expression of a single factor, but it is now known that, in the main, from several to many factors or genes are required for the expression of a single character. Apparently the character "Self" (solid colour) is due to but one gene, but to produce the colour pattern of the Holstein several genes are needed. The inheritance of milk production may require a score or more genes, as is also the case the size, vigour, and a number of other much desired characters.

Illustration of Inheritance

Most of the fundamental laws of inheritance can be illustrated in a cross of Holsteins and Red Polls for two generations. The Holstein is black with white spotting and has horns; the Red Poll is of solid colour, red, and hornless. All F_1s, or first filial generation, are hornless, a solid coloured, and black. If the F_1s are crossed among themselves to produce the F_2s or second generations, it takes 64 animals, on the average, to bring out all the possible genetic combinations of these three characters. These will be distributed as follows:

27 black, solid colour, and hornless

9 black, solid colour, and horned
9 black, spotted, and hornless
9 red, solid colour, and hornless
3 black, spotted, and horned
3 red, solid colour, and horned
3 red, spotted, and hornless
1 red, spotted, and horned

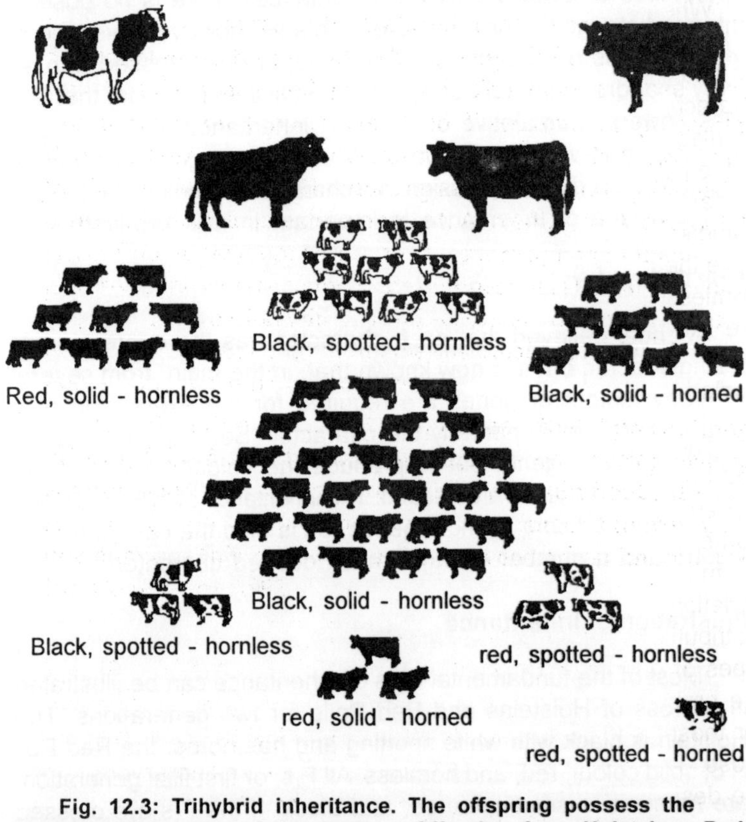

Fig. 12.3: Trihybrid inheritance. The offspring possess the dominant characters of the parents. Offspring from Holstein x Red Polled are hornless, black, and solid of colour. Their offspring (F_2), however, will be of eight different types, in which all the characters of the grandparents (P_1) will appear and in new combinations. On the average, 64 individuals are needed to bring out the types.

From Fig. 12.3 it will be noted that the F_1s are all black, hornless, and of solid colour. The solid colour of the Red Poll is dominant to the white spotting of the Holstein, the black of the Holstein is epistatic to the red of the Red Poll, and the hornless condition of the Red Poll is epistatic to the horned condition of the Holstein.

Homozygous and Heterozygous

When both members of a pair of genes are alike, the condition is known as homozygous; and if they are different, it is said to be heterozygous. The principle of this may be illustrated for the characters horned and hornlessness by letting HH represent the hornless condition in the Red Poll, and hh, the horned condition in the Holstein. Each parent can produce but one type of gamete as far as this character is concerned. For the Red Poll each gamete would have the H, and for the Holstein each one would have the h. the F_1s are heterozygous for horns (Hh), but because hornlessness is dominant to the horned condition, all individuals are like the hornless parent in this particular.

Variation

The hope for improvement of livestock by breeding lies in the fact that there is much variation. While the Holstein and the Red Poll are homozygous for the respective characters of white, spotting, horns, black, hornlessness, red, and solid colour, they are variable for many of their other characters. The general law governing variations is illustrated in Fig. 12.3, which gives the F_2 generation distribution where from two parents appearing alike eight different types of offspring are produced. The factors for milk production are probably more variable in the dairy breeds than the factors for these sample characters illustrated in the Holstein-Red Poll cross. The object of a breeder is to select for homozygosity of the desirable characters and thereby eliminate variation.

Genotype and Phenotype

In order to facilitate discussion it is necessary to know these two terms and what they represent. Phenotype refers to the characteristics of an animal that can be seen; genotype refers to the genetic composition of the animal, part of which is expressed in the phenotype. The phenotype for the three characters, horns, black, and spotted condition, in the Holstein is the same as the genotype. In the F_1 generation of the Holstein-Red Poll cross, however, both the genotype and the phenotype contain the recessive for these three characters. The genotype of an individual can be determined only through the characteristics observed in the offspring. This fundamental conception can be put to practical use in studying the genotype of the breeding animals.

Hybrid and Hybrid Ratios

Hybrid refers to heterozygous individual and is commonly used to designate animals from parents of different breeds. A monohybrid is one with only one factor difference, such as horns and hornlessness. When one factor is based upon dominance and recessiveness, it takes an average four individuals to bring out all of the two types that will result. A cross of the F_1s with each other produces horns to the hornless condition in the ration of 3 to 1. Of these, one is homozygous for hornlessness, two are heterozygous, and therefore hornless, and one is homozygous for horns.

A dihybrid is one in which two factor pairs are involved. Here it takes 16 individuals to bring out the four types, one of which will be double recessive for both factor pairs. Crossing a red hornless individual with a black horned individual, there will be:

9 black and hornless (one of which is homozygous for both pairs of factors)

3 black and horned

3 red and hornless

1 red and horned

A trihybrid ratio has been illustrated in the consideration of the three sets of allelomorphs in the Holstein-Red Poll cross. With an increasing number of factors involved the complexity increases in geometric proportions. For four factor differences it requires, on the average, 256 individuals to get out all possible combinations. Some believe that as many as 18 factor pairs are involved in the inheritance of milk and butterfat production; in that case, the possibility of an infinite number of recombinations exists.

Linkage

Linkage in inheritance exists when one gene goes with another one in the same chromosome. If genes are linked, the characters for which such genes are responsible appear together. In cattle only one linkage of characters is now known and that is in connection with the white heifer disease, a case of sterility which is associated with the inheritance of white colour. In plants many linkages are known, and advantages are taken of this information in breeding. In human beings colour blindness and hemophilia are each linked with sex. The linking of characters in dairy cattle might be very helpful in the breeding programme.

Acquired characters

It has been commonly believed by the laity that inheritable characters could be acquired; thus, for example, pregnant mares were trotted on the race track in order to insure racing ability to the colt. Extensive experimentation, however, has shown that characters cannot be acquired in that way. The germ plasm is set aside from the somatoplasm or body cells and is not dependent on it or influenced by it. The docking of the tails of sheep has been done for many generations without affecting the inheritance of that part of the anatomy.

Mutations

To what extent mutations have played a part in the inheritance of cattle is not known. Undoubtedly there are many cases where the inheritance has been influenced by mutations of one kind or another. There are several cases on record of albino cattle, the appearance of which can best be explained by a mutation of the chromosomes or of the genes carrying the colour factor. Hornlessness also is a mutation and has come in spontaneously in herds that were horned. Very little is definitely known about the effects of mutation on the important practical character of dairy cattle.

With an understanding of these fundamental principles a concerning the physical basis for inheritance and these general laws governing the nature of inheritance one will be better able to understand the reasons for the observed differences in cattle and why apparently new types can spring from old ones.

13

Measures of the Genetic Makeup

The old adage that like begets like is only partially true. It is common knowledge that characters may appear in the offspring that were not apparent in either one of the parents. The red and white Holstein from black and white parents and the horned offspring from hornless parents are examples of this phenomenon. While not much is definitely known about the inheritance of the capacity to produce milk, except that there are many factors involved, it is apparent that here, too, the offspring may vary widely from the production capacity of the dam and the calculated production level of the sire. The offspring may be inferior or superior to either or both of the parents. In the light of modern genetics such behaviour can be explained on the basis of a heterozygous condition of the parents, permitting a recombination of factors in the offspring. Such recombination of many factors may account for wide ranges of variations. This can be illustrated by considering three of the many factor pairs involved in the inheritance of the capacity to produce milk, making the following assumptions:

1. The genes are dominant and recessive.
2. A, B, C represent the dominant genes, and a, b, c represent the corresponding recessive genes.

3. Each parent is heterozygous for two pairs of genes, and double recessive for one pair.
4. The double recessive condition is for a different pair of genes in the two parents.

The genetic makeup of the two parents for the three factor pairs is represented:

Aa	Aa
Bb	bb
cc	Cc

Each parent can produce four different gametes: ABc, Abc, aBc, and abc by one parent, and AbC, Abc, abC, and abc by the other. If the first gametes listed for each parent unite, the resulting individual will have the composition AA, Bb, Cc, or a higher production capacity than either parent. If the last gametes listed for the two parents unite, the resulting individual will have the composition aa, bb, cc, or a much lower production capacity than either parent.

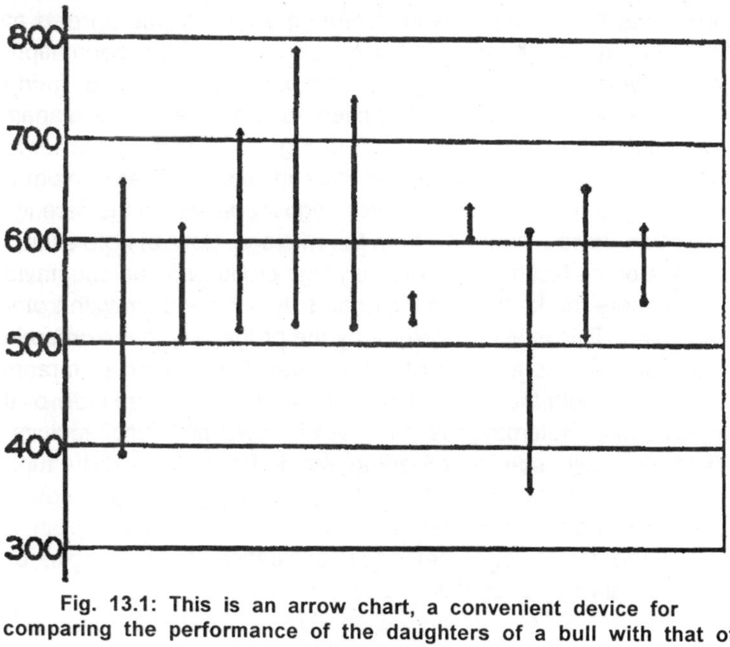

Fig. 13.1: This is an arrow chart, a convenient device for comparing the performance of the daughters of a bull with that of their dams.

The object of the breeder of dairy cattle is to produce animals that are homozygous for all the desirable characters; and to approach such an end he must know not only the phenotype but also the genotype of the breeding animals. The problem, therefore, is one of ascertaining the genotype; the measures for doing this are discussed in the following pages.

Production record of the dam

In the past the milk and butterfat record of the individual, if a cow, or of the individual's dam, if a heifer or a bull, has been the chief criterion in evaluating such an animal for breeding purposes. The milk or butterfat production record of a cow is a phenotypic character - the same as black and white colour- and it does not necessarily represent the genetic makeup. As the black and white animal may possess factors for red, so the high milk production record cow may possess factors for low production. Because of this the offspring from high producing cows may be quite mediocre. A study of this phenomenon has given rise to a law, first propounded by Galton, which is known as the Law of Regression. This law shows that the tendency is for offspring from extreme parents to deviate from such parents toward the average of the population. Gowen, studying correlation between daughter and dam, found that the Law of Regression applied to the inheritance of milk production. This fact is illustrated in Fig. 13.1. Due to the large number of animals involved the lines in this chart are straight. Depending upon the degree of heterozygosity present in the parents, individuals deviate markedly from the average. Special note should be made of the fact that for extremely high production, the daughters deviate more markedly from their dams than is the case with lower production. This is accounted for by the probability that extremely high production is a result of a fortunate combination of factors coming from both the sire and the dam, and that such an individual would be more heterozygous than one with lower production records. While the selection of breeding stock from dams with high production records has aided materially in improving dairy cattle, it falls far short of accomplishing what might be accomplished through the use of better methods in evaluating the breeding stock on the basis of its genetic makeup.

Progeny test

The most reliable means of determining the genetic makeup of an animal is through the performance of the progeny of such an animal. If the progeny test is to be significant, two important considerations must be taken into account: first, the proper matings must be made; and second, there must be sufficient numbers of the progeny to bring out the factor combinations. Progeny from distantly related parents are not so reliable in indicating the genetic makeup of the parents as are progeny from parents of closer relationship. For the inheritance of a complex character like milk production, at least, distantly related parents are more likely to have factors for high production in different chromosomes, and these factors will have a tendency to dovetail or complement one another in such a way that the daughters will be higher milk producers than the dam, and also more heterozygous. Breeders have observed increased milk production from the crossing of certain strains, and refer to this phenomenon as "nicking." The geneticist recognizes the soundness of this hypothesis, and has applied the term "heterosis" to the phenomenon.

The effects of heterosis are recognized in crossbreeding, the offspring usually being much more vigorous than either one of the parents. It is, therefore, evident that mating distantly related parents may not be a test of the genetic makeup of these parents. High producing daughters from a cow may also owe their inheritance to the sire, who may be unusually prepotent; therefore, in order to properly evaluate the genetic makeup of a cow, something should be known about the sire, in regard to his inheritance for milk production. Furthermore, the records of daughters by different sires are of more significance than those of daughters from the same sire. Since the bull's daughters are usually out of different cows, there is no great danger of falling into this error in using the progeny to evaluate his genetic makeup, but the effect of heterosis is equally dangerous in confusing the evaluation of the genetic makeup of the sire. Undoubtedly when a bull has proved to be a sire of good production in one herd and fails in another, heterosis is the basis for the difference. The herd where he was recognized as a sire of high production had the genes for production that would complement or "nick" with the genes that he possessed and thus result in a factorial combination in the offspring for high milk production, while the other herd did not.

Backcrossing

Since the parents and other offspring are likely to have the same genes in common, a better test for the genetic makeup of an animal is to backcross; that is, to breed back the sons to their dams, or the daughters to their sires. When so doing, there is one chance in four that a recessive gene present in both parents and offspring will manifest itself in the F_2s as a double recessive. Inasmuch as only every other one of the offspring will receive the recessive gene from a heterozygous parent, only one out of eight of the F_2s will have a double recessive and thus express a recessive character. Thus, if a Holstein bull is suspected of carrying a recessive gene for red and is backcrossed to his daughters, an average of one out of eight of the calves will be red and white. This emphasizes the need for sufficient number of offspring to prove the genetic makeup of any one animal. For a complex character such as a milk production, where a large number of genes is required for the expression of the character, not so many progeny are needed to determine whether or not the animal is highly heterozygous. If the animal is highly heterozygous, the chances are that the F_2s will receive a number of recessive genes and will be inferior to the parents from the standpoint of milk production.

The ideal test

The ideal test for the genetic makeup of an animal would be the mating of such an animal to one that is double recessive for all characters desired. Thus, to prove whether or not a Holstein carries the recessive red factor; a cross with a red animal would require only an average of two progeny to bring out that character. For a test of heterozygosity for milk production, securing a double recessive animal for the genes involved would be difficult. Undoubtedly, beef animals are lacking materially in factors for milk production; but in crossing a beef animal with a dairy animal other complications are introduced. The beef animal undoubtedly possesses large numbers of genes that are dominant and that are involved in the expression of the character "beefness." In a cross with a dairy animal it seems reasonable to believe that there would be a conflict for expression between the genes for milk production and for beef production, and thus the resulting individual would be a test neither for the genetic makeup of the beef animal nor for that of the dairy animal. It would seem that the best test animal for the genetic makeup for milk production would be one within the same breed that lacks, in so far as can possibly be ascertained, genes for the expression of all the characters that go to make up milk production.

Limitations

Complete analysis of the genetic makeup of cattle is impossible because of the length of the reproduction cycle and the few numbers of offspring from a cow. By the time a record on the progeny from a cow could be obtained, the cow would be about six years of age. Also, the average of five offspring from a cow would be a good number. While a satisfactory number of daughters can be obtained from a bull, the results are partly obscured by the inability to secure the necessary information on the genetic makeup of the cows to which he is mated.

Pedigree

The pedigree in its original meaning is simply an extended record of the ancestry; in that sense any animal could have a pedigree. Among dairy cattle breeders, however, a pedigree is limited to the purebreds, and sometimes purebreds are referred to as pedigreed stock. Then too, the pedigrees, in addition to being mere tabulations of the ancestry, contain varying amounts of information about the individuals appearing in such tabulations. In most cases it contains the records of performance of the individual, if it is a cow, and the records of daughters of both bulls and cows. The writing of pedigrees has become quite a specialty, and a pedigree writer sometimes resorts to the use of phraseology that will connect the records of distant relatives more closely with an animal whose pedigree is being considered. The pedigree can be of great service in estimating the breeding value or genetic makeup of an individual. Most pedigrees, however, do not contain sufficient information to be of great value in this connection. The point can be best illustrated by discussing a pedigree as it should not be. Figure 12.2 is the reproduction of a pedigree which is worthless for evaluating that animal. It will be noted that while a considerable number of animals with records are listed under the sire, they are brought there by the phrase "by brother to the sire of." The animals listed under the sire are such distant relatives of the sire that they have no significance. Similarly, listing a number of animals with records under the dam is to be criticized, as they are "by a brother to that sire of the dam." Practically all of the listing of records in that pedigree can be criticized in the same way. This naturally leads to a discussion of the importance of the various generations in the pedigree.

It is apparent that the most important individuals in the pedigree are the parents, and that the next most important are the grandparents. Only 25 per cent of the genetic makeup of the individual comes from each grandparent. The important evidence, therefore, in the pedigree is that which will give information as to the general makeup of the parents and the grandparents. Here the records of the dam and the two grand dams are of some significance, but relatively small. Far more important evidence is the record of the daughters of the sire and the grand sires and of the dam and grand dams. If all the daughters have been tested and their records are uniformly good, and if there are sufficient numbers of such daughters, then the chances are very good that the individual has the same inheritance. Not only should the production records of the daughters be high, but they should be uniform. If one or more daughters of a bull or a cow have a low milk production record, that should be considered as positive evidence that such an animal has factors for low production; and if it has happened once, there is no assurance that the animal in question has not received the same inheritance.

In evaluating a pedigree, in addition to making sure that the offspring are of uniformly high production, care should be taken to ascertain that the animals listed in the pedigree have not been selected, so that a few of the highest producing offspring are listed while the rest are omitted. It is a rather common practice for pedigree writers to list the highest producing daughters and fail to mention those that have lower records. In addition to this, the breeder frequently selects the most likely cows for testing, leaving untested those that are not so promising. Thus, the information available is not representative of the actual facts.

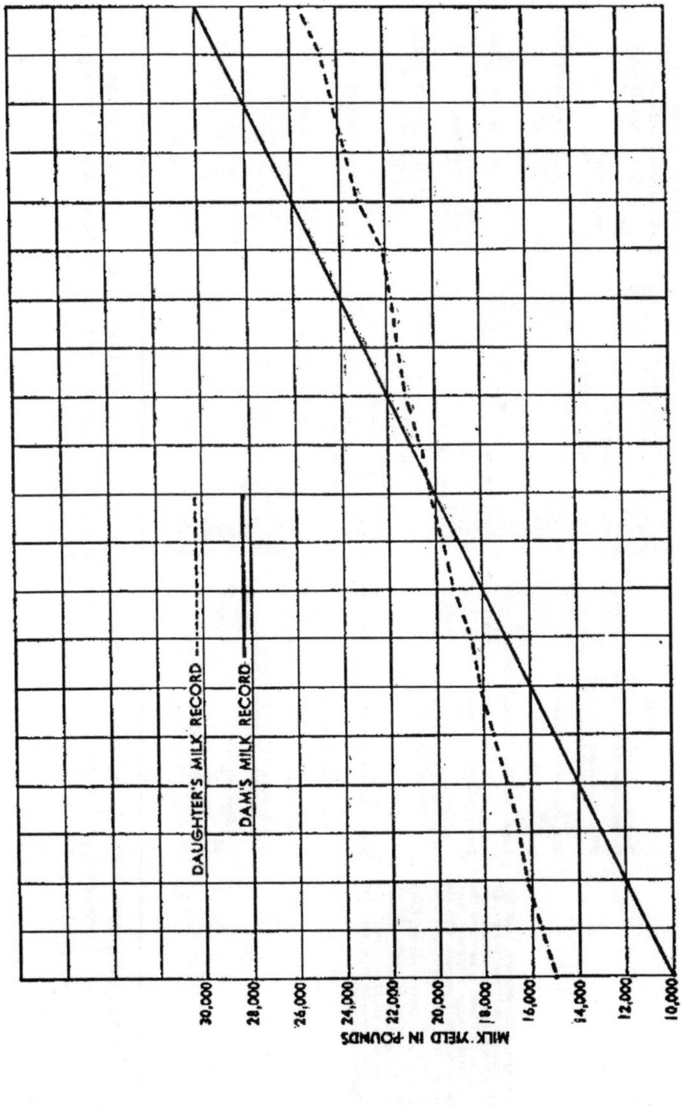

Fig. 13.2: Milk yield of dams and average yield of their daughters.

This youngster has splendid backing. His sire is from a 26 lb. 4 year old and by the 30 lb. bull who is by a brother to two 1,000 lb. cows and from a sister to the breed's greatest long distance sire, Sir Pietertje Ormsby Mercedes, who has 12 daughters that have produced over 1,000 lbs. of butter.

His dam is by a 20 lb. son of King Korndyke Colantha Ormsby, whose daughters are making splendid records in both short- and long-time tests. He is a full brother to a 34 lb. 4 year old with a 1,000 lb. year record.

SIRE

By a brother to the sire of:
Queen Piebe Mercedes. 4y 1389.45
30230 20
(World's Record for class)
Glen Canary De Kol 2d. 4y 1434.36
Milk 25590.20
Bess Pietertje Ormsby Merc. 1235.32
Milk 29053.20
Bess Burke Ormsby. 1146.01
Milk 26044.70
Dinah Pauline Clothilde Ormsby 4½y 1146.01
Milk 24078.10
Queen Piebe Ormsby Merc. 4½y 1136.01
Milk 24123.10
Miss Minita Ormsby Merc. 1078.07
4 others above 1,000 lbs.

DAM

By a brother to:
Miss Korndyke Johanna Rue 4y 30.65
Milk 605.10
Miss Korndyke Haldee Orms. 4½y 30.35
Milk 622.80
Queen Eagle Korndyke Heng. 4y 30.22
Sire is by a full brother to:
Miss Colantha Korndyke Orms. 4½y 34.08
30 days butter 131.40
365 " " 1089.43

GRAND SIRE

By a brother to:
Semi-official records
Miss Korndyke Maid Ormsby 1255.64
Milk 25418.30
Jenny Wren Korndyke Heng. 1050.48
4 from 30 to 39.56 lbs.

GRAND DAM

At 4 yrs., 5 mos.
Butter 26.11
Milk 475.00
At 3 yrs. 2 mos.
Butter 20.86
Milk 388.40
Butter, 30 das. 80.31
Milk 1617.30
At 2 yrs., 3 mos.
Butter 13.09
Butter 289 das. 364.43
Milk 8232.7

GRAND SIRE

By a brother to the sires or dams of:
Irma Johanna Concordia 4½y 37.93
Gypsy Lyons 33.63
Queen Lyons Gelsche Rosewood 33.31
Daisy Colantha Girl 4½y 31.81
9 others above 30 lb.

GRAND DAM

By a brother to:
Grace Fayne 2d's Homestead 35.55
(World's record when made)
Lady Oak 2d's De Kol
8y 34.14
7y 32.19
Jessie Fobes 2d's Maud Homestead 31.17
4 others above 30 lbs.

GREAT GRAND SIRE

6 A.R.O. Daughters
Willow Ridge Korndyke Capitola, 4½y 19.98
2 others above 332 lbs.

GREAT GRAND DAM

Butter 30.44
Milk 579.40
Butter, 30 das. 120.54
Butter, 365 das. 832.05
Milk 19028.30

GREAT GRAND SIRE

22 A.R.O. daughters
14 from 20 to 28 lbs.
3 above 594 lbs.
6 A.R. sons

GREAT GRAND DAM

Butter 19.02
Butter, 365 das. 484.15
3 A.R.O. daughters.
2 above 22 lbs.
1 A.R. son

GREAT GRAND SIRE

14 A.R.O. daughters
3 above 30 lbs.
4 others above 20 lbs.
3 above 521 lbs.

GREAT GRAND DAM

Butter 2½y 20.07
Milk 422.50
Sister to:
Eight from 20 to 27 lbs.

GREAT GRAND SIRE

34 A.R.O. daughters
7 from 20 to 23 lbs.
8 A.R. sons
14 producing daughters

GREAT GRAND DAM

Butter 3½y 17.49
Milk 445.20
Sister to:
Pearl Orms, Burke 30.56

Fig. 13.3: A poor pedigree. There is no information given in this pedigree that is of any value in evaluating the bull. By clever use of phraseology records of good producing but distant ancestors have been brought forward. None of the first two generations have any record of performance.

One other precaution must be taken, and that is to ascertain the type of management that has been used in making the records. If the animals have been forced and given the best of "Official Test" care, a higher production should be expected than if ordinary care has been given the animals while on test. Then, if all the information is available, if all the offspring of the parents of the two first generations have been tested, and if there are sufficient numbers of such offspring from each of the parents-say, three daughters from the cows and 20 daughters from the bull- analysis of the information given should give a reasonably accurate indication of what the probable production inheritance is of the animal in question. In addition to the listing of production records in the pedigree, the type of the individuals may be indicated by its show ring performance or by its type rating.

Bull index

In recent years several attempts have been made to evaluate the genetic makeup of a bull in the form of the so-called "Bull Index." The idea behind the bull index is that by considering the performance of the progeny and their dams, a figure can be arrived at that will be indicative of the milk production transmitting powers of a bull. In all, about ten such indexes have been proposed, each one varying in detail. The Mount Hope index, having been greatly publicized, is perhaps the best known. This is based upon the result of crossbreeding work conducted at the Maine Station. The index for milk and fat percentage is determined by the use of two different formulae. For the Mount Hope index, as well as all other bull indexes, the yearly milk record must be calculated to a mature equivalent. This also must be done with butterfat production.

Mount Hope index - milk

Compute the average mature equivalent of the milk production of all the daughters of a bull and also the average mature equivalent of the milk production of the dams of these daughters, and take the difference between these averages.

If the daughters' average exceed the dams' average, add three-sevenths (or .4286) of the difference to the daughters' average to get the bull's milk index figure.

If the daughters' average is less than the dams' average, subtract seven-thirds (or 2.333) of the difference from the daughters' average to get the bull's index figure.

Mount Hope Index - Butterfat per cent

The index for percentage of buterrfat is obtained by similar operations, but with different fractions.

If the daughter's butterfat average percentage exceeds the dams' butterfat average percentage , add three-halves (or 1.5) of the difference to the daughter's average to gat the bull's butterfat index.

If daughter's average is less than the dams' average, subtract two-thirds (or .6667) of the difference to the daughter's average to gat the bull's butterfat index.

The Holstein-Friesian Association index

The Holstein-Friesian Association calculates the bull index for all bulls having daughter-dam pairs with herd test records. The index is known as an "equal parent index" and is based upon the formula:

Bull's index = dams' average + 2 (daughters' average - dams' average)

The same formula is used for both milk production and fat percentage.

Gifford index

This index, which bears the name of its author, disregards the dams' production. The index is merely an arithmetical average of the daughters' records computed to a mature basis.

Criticisms of the Bull Index

By the use of the Mount Hope index, bulls have been found to have a negative index. In case of equal parent index this situation is possible but not so likely, as the daughters would have to average less than one-half the production of their dams in order to secure values less than zero. The values for the same bull may vary greatly, depending upon whether the Mount Hope, Holstein-

Friesian, or the Gifford indexes are used. If the daughters are lower producers than their dams, the Mount Hope index gives the lowest values and the Gifford index the highest values. If the daughters' exceed the dams', these indexes arrange in a different order.

Aside from the Gifford index, all bull indexes are based upon the assumption that the production record of a cow is an accurate measure of her transmission ability. This is definitely not so, as has been shown previously. The high producing cows are likely to have a favourable combination of factors for high production which have small chances for transmission to the offspring.

Another assumption that lacks proof in its support is that of cumulative inheritance. Work done at the Minnesota Station and elsewhere has shown that the index secured for a bull upon a limited number of his daughters may be very materially different from the index for the same bull derived from another set of daughter-dam pairs. This is what would be expected upon consideration of the fundamentals of inheritance. If the factors responsible for milk production are dominant (and there are good reasons to believe that they are), then the Gifford index or the mere arithmetic average of the bull's daughters would be indicative of his potential level of production. Studies at the Minnesota Station seemed to support this. No correlation was found between the dam's records and the daughters' records from the same bulls, when the bulls were apparently of as high or higher inheritance than that of the dams. If the hypothesis of dominance and recessiveness is true, the arithmetical average of the daughters as an index of the bull's would be in error when the dam possessed a higher level of inheritance than the bull. Positive conclusion as to the value of bull indexes in evaluating bulls must be withheld until more convincing information is at hand. In the meantime, the breeder should have an open mind toward the bull index, but should not depend too much upon it in giving direction to his breeding programme.

The breeder of today must familiarize himself with all that is known about inheritance of characters in dairy cattle, learn how to test his herd for their genetic makeup, and use the system of breeding that is best adapted to his needs. Depending alone upon any one formula or single set of factors to give direction to the breeding programme where inheritance is apparently so complex as in dairy cattle, is fraught with great danger.

14

Known Inherited Characteristics in Dairy Cattle

While as yet comparatively little is known about inheritance in cattle, there are a number of characters the nature of the inheritance of which is known. Many of these characters are of economic importance, while others are mainly of interest for what they may contribute to the general knowledge of inheritance. A consideration of the more important of the known inherited characters of dairy cattle is essential for one interested in the breeding of dairy cattle. The value of a knowledge of the nature of the inheritance of the characteristics that are of economic importance is obvious. A knowledge of the nature of the inheritance of characters not of economic importance finds value in that it contributes to one's concept of how inheritance behaves in cattle. The characters for which the nature of the inheritance is more or less known fall into the following groups:

1. Inheritance of colour
2. Inheritance of miscellaneous characters
3. Inheritance of lethal factors
4. Inheritance of characters affecting production

INHERITANCE OF COLOUR

The inheritance of colour in cattle is governed by a large number of factors. These can be grouped into two classes: namely, a group of factors that influence the pigmentation of the hair, and a group of factors that influence the colour pattern.

Factors that Influence Pigmentation

In cattle there are all degrees of shades of colour, ranging from a jet black down to white, which is a complete absence of colour pigment. These colours and shades are due to several different types of inheritance. These types of inheritances may be divided into four different groups, as follows:

1. Where the darker colour is dominant or epistatic to the lighter colour.
2. Where the darker colour is inhibited from showing even though a gene for such a colour may be present.
3. Where there is a mixture of two or more colours.
4. Where the mechanism for colour production is lost.

Dominance of Darker colours

Unless there are other interfering factors, the rule is that the darker colour is dominant or epistatic to the lighter colour. Thus, the red of the Red Poll is dominant to the yellow of the Jersey or Guernsey, and the black of the Angus or Galloway is dominant to the red of the Red Poll.

Factors inhibiting darker colours

Failure of a darker colour to express itself even though it is present in the genetic makeup of an animal is observed in many cases. It may take form in a complete suppression of colour in parts of the body or the entire body, or it may lighten the coat colour in various degrees. Dominant white spotting, to be discussed under colour patterns, may be considered as one form of complete suppression of pigment in certain areas of the body. The black West Highland cattle of England become dun in the presence of a dilution factor (D), which acts upon the black to make it several shades lighter. A similar factor is found to act upon the red of the Hereford to dilute it to a yellow. In the Jersey, Ayrshire, and Guernsey there is an intensity factor (I) which, when present, intensifies the colour or makes it darker. The recessive (i) might be said in all probability to dilute the intense black of the Holstein and Angus. In the Ayrshire and Jersey there is a peculiar modifying factor (ML) of the black spotting (Bs). This factor intensifies the black colour. M, representing much black, is dominant in the male; and L, representing little black, is dominant in the female. Thus a male of ML composition is black, and a female of that composition is red. The black females are homozygous for M. There are many other factors influencing the degree of pigmentation in cattle. Later work, undoubtedly, will bring to light many factors influencing this phenomenon.

Mixture of Colour

There are some cases where two colours may appear in the same animal. While this is also considered under colour pattern, it must be mentioned here since it affects the degree of pigmentation of the hair. The most commonly noticed of these is brindling (Br). This is a character manifested by alternating bands of black and red hair. The nature of the inheritance is discussed under colour pattern. The black spotting (Bs) in Ayrshires and Jerseys permits the black to be expressed upon red. In the Guernsey, too, is found a condition where jet black spots of various sizes may appear on the red.

Loss of Colour-albinism

An interesting mutation is that of a loss of the capacity to develop pigment in the hair, skin, and other parts normally pigmented. This condition produces albinos, of which there are a number of cases on record for cattle. Experiments with albinos at the University of Minnesota have shown that while albinism is due to a single recessive gene in the homozygous condition, all other genes for colour or colour patterns fail to express themselves except for a peculiar character referred to as a ghost pattern. When the gene for black (B) is present in the albino, a pattern of the nature of that aspect for a black and white animal can be seen under proper lighting conditions. The darker pattern is not caused by pigment but is due to a hair structure in which the medulla is absent. This hair structure absorbs more light than the normal hair with medullas to produce the ghost pattern. It is thought that albinism is due to the loss of a gene essential for the conversion of tyrosine into the pigment.

Colour Patterns

While much work has been done in the study of inheritance of colour patterns, the final word has not as yet been said on the nature of this type of inheritance. The general behaviour of the major features is quite definitely known, but many of the factors for minor variations are not so well known. For discussion, the inheritance of colour patterns may be divided into four groups:

1. Self (S) and recessive white spotting (s)
2. Dominant white patterns
3. Black spotting
4. Mixed colours

Each one of these groups has a number of modifying factor which will be discussed in connection with the main thesis.

Self and recessive white spotting

Recessive white spotting (s) is an allelomorph of self (S). An animal that is self is solid of colour unless there are some other modifying factors present, as is usually the case. Self is dominant to recessive white spotting. The heterozygous self (Ss) animal shows the same characters as the homozygous (SS) one. For the recessive white spotting to show the animal must be homozygous, and such an animal will breed true. The Angus, Galloway, and Red Poll are representative examples of the selfed animal (SS) even though they are modified by a dominant inguinal white (In). If this factor is present, white will be found in the inguinal region.

Recessive white spotting is recessive as the name indicates, and is found in the Holstein, Shorthorn, Jersey, Guernsey, and Ayrshire. It is responsible for the white areas of the body, tongue, nose, lining of the mouth, and white of the eyes and the legs. The white areas on the body and legs vary greatly in extent. This variation is accounted for by a single pair of modifiers, little white, Lw lw. Lw is the not completely dominant to lw. This permits three types of modification of the extent of white spotting, depending upon the combinations. Thus, the Lw. Lw animal will have very little white; the Lw lw will have a medium amount of white; and the lw lw animal will have a large amount of white. With the natural somatic variation, these three will account for all the degrees of white spotting that is observed. The Ayrshire and the Holstein undoubtedly possess both of the factors, while the Guernsey and the Jersey possess but the Lw.

A second modifying factor of recessive white spotting is known as the pigmented leg factor (Pl). This factor is responsible for the pigmentation below the knees, which usually begins at the hoofs and extends upward. It is also responsible for a spotting about the head. Being a dominant gene, whenever an animal possesses it in either or both of the chromosome pairs, the character will be manifested. The gene is very common in the Ayrshire and Shorthorn, and may be present in some Guernseys and Jerseys. Holsteins with the Pl factor cannot be registered. The small black spots sometimes found on the legs of Holsteins are not due to Pl factor, but more probably to another factor known as the distal leg (Dl) factor.

Dominant White

There are at least five dominant white genes in cattle. All of these will find expression in either a recessive white spotted animal or a selfed animal. They are the White Park cattle of England (Wp), the Hereford pattern (SH), the Dutch Belted (SD), the colour-sided pattern (SC), and the Inguinal white (In). Of these the SH, the SD, and the SC are allelomorphs of the self and recessive white spotting. Therefore, only two of these genes can be present in any one animal.

The Hereford pattern (SH) is dominant; it produces a white head, feet, ventral side of the body, and tip of the tail, and a strip of white of varying size over the shoulder running parallel with the length of the body. The SH gene may be said to be responsible for both the white and the pigmented part of the pattern. It is incompletely dominant to self and completely dominant to recessive white spotting. A cross of a Hereford with an Angus produces an F_1 where the white is diminished. When the Hereford is crossed with a Holstein, there is no diminution of the white. Among the Herefords there is a great deal of variation in the amount of white and pigmented areas. This is accounted for by a number of modifying factors. One is the Lw factor, which behaves like the same factor in the Holstein. Another is the white restrictor (Wr), which restricts the amount of white on the dorsal part of the neck and shoulder. A third is the red eye (Re) which is completely dominant to its recessive (re); it is responsible for the red hair around the eyes.

Dutch Belted (SD) is responsible for the white belt encircling the chest. It is completely dominant to recessive white spotting and incompletely dominant to self. A cross of a Dutch Belted with an Angus produces an animal with a narrower belt. There are, undoubtedly, factors modifying the Dutch Belted pattern; none, however, have been studied sufficiently to warrant giving them genetic symbols.

Colour sided (Sc) is the factor responsible for a wide white stripe along the backbone and another along the belly and brisket, which gives the animal the appearance of having a stripe of colour along each side. There is no purebred American breed possessing this character. In Norway, however, there are two breeds, the Telemarks and the Troenders. It is also found in the Yak and Zebus. This factor is incompletely dominant to self and completely dominant to recessive white spotting.

Inguinal white (In) is a dominant gene, epistatic to self. It is responsible for the white hairs in the inguinal region. In recessive white spotting it cannot be ascertained because recessive white spotting usually is responsible for white in the same region. The Holstein, which is homozygous for recessive white spotting, possesses this factor, for when the Holstein is mated to self animals free from inguinal white the character appears in the F_1s.

Black Spotting Patterns

The inheritance of two black spotting patterns is known. These are black spotting (Bs) and pigmented skin (Ps). The black spotting factor is found in the Jersey, Ayrshire, Brown Swiss, and in some cases probably the Holstein. The black spotting factor manifests itself by producing black hair on lighter pigmented areas. It also causes black pigment in the skin, hoofs, nose, tongue, mouth, and eyes if the animal is self. As has already been stated, black spotting is dominant and is modified by the much black (M) which is dominant in the male and produces a more intense pigment, and by little black (L) which is dominant in the female and produces red.

The pigmented skin factor produces skin spotting without pigmentation of the hair. This factor is dominant and is best observed on denuded parts of the body, such as the nose; however, it may appear on any part of the body. It is the factor that is responsible for the black nose in Guernseys, which is considered undesirable. The fact that a Guernsey may have a clear nose does not necessarily mean that she is free from the pigmented skin factor, because the gene may manifest itself by pigmentation on another part of the body. This factor is also found in the Shorthorn and the Hereford.

The author has also observed jet black spots on the red areas of Guernseys. The nature of this inheritance is not known, but it probably behaves as a dominant gene in very much the same way as the black spotting factor. The clean-cut demarcation between the black hair and the red hair would suggest that it is a different factor than black spotting (Bs), where the black gradually fades out to red.

Mixed Colours

There are two types of mixed colours, both of which are well known and satisfactorily worked out from a genetic viewpoint. These are the brindle and the roan. Brindle is a character where narrow stripes of black hair show on a background of red. Two genes are involved in its expression; one is the dominant black spotting (Bs) gene which must be present, and the other is the dominant brindling (Br) gene. The Jerseys carry the Bs gene to a large extent but do not possess the Br gene; consequently, no brindling is found in purebred Jerseys. The Angus carries the Br gene, but it does not possess the Bs gene; and even if it did, the brindling would not manifest itself, since they are selfed for black. If Jerseys and Angus are crossed, brindling may appear in the F_2 generation, one of each of the important genes coming from each of the parental types. A limited amount of bridnling occurs in the Guernseys. This would indicate that the Guernsey possesses the gene for brindling and also the black spotting gene. In the Guernsey the brindling is usually confined to the head and neck, but in scrubs it will be extended to the entire body.

Roaning is a condition where white hair is interspersed with pigmented hair. If the pigmented hair is red, it is known as red roan. If the pigmented hair is black, it is known as blue roan. The inheritance of this character is quite complex and is not so well known as most of the other colour inheritances. It is generally agreed upon that factor N is needed; in the homozygous condition it produces white by inhibiting the expression of red. In the double recessive (nn) form the animal will be red. In the heterozygous (Ns) form the animal will be roan. That this condition is necessary for roaning is generally agreed upon; however, there are other factors which modify the character roaning which are not so well agreed upon.

Ibsen explains the modifying factor tentatively by postulating a dominant roaning modifier (Rm) which acts upon the heterozygous (Nn) to produce a roan. The recessive rm rm would produce a red. If only the heterozygous condition Nn were necessary for roaning, all matings of white and red in the Shorthorn breed would be roans; but this is not so. Ibsen's postulation would account for the exceptions of red and white Shorthorn crosses in producing roans.

Colour Factor in Different Breeds

The colour factors in the different breeds are as follows:

Holstein

On the basis of what is now known, the colour formula for the Holstein is as follows:

BB dd Il nn ps ps ss Lw lw pl pl WW Wn Wn Wp Wp

Bb Ps ps lw lw

bb Lw Lw

The Holstein is variable for pigmented skin where individuals may be double recessives or possess the dominant pigmented skin gene, and for the little white modifier of recessive white spotting. The Holstein is the least variable of any of the dairy breeds in the fundamental colour factors. There is a recessive red. Animals having this recessive factor cannot be registered; whenever a red and white Holstein calf is dropped, it is a loss to the breeder of purebred Holsteins.

Jersey

On the basis of the present knowledge, the colour formula for the Jersey is as follows:

bb br br Bs bs ML dd ii nn SS Lw Lw ww Wn Wn wp wp

Bb LL Dd ss

MM

The Jersey is variable for black, as it may be either red or black; for black spotting; for black spotting modifier; for dilution; and for self, as it may be either solid coloured or white spotted and may be variable for the recessive white spotting factor (LW).

Ayrshire

The formulà for the Ayrshire on the basis of present knowledge is as follows:

Bb Br br Bs bs ML dd II nn Ps ps ss Lw lw Pl pl WW Wn Wn Wp Wp

bb br br bs bs MM

BB Br Br Bs Bs LL Ps ps Lw lw pl pl

Ps Ps Lw Lw Pl Pl

The Ayrshire is the most variable of the diary breeds for colour genes. It may be heterozygous for the genes affecting black, brindling, black spotting, black spotting modifiers, pigmented skin, recessive white spotting modifiers, and pigmented legs.

Shorthorn

The colour formula for the Shorthorn is as follows:

bb bs bs dd II Nn Rm rm Ps ps ss Lw lw Pl pl WW Wn Wn wp wp

nn Rm Rm Ps ps lw lw Pl pl

NN rm rm Ps Ps LW LW Pl Pl

The Shorthorn is variable for the roaning factors (N and Rm), pigmented skin, and the recessive white spotting modifier, little white, and pigmented leg.

Guernsey

The colour formula for the Guernsey is as follows:

bb bs bs dd ii nn Ps ps ss Lw lw Pl pl WW Wn Wn wp wp

Bs bs? ps ps lw lw Pl pl

Ps Ps Lw Lw Pl pl

The Guernsey varies in its inheritance of genes for pigmented skin and white spotting modifier. Guernseys may, in some cases, possess genes for pigmented leg and black spotting.

The variables are:

Ps ps

Lw lw

Pl pl

Bs

Brown Swiss; Dutch Belted

There is not enough known about either the Brown Swiss or the Dutch Belted to warrant a colour formula.

INHERITANCE OF MISCELLANEOUS CHARACTERS

Horns and hornlessness. The nature of the inheritance of the hornless condition was one of the first genetic factors worked out for cattle. At first it was assumed to be a simple. Mendelian dominant-recessive phenomenon, in which the hornless condition was completely dominant to the horned condition, or a dominant inhibiting factor. More recently, it has been shown that the inheritance cannot be explained by a single factor, for in the F_2's and F_3's, scurs often appear. Ibsen postulates that all cattle are homozygous for horns and that, in addition, Polled cattle carry a dominant gene (P) which is completely dominant to its recessive and epistatic to the horned condition. Crosses between homozygous polled and horned cattle produce mostly polled offspring, but some (mostly males) are either scurred or horned. To account for this, Ibsen postulates two other genes Ha (African horns) and Sc (scurred) as being involved. In the male Sc Sc or Sc sc is epistatic to P, and all males carrying the factor are scurred. In the female sc must be homozygous to be epistatic to P. Ha probably behaves similarly. Males carrying P are horned whether they are homozygous or heterozygous for Ha.

Notched Ears

In the Ayrshire and Jersey breeds a condition of a notch of varying sizes in the lower part of the ear has been observed. From a study of a number of matings, it seems to be due to a single Mendelian dominant gene. Bulls with "notched ears" and apparently heterozygous, transmitted the character to approximately one-half of their offspring.

Night Blindness

This is a defect found in Shorthorns, which makes it impossible for them to see in lights in which other cattle can see perfectly. The defect is one which affects the rods and cones of the retina, and behaves in such a way as to lead to the conclusion that it is due to a single recessive gene.

Umbilical Hernia

Umbilical hernia has been observed in dairy cattle for along time. Not until recently, however, has there been any concerted attempt to ascertain the nature of its inheritance. The problem has been made difficult by the fact that it affects, in the main, only the males, and frequently those that may have the inherited character do not show it, because environment is a factor in its expression. There can be little question that the factor is recessive and that perhaps only one gene is involved.

Polydactyly

Polydactyly is a condition in cattle where more than two toes are found. While it is not very common, it has been found sufficiently often to have made possible a study of its genetics. The character is recessive and probably only one gene is involved in the expression of the character.

Screw tail

Screw tail or a kink in the tail is a condition that has been observed and studied in the Red Polled cattle. It manifests itself by a kinklike condition of the tail which is effected by a fusion of one or more pairs of adjacent coccygeal vertebrae. It has been shown to behave as a simple recessive Mendelian character.

Wry tail

Wry tail, a condition in which the tail is set over to one side of the body, has been described in the Jersey. This likewise behaves as a simple recessive Mendelian character.

Defective Teeth

Defective teeth, a hair defect, and several other minor characters have been studied; and nearly all of them appear to be due to recessive genes.

Udder Abnormality

An udder abnormality which is inherited as a single recessive Mendelian character has been described in the Guernsey. The udder is usually poorly shaped, is of about equal development on both sides, but there is only one teat on the left side.

INHERITANCE OF LETHAL FACTORS

A lethal, as the name indicates, is a factor that causes death of the individual. Strictly speaking the lethal should produce death at or before birth. Sublethal should apply to the factors that do not cause death until some time after birth. At the present time about 25 lethals and sublethals are known for cattle. This is more than for any other species, and there are undoubtedly still more to be discovered. Since most lethals are due to a single recessive gene, it is obvious that in the mating of animals each possessing the gene, one out of four of the progeny will be affected; two will carry the gene; and one will be free from it,. The loss in calves in a population in which one or more lethal genes are present can be large. The more important of the lethal factors will be briefly discussed.

Achondroplasia

There are three types of achondroplasia, all dealing with some abnormality of the cartilage as it forms bone. Flat, long, and irregular bones may be involved.

Achondroplasia 1

Achondroplasia 1 was the first lethal factor to be discovered in cattle. It is also known as "bulldog head" because of the shape and size of the head. The gene is incompletely dominant. In the homozygous condition the fetus becomes a monster and is usually aborted at from three to eight months of gestation. In the heterozygous condition the legs are shortened. The Dexter breed is a heterozygote for this gene. In mating Dexters one-fourth of the offspring are aborted as "bulldog" calves, one-half are normal Dexters, and one-fourth are normal legged animals known as the Kerry breed. The Kerrys breed true but the Dexters split into the three phenotypes. The gene for achondroplasia has been found in Jerseys.

Achondroplasia 2

Achondroplasia 2 differs from the other form in that the affected calves are usually carried to normal term and may live for a few days. There is also some difference in the malformation in which the lower jaw protrudes beyond the upper jaw. The gene is present in the Telemark cattle of Norway where it was first described. It has also been found in the Holstein, Jersey, Guernsey, and Ayrshire breeds.

Achondroplasia 3

Achondroplasia 3 is found in the Jersey breed, having been discovered by workers at the California Station in an inbreeding project. The heads of the affected individuals are short and wide, the lower jaw protruding, and the palate usually is cleft. Sometimes the legs are shortened and the pasterns flexed. Affected individuals usually die shortly after birth but an individual may live up to fourteen months.

Short spine lethal

This condition has been observed only in the Oplandske breed of cattle of Norway. It is characterized by a fusion or absence of a number of the vertebrae of the neck, back, and tail, producing an exceedingly short neck and body. Other parts of the body are normal. It behaves as a simple recessive character, since 25 per cent of the offspring of heterozygous parents are affected.

Amputated Leg Lethal

Amputated leg lethal has been found in the Holstein breed of Sweden. It is a complementary gene of the short spine, as the bones not affected by the short spine are affected by this factor. The legs are shortened, and the feet and lower parts are entirely missing. The lower jaw is vestigial or entirely missing, and the upper jaw is shortened or curved back under in the position where the lower jaw normally would be. This, too, behaves as a simple recessive Mendelian character.

Hairless Lethal

Hairless lethal has been reported only in the Holstein breed of Scandinavia. The calves, born at the normal time, are entirely lacking in hair and live for but a short time. Like the other lethals described, it, too, is apparently due to a simple recessive gene.

Epithelial Defect

The epithelial defect, which is lethal, is manifested by a defective epithelium noted at the birth of a calf. The skin below the knees is denuded, and the mucous lining of the nostrils, mouth, tongue, palate, and cheeks also is affected. One or more of the claws is underdeveloped, and the integuments of the muzzle are defective. This condition has been described for the Holstein breed in America, and at least one Shorthorn calf has been reported that answers to the description of this congenital defect. In all cases where the defect has been known in the Holstein breed, the ancestry can be traced back to the bull Sarcastic Lad through at least two lines.

Impacted Molars

A lethal has been reported for the Milking Shorthorn in which the mandible is shortened and the premolars are impacted in the jaw bone. The molars are irregularly placed and the jaw bulges or is broken on the lateral surface. The calves are dropped at normal time but die during the first week. This lethal is also due to a simple recessive factor.

Additional Lethals

The following are a list of additional lethal or sublethal factors that have or seem to have a genetic basis.

General ankylosis

All joints are ossified to prevent flexion at the joints. Found in Black and White lowland cattle in Germany.

Ankylosis of lower jaw

The lower jaw is fused with the upper jaw at point of articulation. Found in Lyndal breed of Norway.

Agnathra

Partial or complete absence of the lower jaw. Found in Jerseys in the United States.

Hydrocephalus

Enlarged skull filled with a fluid; reported in Holsteins in Michigan.

Skull defect

The bones in the skull failed to close exposing the brain to trauma. Jersey, United States.

Micromelia

Short legs differing from the amputated leg condition. Found in Russian cattle.

Deformed limbs

All legs markedly deformed. Found in Friesian cattle in Russia.

Missing Phalanges

One or more of the phalanges absent. Found in Swedish cattle.

Mummification

Fetuses mummified in the uterus before birth. Found in Danish Reds.

Lameness

Calves, unable to stand, die in a day or a few days after birth. Found in Red Danish Breed.

Muscle contracture

Spastic contraction of extensor muscles of neck and limbs. Found in Norwegian, Danish Red, and Holstein breeds.

Closed nostrils

Membrane closure of nostrils producing suffocation. Found in Mountain breed of Croatia.

Artresia Ani

The anus is closed. Surgical opening does not prevent death. Found in Indian cattle.

Congenital spasms

Found in Jerseys as the result of continued inbreeding.

Congenital dropsy

Generalized hydration of the body. Found in Swedish breeds.

Sex-linked lethal

Males affected die. No specific lesions observed. Found in Angel cattle.

INHERITANCE OF TWINNING

There is positive evidence that twinning is an inherited character. According the recent figures, twins represents about one-half of 1 per cent of the calvings, and 1 per cent of the total number of calves. The per cent of twinning varies with different breeds. In Sweden it is found more frequently among the Holsteins than in the Red and White breed, and in this country it is much more frequent in the dairy than in the beef breeds. In the Kansas Station's Holstein herd the twinning percentage was 8.84 per cent, indicating that in this herd the factors for twinning are present quite generally. Because twinning is not a desirable character in cattle, no one has ever bred for this character. As a result not much is known as to how successful one would be in attempting to establish a herd having the twinning character quite general. With sheep, where selection for this character has been general because of the desirability, flocks have been established that have been quite pure for the character.

As environment is an influencing factor in the production of twins, the exact nature of the inheritance is not determined. Animals that may have the factors for twinning may not necessarily produce twins because of a number of possible interfering conditions. The competition for the survival of the implanted embryos is great. A cow that many have the inheritance for secretion of two or even more ova at each ovulation may never carry more than one fetus to normal term because of the many hazards encountered.

Formerly it was thought that monozygotic twins rarely if ever occurred in cattle. It is now well established that identical twins occur with sufficient frequency to make their use practical in research work of nearly all kinds. The frequency of identical twins is not definitely known but estimates are that they occur about once in each one thousand parturitions. Hundreds of monozygotic cattle twins have been inspected by the author. They may possess mirror imagery or be alike.

Freemartin

When a heifer is a twin to a bull, it is known as a freemartin. Ninety-two per cent of all freemartins are sterile because of the inhibitory effect the embryonic male hormones have upon the development of the female reproductive organs. Freemartins, like all twins, are much smaller at birth than singletons. They average from 70 to 80 per cent of the normal weights of single-born calves. With freemartins, as well as with all twins, about five times as many are stillborn as are singletons. They, too, have less vitality; the records show that 12½ per cent of twins die as young calves, whereas the average losses for all calves is about 4.2 per cent, under the same environmental conditions.

INHERITANCE OF FACTORS CONCERNED WITH PRODUCTION

There are so many factors involved in inheritance of milk and butterfat production that the knowledge as to the nature of the inheritance is speculative. The theories concerning the inheritance of milk and butterfat production have been evolved largely form circumstantial evidence or meager data and must, therefore, be

Fig. 14.1: A set of Jersey-Brown Swiss Cross is pictured here.

held subject to such changes as new evidence may determine. Before considering the theories and what is known about these most important characters, it is well to consider the physical basis for milk and butterfat production.

In order to produce milk, the cow must have the mechanism which manufactures milk; a large number of factors undoubtedly are involved in the development of this mechanism. Then efficient use of the mechanism must be made, and other factors are necessary for this. Under the head of the factors for the development of the mechanism may be considered factors influencing the size of the animal, the capacity for feed, the metabolism of feed, the size of the udder, and the quality of the udder. Factors affecting efficient use of the mechanism may be divided into those affecting milk production, fat production, and persistency. In addition to these considerations the practical dairyman is interested in the inheritance of type, longevity, breeding efficiency, and vigour.

Size

A number of people have shown that size is correlated to a certain degree with production. There is evidence that large animals may not be so efficient as some smaller animals, yet there is a limit to the smallness of the animal for profitable production. In the case of the inheritance for size there are so many factors involved that nothing specific about individual factors is known. That size is inherited is supported by a large amount of evidence. Different breeds are characterized by differences in size, and since all breeds at one time originated from the same common ancestry, different factors for size have been retained by different breeds in their development. The larger breeds must have a number of factors for size that are absent in the smaller breeds. The effect of selection for size factors is also evidenced in strains and families within the breeds. There is ample evidence in the records of practical breeding to show that by selection people have established strains and families of cattle that are noted for much larger size than is normally found within the breed.

Crossbreeding has furnished a clue as to the possible nature of some of the factors involved in size. The F_1s in crossbreeds where the parents vary greatly in size are intermediate, but they tend to be closer to the size of the larger parent. Thus, a cross of Jersey and Holstein produces individuals that are intermediate but more nearly the size of the Holstein than of the Jersey.

Inbreeding experiments have commonly resulted in reduced size of the inbred animals. This fact, together with the fact that in crossbreeding the offspring are closer to the size of the larger parent than the smaller parent, indicates that a number of the factors responsible for size are dominant. From the larger number of variations in degree of size between individuals within a breed and between breeds it is apparent that a large number of genes are involved in the inheritance of size.

Capacity for Feed

Dairy animals vary greatly in their capacity for handling feed. A portion of the ability to handle large amounts of feed can be accredited to development, since animals that have been heavily fed will be able to consume more feed than those which have been lightly fed; yet most of the ability to handle feed is due to inheritance. The differences in the ability of animals to consume roughage is the most pronounced. At the Minnesota Station variations in the ability of animals to consume roughage were found to be from two and one-half to four pounds of hay per 100 pounds of live weight per day. Daughters of one bull had uniformly large capacity for handling of roughage regardless of their dam's capacity. While no work on the specific inheritance of a capacity for feed has been reported, such inheritance is probably due to many factors, some of which, from the influence observed of one parent upon the daughters, would appear to be dominant. This variation in the ability of dairy cattle to handle roughage is an important economic factor in the breeding of dairy cattle.

Roughage yields more nutrients at a lower cost per acre than do the cereals. Cows that surpass in their ability to use large amounts of roughage have a distinct economic advantage over those that are lacking in this respect.

Udder Size

A large udder is one of the essential prerequisites for high production, although large udder size is not a guarantee of high production. Development of the udder is due to the action of hormones, for which there are probably several hereditary factors. The ultimate size of which an udder may be developed by the action of these hormones is undoubtedly dependent upon some other inherited factors. How many factors are concerned in the udder development is not known, nor is the nature of any of the factors known. In crossbreds of beef and dairy breeds, the udders of the F_1s are a little larger than half way intermediate between the two parents; this would indicate that at least some of the factors for udder size are dominant, although it is possible that the effect of heterosis may be a contributory factor to the observed fact. To offset this, it is possible that the beef breeds contribute some factor or factors which inhibit the growth and development of the udder.

Quality of Udder

It is well known that there are great differences between individuals in the quality of udders. It is also common knowledge that the udder of poor quality produces more than does one of poor quality. The poor quality is due to a relatively large amount of connective tissue and a corresponding lesser amount of secreting tissue. Again, the nature of the inheritance of "quality of udder" is as yet speculative. It has been generally observed that there is a tendency for dams with poor quality udders to pass this characteristic on to the daughter. Bulls are also known to have passed this characteristic on to their daughters. Breeders who have persistently selected for good quality of udders have attained a reasonable degree of success, but the slowness with which success is attained lends support to the contention that the inheritance of quality of udder is complex.

Activity of the Milk Making Mechanism

It is common knowledge that cow with large udders of good quality may sometimes be rather poor producers.

There are several possible causes, of genetic origin, for the udder to fail to secrete the maximum amount of milk per unit of tissue provided the nutrient intake is adequate to support higher levels of production. One is a failure of the endocrine system to supply the necessary hormones in optimum amounts. Another is the failure of adequate blood supply to the gland; a third is the lack of the individual cells to respond to greater production; and a fourth is the failure to get all the milk out of each milking.

Endocrine activity, in relation to udder development and milk secretion, is very intricate and complex and far from being fully understood. It is known, however, that prolactin, a hormone secreted by the anterior pituitary, is essential for milk secretion. It has also been demonstrated for both cows and goats that production in some animals may be greatly increased by injection of prolactin. This indicates that secretion of this hormone in quantities not sufficient to maintain high activity of the secretory tissue is sometimes a factor. Goats have been found that increased milk production up to 262 per cent. In cows, many workers have obtained increases in milk production following the administration of prolactin, including one case in which the author obtained more than 60 per cent increase. For the most part, however, increases in this species seldom exceeds 25 per cent and often no augmentation is obtained. The thyroid is also definitely concerned with maintaining milk secretion, since ablation of this gland causes cows to dry off and feeding of thyroxin increases both milk and fat production. In some cases, at least, it would appear that lack of inheritance for the secretion of the required amounts of thyroid substance is a limiting factor.

It has been shown that about 400 volumes of blood must pass through the udder of cow for each volume of milk produced. Any constriction of the vascular system or failure of its optimum development would therefore limit production of milk. Ergot, which constricts the vascular system, has been shown to have a marked depressing effect upon milk secretion. It is theoretically possible that the individual cells lack the capacity for producing optimally regardless of how well they may be supplied with the necessary precursors and hormones. No evidence as yet exists for support for rejection of such a hypothesis.

Failure of the cow to respond to the milking stimulus with a complete let-down of milk has been demonstrated to be an important factor influencing the level of production.

Since a definite amount of nutrients is required for any given amount of milk of a certain fat percentage, it is evident, too, that the animal must have inherited capacity for handling enough feed to take care of the nutrient requirements for production. As has been previously stated, lack of inheritance for food capacity is frequently the limiting factor for high production.

Milk and fat production

In general, there are two views as to the nature of milk and fat inheritance. One is that there is a large number of dominant and recessive Mendelian factors, and the other, supported by a number of people, is that milk production is the result of an inheritance that is cumulative; this means that each gene of the pair contributes toward the expression of a character. The hypothesis that the majority of factors for milk production are dominant finds much support. As has been previously indicated, recessive characters are easier to establish, for when a character is expressed, the animal is homozygous for such a character. In cases where the characters are the result of dominant genes, the undesirable recessive gene may be present; it cannot be ascertained from the type of the individual, and can only be described through inspection of the progeny.

Experiences that dairymen have had in the mating of heavy producers, when some of the offspring are decidedly inferior to one of the parents, would lend support to the hypothesis that the characters for milk production are dominant, and that high producers may carry many recessive factors for low production. Researcher has added more evidence to the probability of the dominant-recessive hypothesis. After studying the distribution of production in mixed

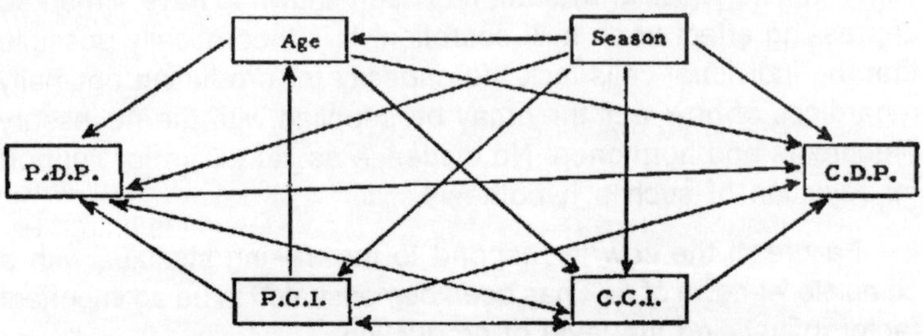

Fig. 14.2: Diagram showing the complex interactions between the age of calving, preceding (P.C.I.) and current calving intervals (C.C.I.), preceding (P.D.P.) and current dry periods (C.D.P.) and the season of calving. The line of action is indicated by arrows.

breeding, he postulated that such distribution could be accounted for by 18 Mendelian factors acting on the basis of dominance and recessiveness. Evidence for the cumulative hypothesis finds support in the observed production as a result of cross-breeding. Where beef breeds are crossed with dairy breeds, the F_1s are intermediate, with the milk production being nearer the level of the high producing parent and the fat percentage nearer the level of the low testing parent. Crosses of extremes within the dairy breed have not been intensively studied, but apparently there is some evidence that this, too, results in production levels intermediate between the two parents. With the crossbreeding of beef breeds and dairy breeds, the results can be questioned on the basis that, since the beef breeds have factors for beef production which may be epistatic or dominant to the factors for milk and fat production, such crosses cannot reveal the true nature of the inheritance of factors for milk and fat production. It is possible that a combination of dominant and recessive factors and cumulative factors are responsible for milk and fat production.

More evidence for the support of the dominant hypothesis lies in the performance of prepotent sires, where the daughters are invariably of a production level that would be more nearly that of the sire. At the Minnesota Station, no correlation was found between the dam's record and the record of the daughters of such bulls although the dams varied materially. It would appear that the daughters' inheritance for production had come mainly from the sire. This may be explained by postulating dominance of the factors for milk production and that the sire was relatively homozygous. There are also many records of bulls siring daughters whose production levels are consistently lower than their dam's. This is more difficult to explain unless one postulates their possessing dominant inhibitory factors.

The only conclusion that can be positively drawn is that the inheritance of butterfat and milk production is extremely complex.

Fat percentage

The question of whether fat percentage is an inherited character is at the present debatable. The fact that different breeds are characterized by fairly definite fat content of the milk has lent support to the hypothesis that percentage of fat is a definite inherited character. Fat percentage is merely the ratio of fat to milk; and if it is a definitely inherited character, that which influences one should influence the other to the same extent. This is not so. Certain high fat feeds will increase the fat content of milk without affecting the amount of milk. The fact that with the advance of lactation the daily milk production drops more rapidly than the daily fat production, resulting in an increased fat percentage, must be taken as evidence against the inheritance of fat percentage. Another argument against such an inheritance is based on the well-known wide daily variations of fat percentage. Recent advances in the knowledge of the physiology of milk secretion indicate that milk fat is synthesized independently of the other ingredients of milk; this should be considered as additional evidence opposed to the inheritance of fat percentage as a definite character.

Rather than to consider fat percentage as a definite inherited character, it would seem more logical to consider the inheritance of capacities for milk and fat production separately. By postulating a few factors affecting milk and fat production separately, all the variations in fat percentage can be explained.

Persistency

Persistency, or the ability to maintain a high daily milk flow throughout the lactation period, is one of the very important characters essential for economic production. That persistency is an inherited character cannot be doubted. Beef breeds, in the main, lack persistency, frequently going dry after five or six months of lactation. Crosses between beef breed and dairy breeds are intermediate in persistency.

A hormone prolactin, secreted by the anterior pituitary body, is necessary for the initiation of lactation. Recent work indicated that a continued secretion of this hormone is necessary to maintain milk production. Injection of the hormone into lactating animals with poor persistency records resulted in marked improvement. This would seem to indicate that the inheritance of the factors for persistency are concerned with the anterior pituitary body. Attempts at determining the nature of the inheritance have met with little success and have indicated only that it is, in all probability, a complex inheritance.

No characteristic is more subject to variation due to environmental influences than is persistency. It is therefore more difficult to ascertain the genetic influence on this characteristic. Several studies have shown, however, that the slope of the lactation curve is markedly influenced by heredity. Swedish workers have estimated that from 15 to 30 per cent of the variations encountered in persistency is determined by heredity. These same workers have estimated that heredity accounts for 30 to 40 per cent of the variation in milk or butterfat yield for 300 days and from 70-80 per cent of the butterfat percentage. The rest of the variation for these characteristics is assumed to be due to environmental factors. Studies at the Minnesota Station indicate that heredity played a major role in accounting for the variation in persistency.

Type

Selecting and breeding for type is one of the oldest objectives of breeders. As the character "type" involves all of the body conformations and proportions of body parts, it is reasonable to assume that it involves the most complex inheritance of any of the dairy characters. There is conclusive evidence that many factors are required for a single part of the body. Since literally scores of parts of the body are involved in the whole animal, and since for the correct type each part not only must be shaped correctly but also must be proportionate and in harmony with every other part, it is easy to visualize hundreds of factors as being involved. In spite of the great complexity of the inheritance of type, there are records of many successes of breeders in securing herds of superior type. While many matings of parents of superior type have resulted in offspring of poor or mediocre type, there are also many examples of animals that breed practically true for excellent type. The fact that in the Jersey, Guernsey, and Holstein breeds three direct generations have won Grand Championships at the National Dairy Show, must be taken as *prima facie* evidence that good type is transmitted. That good type animals are not always secured from the breeding of superior types does not detract from the fact that good type is inherited, but contributes to the contention that the inheritance is very complex and that in all probability there are more factors involved in its inheritance than in any other.

Vitality and Vigour

Like other important characters of dairy cattle, the inheritance of vitality and vigour is not known. There is, however, plenty of evidence that a large number of factors are involved and that vitality and vigour can be bred by proper selection. In plants, where more genetic work has been done than with animals, it is found that a large number of factors are involved in vitality. Vitality and vigour are the first characters to be lost in inbreeding; this lends support to the contention that the mere absence of one of the many dominating genes for vigour and vitality may be responsible for the loss of this character. As loss of vigour and vitality is generally observed in the inbreeding of dairy cattle, it is apparent that cattle are heterozygous for many of the factors involved. The occasional weak offspring from vigorous parents can be accounted for by a combination of recessive factors for vigour from heterozygous parents.

Resistance to Disease

With most highly infectious diseases of cattle it is questionable whether there is any material inherent resistance. For other diseases it has not been proved whether there is inherent resistance among individuals. On the basis of what is known in plant breeding it is reasonable to believe that there may be individuals among cattle which have a higher degree of resistance to some diseases than others. Plant breeders have established many varieties of plants resistant to devastating diseases. When more is known of possible individual resistance to disease in cattle another tool becomes available for use of the breeder in improving cattle.

Milking Factors

There are at least two types or inherited characteristics that effect milking. One is hardness of milking and the other is the promptness and completeness with which the cow responds to the milking stimulus.

Because of the hardness of milking, cows may require from one minute to more than 15 minutes for removal of the same quantity of milk. It is not uncommon to find cows that require 10 more minutes per day than the normal for milking. Assuming such cows are milked 300 days each lactation, a total of 50 hours more are required for milking time. Studies now in progress by the researcher have demonstrated that hardness of milking is inherited. Daughters from hard milking cows tended to be harder milkers than the normal. The variations found in these studies indicate that several genes are involved in the inheritance of the hardness or ease with which cows milk.

Limited studies indicate that failure of cows to respond with a complete let-down of milk at each milking may be a major factor in some cases of poor persistency. A characteristic of these cows is great variations in the amounts of milk obtained from milking to milking and probably infrequency of complete emptying of the udder. Studies of one such cow and her three daughters emphasize the depressing effects of this abnormality upon production and indicate that it is inherited. When this cow was handled so she responded with a complete let-down of milk, at each milking she increased her milk production by over 60 per cent for a lactation period of 305 days. That the abnormal behaviour is inherited is supported by the fact that two of the three daughters presented similar idiosyncrasies.

DIFFICULTY IN DETERMINING GENETIC ROLE IN PRODUCTION

The total production of a cow is the sum of the interaction of many factors, part genetic and part environmental. The difficult problem for the student is that of segregation of the genetic from the environmental factors. Aside from feeding and management other factors are graphically illustrated in Fig. 14.2 with arrows indicating the direction of the interplay.

The use of monozygotic or identical twins will enable research workers better to arrive at environmental influences, since in this case the heredity is kept constant within pairs.

15

Systems of Breeding

Systems of breeding are classified upon the basis of closeness of relation of the animals mated. A knowledge of these systems and of what can be achieved through the use of any of them is of considerable value to the breeder of dairy cattle. Although very little experimental work has been done to give us adequate data for complete evaluation of the different systems of breeding, a discussion of these systems and of their uses and values in the breeding of dairy cattle will follow. The systems of breeding generally recognized are crossbreeding, outcrossing, linebreeding, inbreeding, and brading up. In addition to a discussion of the systems of breeding, it is both of interest and value to consider the methods used by the noted breeders of the past.

CROSSBREEDING

Crossbreeding is the mating of either purebred or grade animals of two distinct breeds. It is obviously not available to the breeder of purebred cattle, and can be used only in the beginning by one who wishes to establish a herd of high grades. Crossbreeding has been resorted to by dairymen to a considerable extent under the following conditions: in the beginning of a grading-up programme; when it is deemed advisable to raise beef types from dairy animals; in attempts to combine the high fat content of the milk of Jerseys or Guernseys with the large milk yield of low fat content of the Holstein; and to increase the fat content of the milk to meet market demands. Crossbreeding has also been resorted to for experimental purposes to determine the nature of the inheritance of milk, fat percentage, and beef characteristics.

Crossbreeding for Grading up

The owner of a mixed herd who desires to grade up such a herd by the use of a bull of a certain breed, naturally will secure crossbred stuff. As such an owner continues to use bulls of the same breed, he gradually develops a herd having all the characteristics of the breed which the bulls represent, and the undesirable characters of the crossbreds will be gradually eliminated. Thus, the problem of having a herd lacking in uniformity due to the interaction of the characters of the two breeds that are crossed is only a temporary one and need not be given serious consideration.

Crossing Dairy Cattle with Beef Bulls

Beef bulls have been used to a considerable extent on cows of dairy breeding for the purpose of improving the beef qualities of the calves. Beef bulls of dominant colour and colour patterns are preferred because the offspring will then be uniform in that respect. Angus crosses will be solid black and Hereford crosses will have the Hereford pattern, but Holsteins and Jerseys when crossed will be black instead for red. Since the offspring of these crosses are sold for beef, there is no further breeding problem to be encountered. Studies of beef-dairy crosses at the Maine Station showed that the inheritance of beefiness is intermediate between the dairy and beef types; for Angus-Jersey crosses the forequarters resembled more nearly the beef type, while the hindquarters were more like the Jersey type. Similar experiments at the Wisconsin Station corroborated the work of the Maine Station. It is therefore apparent that the use of beef bulls on dairy type cows will produce offspring of considerably greater value for beef purposes.

Crosses to Increase the Fat Content of the Milk

In certain markets the demand for higher fat percentage of the milk, with resulting premiums for milk of high fat content, has forced dairymen to use bulls of the high testing breeds on Holstein cows. This has resulted in a mixture of colours that is generally undesirable. If a bull of the same breed is used on subsequent crosses, there will ultimately be a switching of the breeds, because gradually the blood of the high testing breed will be increased to such an extent that only its characteristics will remain.

Several experiments involving the crossing of different dairy breeds have shown that in general the offspring are intermediate between the two parents for fat percentage and amounts of milk. In general the milk yield of the hybrid will be somewhat nearer to the level of the high producing parent and the fat percentage nearer to the level of the low testing parent. This had led some to conclude that the factors for milk production are partially dominant, and that those for fat percentage are more recessive. If bulls of different breeds are used alternately in crossbreeding, problems of lack of uniformity in types and particularly in colours are encountered. It is also to be expected that a certain amount of segregation will make for great variability in the fat content of the milk as well as in the amounts of milk. In this case fat per cent and amount of milk will vary inversely. On the basis of the amount of evidence that is now available the desirability of crossbreeding is questionable.

Cross-breeding for Experimental Purposes

Two types of crosses have been made for the purpose of studying inheritance. One is the cross of beef and dairy types, and the other is the cross of extremes in the dairy breeds. These crosses yield valuable information on the inheritance of certain characters, such as colour and the horned condition. The validity of the results in interpreting the nature of the inheritance of such complex characteristics as milk and butterfat production and beef is questionable. In beef-dairy crosses it is reasonable to assume that a large number of the factors responsible for either one of these crosses are not allelomorphic, and that undoubtedly factors for both milk and beef production are dominant or epistatic. It is therefore probable that there will be a conflict for expression of these characters in the hybrid, resulting to a certain extent in an incomplete expression of both sets of characters. This conflict would give the appearance of an intermediate inheritance, which is as has been observed. Crossing of dairy breeds, while uncomplicated by the factors for beef production, is also subject to criticism as a means of studying the inheritance of amounts of milk and fat percentage.

Since all the dairy breeds are fairly well specialized for certain characteristics and since no crossing between the breeds has taken place for a long time, heterosis can be expected to be a factor in the hybrids. This would invalidate the data as a means of studying the inheritance of milk and fat percentage. In nearly all the crossbreeding experiments of different dairy breeds it has been observed that the hybrids have milk yields closer to the level of the high milk-producing parent and a fat percentage closer to the low testing parent. Fat percentage has been interpreted as being an inheritable character, when possibly it is the result of two inherited characters. It is possible that instead of fat percentage being the inherited character, the capacity for total fat production is the inherited character and the fat percentage is the ratio between the two inherited characters. This finds some support in the fact that the fat production of the hybrids is about that of the high producing parent; with an increasing amount of milk inherited from the higher milk-producing parent there will naturally be a decline in the fat percentage. This interpretation, too, lends support to the hypothesis that factors for milk production are dominant. It is clearly evident that more experimental work is necessary before positive conclusions can be arrived at.

Crossbreeding for Commercial Herds

The Bureau of Dairying has carried on experiments with reciprocal two-breed crosses for Jersey × Holstein and Holstein × Red Dane and one-way crosses of Jersey × Guernsey, Holstein × Guernsey, Red Dane × Jersey, and Red Dane × Guernsey of which 50 crossbreeds have completed production records of 365 days, milked three times daily. All parents were purebred. The first records of the crossbreds are compared with the first record of their dams in Table 15.1.

One of the problems in a crossbreeding programme is what to do with the crossbreds. If bred back to either of the parental breeds much of the supposed benefits from crossbreeding would be lost.

Table 15.1: The first records of the crossbreds are compared with the first record of their dams

	Milk	Butterfat		Age	
	Pounds	Per Cent	Pounds	Years	Months
50 two breed crosses, average	12, 958	4.56	586	2	2
50 dams, average	10,253	4.57	445	2	4
Average difference	+ 2,705	-.01	+141		
Number daughters better than their dams	41	20	47		

Introduction of a third breed is suggested, after which, theoretically, either of the first two parental breeds may be used without much loss in heterosis. To date 27 three-breed combination cows have completed 365 records on three-times-daily milking that can be compared to their dams as shown in Table 15.2.

Table 15.2: Records on Three-times-daily Milking

	Milk	Butterfat		Age	
	Pounds	Per Cent	Pounds	Years	Months
27 three-breed crosses, average	13,130	4.64	618	2	2
27 two-breed dams, average	13,165	4.62	604	2	2
Difference	-35	+.02	+14		
Number of daughters better than their dams	17	11	17		

It will be noted that in the two-breed cross a significant increase in both milk and butterfat production was obtained. In the three-breed cross the production level was maintained.

Outcrossing

Outcrossing is the term applied to the system of breeding

within a breed, the parents being selected from distantly related strains. Many people believe that outcrossing produces better results than closer breeding. Some breeders believe that crossing certain strains produces better results than the crossing of other strains, and refer to this phenomenon as "nicking." Whether this is the case cannot be positively stated for lack of experimental proof; however, the possibility of its being true finds support, at least theoretically, in the science of genetics. It is hypothetically possible that factors for both fat and milk production are found in different loci in two strains; and by mating such strains there would be a complementary effect of the factors from both parents.

Linebreeding

Linebreeding is the mating of two animals to concentrate on the qualities of some superior ancestor. As in inbreeding, the two sides of the mating are common in this respect; but linebreeding differs from inbreeding in that the other ancestors of the two animals are more distantly related or unrelated. The linebred animal, therefore, is not referred to merely as being linebred, but linebred to a certain individual, such as a "Linebred Sophie 19th." Linebreeding is practiced with the idea of holding together and getting in as pure a form as possible the desirable traits of either a superior sire or dam. It has definite limitations in that linebreeding cannot be carried on to one individual for many generations without also involving linebreeding to other descendants of the original ancestor. When this stage is reached, the system changes from that of linebreeding to inbreeding. As contrasted to outcrossing, linebreeding reduces the number of ancestors, but not so much as does inbreeding. Linbreeding with a reasonable amount of selection naturally tends to increase the uniformity of the herd, although not so rapidly, perhaps, as does inbreeding. By linebreeding one avoids, to a certain extent, a good many of the disastrous results encountered in inbreeding, such as loss of fertility and vigour. It is largely through linebreeding that families are established.

Inbreeding

Inbreeding is a system of mating closely related animals, such as brother and sister, son and dam, or sire and daughter. Two purposes may be accomplished by this system of breeding.

One is to test the genetic makeup of the parents, and the other is to produce a more uniform herd by limiting the factors to those within a family.

As has been previously indicated, it is desirable to test the genetic makeup of the parents, and one of the most effective ways of doing this is through backcrossing the offspring to the parents. This is particularly important to the breeder of purebred cattle who is desirous of eliminating from his strain undesirable recessive characters. Animals that are found to have undesirable recessive characters may then be eliminated.

The breeder who has unusually superior stock with characters that he is very desirous of perpetuating and has difficulty in finding nonrelated stock of equal merit, can best perpetuate what he is working for through inbreeding. Frequently, too, a sire has proved to be unusually superior and rather than let his qualities be lost when he can no longer be used for general service, it may be advisable to breed him to his daughters, thus practicing inbreeding.

Inbreeding is not to be recommended to the inexperienced breeder. Merely to inbreed, even when relatively superior animals are used, does not guarantee establishment of uniformity. In order to improve upon a herd by inbreeding, the breeder must follow a plan of rigorous selection to eliminate those individuals possessing undesirable characters.

Dangers of inbreeding

Inbreeding as a general system to be used by the average cattle breeder is fraught with a great many dangers. Inbreeding for a considerable length of time invariably results in loss of vigour, size, and fertility. If there are any lethal or sublethal factors present, the losses will be heavy when inbreeding is practiced. Plant breeders have experienced the same difficulties in the inbreeding of corn; but by crossing two simultaneously inbred lines they have found that vigour is restored, and if proper selection has been made in inbreeding, a superior line is frequently established. While many breeders have noted the deterioration of their inbred lines, there is no record of anyone having practiced inbreeding of two lines of dairy cattle simultaneously and then crossing them.

The United States Department of Agriculture furnishes one of the best examples of the results from inbreeding where daughters from grade cows of average production were inbred to good purebred sires of the Holstein and Guernsey breeds. Inbreeding Guernseys for two generations resulted in lower birth weight of the calves, increase in the incidents of deformity of the calves, and a decrease in the mature weight of the inbred animals. The milk production level of the 50 and 75 per cent inbred daughters was about the same as that of the foundation cows, but the butterfat production was increased with the inbreeding because of an increase in the fat percentage of the milk. The variability of the inbred animals for both milk and fat production was lessened with the degree of inbreeding. For the Holsteins there was no decrease in fertility, but there was marked decrease in the birth weight of calves with the intensity of inbreeding. The calf mortality increased, and the rate of growth was slower, resulting in the mature inbred cows being smaller than their foundation cows. The milk production increased and the per cent butter production decreased- the opposite of what happened in the inbreeding of Guernseys. As with the inbred Guernsey, the variability decreased among the inbred Holsteins.

Measures of Inbreeding

There are definite formulae for measuring the amount of inbreeding, which is ultimately expressed in per cent. The formula advanced by Sewall Wright is:

$$F_x = \left((½)^{n+n'+1}(1+F_a)\right)$$

F_x represents the coefficient of inbreeding of the individual, n equals the number of generations from the sire, n' is the number of generations from the dam to the common ancestor, and F_a represents the inbreeding of the common ancestor. Figure 12.3 illustrates the method of calculating the coefficients of inbreeding for different matings. The coefficient of inbreeding for three generations of brother and sister mating equals 50 per cent. This means that such an inbred animal is 50 per cent less heterozygous than the original parent stock.

Grading up

Grading up is the successive use of purebred bulls of a certain breed on nonpurebred herds. Assuming that the original cows are a different breed than that of the bull, the first cross would have 50 per cent of the inheritance of the breed of the bull; for the second cross this would rise to 75 per cent, and for the third cross to 87½ per cent. Each additional cross would approach toward 100 by one-half of the previous increment. After the fourth or fifth cross, the grades would have most of the characters of the breed which the bull represents, and from many standpoints would be almost as good. While the purity of the breed is closely approximated, grades cannot be registered. There are good reasons for the undesirability of registering grades that theoretically are almost 100 per cent purebred. A grade would be likely to carry many undesirable recessive characters that would appear in mating *inter se*. The difficult of ridding a breed of a single undesirable recessive character is well known to the breeders of Holsteins, where the red recessive crops out relatively frequently in spite of many years of breeding and selection for black and white. With the intermating of grades, no matter how "high," there would be many similar characters. There have been many successes in developing grade herds of high production and excellent type from scrubs or non-descripts by the use of two or more successive purebred bulls. Specific examples of such accomplishments are given in the next chapter. In the grading-up programme the greatest increases in production are noted in the first cross. As the average production of the herd increases, further improvement in production becomes increasingly difficult.

Methods used by Noted Breeders

Toward the end of the eighteenth century and the beginning of the nineteenth century there was a great movement in England for the improvement of cattle, particularly Shorthorns, that the resulted in outstanding accomplishments by a number of men who now are recognized as some of the greatest breeders of all times: The Colling Brothers, who started their breeding operations about 1780, Booth, who began to breed Shorthorns about 1790, and Amos Cruickshank, who developed the famous Scotch type of Shorthorns beginning in 1837, are a few of the very outstanding breeders who were credited with the development of the beef characteristics of the modern Shorthorn breed. Thomas Bates, who began breeding Shorthorns just before the beginning of the nineteenth century and selecting for dairy capacities, used methods similar to those of the other breeders; his methods are of more interest, however, to students of dairying.

Bates is credited with establishing the milking strain of Shorthorns. He first selected individuals with superior dairy

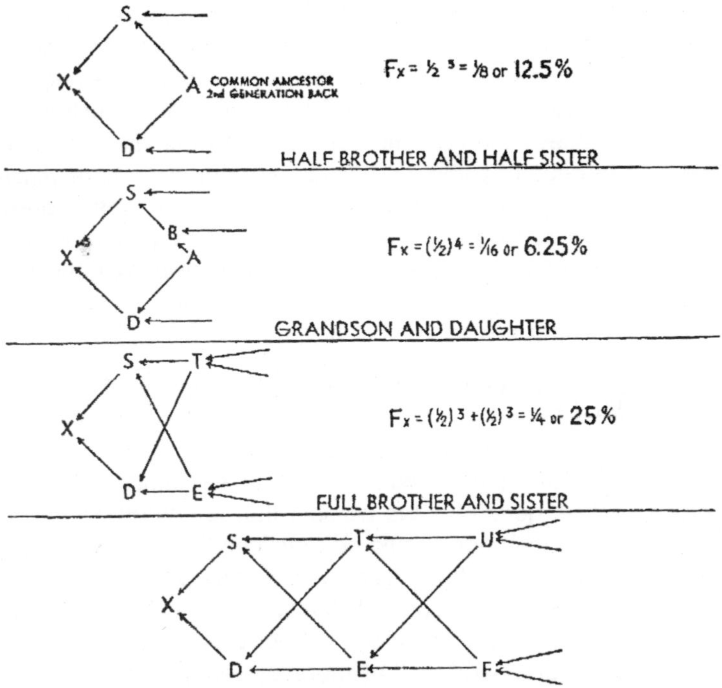

Two generations of brother sister mating

Sire and dam connected thru six independent chains

STD	STUED	
SED	STFED	
	SEUTD	Fx = 3/8 or 37.5%
$2(½)^3$	SEFTD	
	$4(1/5)^5$	

Fig. 15.1: Diagrammatic representation of inbreeding for various related matings.

characteristics and mated them. These matings were followed by inbreeding, and it was through his intensive inbreeding programme that Bates succeeded in fixing the dairy characteristics in the Shorthorn breed that are manifest to this time. He experienced many of the disappointments in inbreeding that are usually encountered. Some of his inbred animals became sterile, and there was a marked loss in vigour. Both of these faults were overcome, however, by judicious outcrossing of carefully selected animals for the characters he was attempting to establish.

Outstanding breeders in other breeds of cattle have practiced very much the same methods. Their successes have not been so outstanding, because they began with a better developed foundation stock than did early English breeders. It is much more difficult to achieve marked improvement with our modern well-developed breeds of cattle than it was a hundred or more years ago when cattle were not so well developed. While these earlier breeders knew nothing of the science of genetics, their practices are certainly supported by the facts made known by genetics.

Modern breeding

At this point we are ready to consider the methods of breeding that should be followed in the improvement of the various herds and breeds of cattle. While there has been a marked improvement in all the breeds of dairy cattle, there is still much room for improvement. In general it can be said that to improve herds of today, the same methods should be practiced that the old master breeders used. One of the major contributions of the science of genetics is the lending of support to the soundness of the methods used by the old breeders. The modern breeder has a big advantage over the older breeders, in that more evidence is available to measure the genetic makeup and breeding value of dairy animals. Although there are not nearly enough records, there are infinitely more records of production than there were years ago.

The most essential requisite for more intelligent breeding is the adoption of a sound testing programme in which all of the offspring of a sire are tested. Without the adoption of such a programme the breeder of today cannot hope to make much progress. He must have available these records in order to select his breeding stock intelligently. Then and only then, by using the records as tools in rigorous selection for the characters toward which he wants to breed and by judicious use of inbreeding, linebreeding, and outcrossing, will he be able to formulate a breeding programme that will ultimately produce superior strains.

Modern genetics permits a concept of establishing a pure line for high milk and butterfat production. Such individuals would be homozygous for all of their genes affecting milk and butterfat production. When such animals are obtained, nothing but uniformly high production can result from matings *inter se.*

The adoption of this concept of establishing a pure line for high production as a goal is to be recommended to all breeders and research workers as one that is likely to be productive of results. With this as an objective the problem becomes one of setting up a system of breeding that will eliminate the undesirable characters and retain all the desirable characters now in cattle.

16

Selection and Care of the Herd Sire

Importance of the herd sire. The selection of the herd sire is by far the most important decision a breeder has to make. While the evidence indicates that the sire and the dam contribute equally to the inheritance of the offspring, the sire has many more offspring than the dam, and therefore his influence from a hereditary standpoint is much greater than that of a cow. The popular statement that "the sire is half of the herd" is correct to the extent that he is the sire for the whole herd. A superior bull can be responsible for a greatly improved herd, while a poor bull can ruin a herd. The variation in the ability of bulls to sire production is well illustrated in Table 16.1.

Table 16.1 gives the result of the analysis of 1,000 purebred bulls, showing the per cent of the bulls that increased the average production in herds of various production levels. It will be noted that as the herd averages increase, the percentage of bulls siring daughters superior to their dams in production decreases with the increased average production of the cows to which they are mated. All bulls mated to cows producing less than 200 pounds of fat, sired daughters superior to the cows; and all bulls mated to cows producing more than 600 pounds of fat, sired daughters inferior to their dams. This table also illustrates the increasing difficulty of selecting satisfactory bulls for herds of high producing cows.

Table 16.1: Analysis of 1,000 bulls mated to cows of varying production levels

No. of Sires	Bred to Cows Producing	Per cent of Sires Increased Production	Per cent of Sires decreased Produciton
10	Under 200 lbs. fat yearly	100	0
142	200 to 300 lbs. fat yearly	86	14
487	300 to 400 lbs. fat yearly	73	27
305	400 to 500 lbs. fat yearly	42	58
47	500 to 600 lbs. fat yearly	28	72
9	600 to 700 lbs. fat yearly	0	100

Figures from the Grand Rapids, Minnesota, Branch Station not only illustrate what can be accomplished by using good purebred bulls, but also show that improvement is rather rapid from the lower levels of production and much more difficult and slower as the average production of the herd increases. The data presented in the Table 16.2 represent the increased production by years from scrub cows by the use of purebred Guernsey bulls.

Another illustration of what can be accomplished by the use of purebred bulls is furnished by the Iowa Station, where purebred bulls of the Holstein, Guernsey, and Jersey breeds were mated with scrub cows. The results are represented in Tables 16.3 and 16.4. Table 16.3 gives the average production of milk and fat for the original scrub cow and the two succeeding generations. Table 16.4 gives the increase in per cent over scrub cows; from this table it can be seen that while there is considerable variability in the degree of increased production, in all cases the production was greatly increased by the use of purebred sires. It may also be added that while the first generation was variable from the standpoint of colour and type, the second generation was noticeably of much more uniform type, taking on more of the characteristics of the breed of which the sire was a representative. There are numerous other examples of what has been accomplished through the use of good sires. It must be stated, however, that there are also many examples of the sire having been responsible for great decreases in production, often leading to the ruin of the herd. One bull at the University of Minnesota Station was responsible for a decrease of 38 per cent in the butterfat production of his daughters as compared with their dams.

Table 16.2: Results from using purebred Guernsey bulls for 20 years, beginning with common cows and grading up

Year	Average pounds of milk per cow	Average pounds of butterfat per cow	Average per cent of butterfat	Average per herd
1904	4,700	196	4.2	4,700 pounds of milk 196 pounds of butterfat
1911	5,301	226	4.7	
1912	5,371	236	4.4	Six-year average, 1911 to 1916, inclusive:
1913	5,313	227	4.4	5,584 pounds of milk
1914	5,519	259	4.7	256 pounds of butterfat
1915	5,721	280	4.9	
1916	6,281	301	4.8	
1917	7,184	358	5.0	
1918	6,502	313	4.8	Eight-year average,1917 to 1924, inclusive:
1919	7,152	333	4.7	6,968 pounds of milk
1920	6,972	341	4.9	338 pounds of butterfat
1921	6,757	332	4.9	
1922	6,797	331	4.9	
1923	7,542	362	4.8	
1924	6,841	331	4.8	

Factors to Consider in Selecting a Bull

Bulls may be selected for one or more of the following considerations:

1. Type of the animal.
2. Pedigree.
3. Consideration of progeny performance.

Table 16.3: Results from the use of purebred sires for two generations on scrub cows

Group purebred sire used	Dams		Daughters		Grand-daughters	
	Milk Pounds	Fat Pounds	Milk Pounds	Fat Pounds	Milk Pounds	Fat Pounds
Holstein	3,782	176	6,839	274	11,127	420
Guernsey	3,687	168	5,102	241	5,810	301
Jersey.	3,463	168	5,009	264	5,411	287
Average	3,660	172	5,999	261	8,402	358

Table 16.4: Percentage of increase in production of the two generations of grades over their scrub dams

Group	Increase in production			
	First generation		Second generation	
	Milk	Fat	Milk	Fat
Holstein	81%	55%	94%	138%
Guernsey	38%	43%	58%	74%
Jersey.	45%	57%	56%	71%
Average	64%	52%	130%	109%

Type

Type should be given serious consideration because of the desirability of having a bull of good type and also because type is inherited. Frequently it is the only consideration taken into account in selecting a bull; this cannot be justified. Many bulls of excellent type are sires of offspring that are mediocre in this respect, and no evidence exists that there is any marked correlation between the type of a bull and the production of his daughters.

Selection on the basis of type is even less reliable for the young bull, as there may be marked changes in the body conformation with development. A young animal of inferior type may improve with age; and conversely a young bull of good type may become poorer in this respect with increase in age.

The Purebred Dairy Cattle Association has prepared a score card for the dairy bull of all breeds which has the approval of the American Dairy Science Association. That score card with comments on special breed characteristics and evaluation of defects is reproduced here (Table 16.5).

Ayrshire characteristics

Colour - Red of any shade, mahogany, brown or these with white, or white, each colour clearly defined. Distinctive red and white markings preferable; black or brindle markings strongly objectionable.

Table 16.5: Dairy bull score card
Ideals of type and breed characteristics must be considered in the application of the terminology of this score card.

Based on order of observation		Perfect score	Bull under observation	Official score
1. GENERAL APPEARANCE		30		
Attractive individuality, revealing vigour, masculinity with a harmonious blending, and correlation of parts. Impressive style and attractive carriage with an active, well-balanced walk	20			
Breed characteristics (see below)				
Head masculine, medium in length, clean-cut; broad muzzle with large open nostrils; lean, strong jaw; full, bright eyes; forehead broad between the eyes and moderately dished; bridge of nose straight; ears medium size and alertly carried.	–			
Shoulder blades set smoothly against chest wall and withers, forming neat junction with the body.				
Black strong and appearing straight with vertebrae well defined.				
Loin broad, strong, and nearly level.				
Rump long, wide; top-line level from join to and including tail head.	10			
Hips wide, approximately level laterally with back, free from excess tissue.				
Thurls wide apart.				
Pinbones wide apart and slightly lower than hips, well defined.				
Tail head slightly above and neatly set between pinbones.				

Based on order of observation		Perfect score	Bull under observation	Official score
Tail long and tapering with nicely balanced switch.	-			
2. DAIRY CHARACTER		35		
Animation, angularity, general openness, and freedom from excess tissue.				
Neck masculine and long, with moderate crest blending smoothly into shoulders. Clean-cut throat, brisket, and dewlap.				
Withers well defined and wedge-shaped with the dorsal processes of the vertebrae rising slightly above the shoulder blades.				
Ribs well arched, wide apart, rib bone flat, wide, and long.				
Flanks arched and refined.				
Thighs when viewed from the side, flat; when viewed from the rear, wide apart. Well-cut-up between the thighs.	35			
Skin of medium thickness, loose and pliable. Hair fine.				
Testicles both normal. Scrotum, normal.				
Rudimentary teats wide apart, squarely placed and in front of scrotum.				
Mammary veins large, long, and well defined.	-			
3. BODY CAPACITY		20		
Relatively large in proportion to size of animal, and deep at the flank, providing ample digestive capacity, strength, and vigour.	10			

Based on order of observation	Perfect score	Bull under observation	Official score
Barrel deep, strongly supported, ribs wide apart, and well sprung.Heartgirth large, resulting from long, well sprung foreribs, wide chest floor between front legs, and fullness at the point of elbow. 10			
4. LEGS AND FEET	15		
Forelegs medium in length, straight, wide apart, squarely placed. Feet short, and well rounded, with deep heel and level sole. 5			
Hind legs when viewed from the side, nearly perpendicular from back to pastern. When viewed from the rear, legs wide apart and nearly straight. Bone, fat and flinty tendons well defined. Pasterns, of medium length, strong, and springy. Hocks cleanly moulded. Feet same as above. 10			
Total	100		

Size - A mature bull in breeding condition should weigh about 1,800 pounds.

Horns - Inclining upward, medium size at base, refined, medium length, and tapering toward tips.

Guernsey characteristics

Colour - A shade of fawn with white markings clearly defined, black or brindle markings objectionable. Skin should show golden yellow pigmentation. When other points are equal, a clear or buff muzzle will be favoured over a smoky or black muzzle.

Size - a mature bull in breeding condition should weigh about 1,700 pounds.

Horns - Inclining forward, medium size and yellow at base, refined, medium in length, and tapering toward tips.

Jersey characteristics

Colour - A shade of fawn, with or without white markings.

Size - a number bull in breeding condition should weigh about 1,500 pounds.

Brown swiss characteristics

Strong and vigorous. Size and ruggedness with quality desired. Extreme refinement undesirable.

Colour - A shade of brown varying from a silver to a dark brown. Hair inside ears is a lighter colour than body. Nose and tongue black with a light coloured band around nose. Colour markings which bar registry are: white switch, white on sides, top head or neck and legs above knees or hocks. White on belly or lower legs objectionable.

Size - A mature bull in breeding condition should weigh about 1,900 pounds.

Horns - Inclining forward and slightly up. Medium size at base, medium length, tapering toward black tips.

Holstein Characteristics

Colour - Black and white markings clearly defined. Colour markings which bar registry are solid black, solid white, black in switch, black belly, black encircling leg touching hoof, black from hoof to knee or hock, black and white intermixed to give colour other than distinct black and white.

Size - A mature bull in breeding condition should weigh about 2,000 pounds.

Horns - Inclining forward, incurving, medium size at base, refined, medium length and tapering toward tips.

Pedigree

The value of a pedigree as an instrument in evaluating diary animals has been described previously. It was pointed out that the pedigree containing ample information about the ancestors and close relations of an animal is of great value in evaluating such an animal. Most pedigrees, however, do not contain sufficient

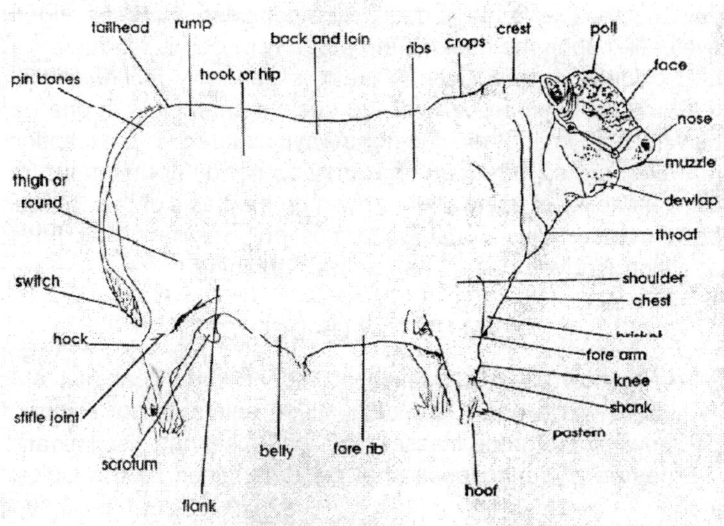

Fig. 16.1: Parts of the dairy bull

information, either because much of the information that is needed is left out by the pedigree writer or because not enough of the ancestors have production records. The breeder who follows out a certain line of breeding finds additional value in the pedigree. For commercial reasons breeders often find it advantageous to follow certain lines of breeding that have been publicized and come into popular demand. Following such lines in a breeding programme facilitates sale of surplus stock at better prices. While in some cases it is unfortunate that such a situation should exist in that it may interfere with a constructive breeding programme, nevertheless it is a reality that must be recognized. For the most intelligent selection the pedigree must always be taken into account. If it contains a complete record of all the necessary information about the ancestors and close relations, it can be an instrument that is reasonably accurate in the evaluation of the bull. Its use merely to follow certain blood lines, however, contributes very little to a constructive breeding programme.

Progeny performance

Evaluating animals on the basis of progeny performance is the most reliable of any method that is available to the breeders of dairy cattle. The fundamentals to be considered in selecting and evaluating upon the basis of the progeny performance have been fully discussed previously. While it is generally recognized that if a bull has sired progeny of the desired characters in one herd he will do so in another, it is not always assured. The exceptions, however, are so infrequent that they do not deter materially from the desirability of using sires proved on the basis of their progeny performance. This consideration is so important that further attention is given under the following heading.

EVALUATION OF DEFECTS

In a show ring, disqualification means that the animal is not eligible to win a prize. Any disqualified animal is not eligible to be shown in the group classes. In slight to serious discrimination, the degree of seriousness shall be determined by the judge.

Eyes

1. Total Blindness: Disqualification.
2. Blindness in one eye: Slight Discrimination.

Wry face

Serious discrimination.

Parrot jaw

Serious discrimination

Shoulders

Winged: Serious discrimination.

Capped hip

Slight discrimination.

Tail setting

Wry tail or other abnormal tail settings: Slight to serious discrimination.

Legs and Feet

1. Lameness- apparently permanent and interfering with normal function: Disqualification.
   - apparently temporary and not affecting normal function: Slight discrimination.
2. Bucked knees, blemished hocks, crooked hind legs, weak pasterns: Serious discrimination.
3. Evidence of arthritis, crampy hind leg: Serious discrimination.
4. Enlarged knees: Slight discrimination.

Absence of horns

No discrimination.

Lack of size

Slight to serious discrimination.

Testicles

Bull with one testicle or with abnormal testicles: Disqualification.

Overconditioned

Serious discrimination.

Temporary or minor injuries

Blemishes or injuries of a temporary character not affecting animal's usefulness: Slight discrimination.

Evidence of sharp practice

Animals showing signs of having been operated upon or tampered with for the purpose of concealing faults in conformation, or with intent to deceive relative to the animal's soundness: *Disqualification.*

Proven sire

A proven sire is a sire having daughters with production records from dams with production records. The question as to the number of tested daughters that a sire needs in order to be proven is as yet somewhat controversial. Various arbitrary numbers of daughter-dam pairs that are needed to pronounce a bull as being proven have been suggested. Davidson published data that indicated that the first six daughters are the smallest number that could be used as being reasonably reliable in indicating the production the bull will sire. Guiford, however, indicates 10 pairs as the least number from which the average production of future progeny can be predicted with reasonable reliability. Copeland has studied this problem by working the coefficients of correlation between different numbers of daughter-dam pairs with the average yields of all subsequent daughters. His results are presented graphically in Fig. 16.2. The predictions based upon 6 daughter-dam pairs were found to deviate by more than 50 pounds of fat from the actual average production of subsequent daughters. When 10 pairs were used, the deviation dropped to 45 pounds; and when 15 pairs were used, it dropped to 35 pounds.

A striking example of what good proven sires will accomplish is furnished by Table 16.6 in which the performance of 426 proven sires used in artificial breeding associations on January 1, 1948 are analyzed.

Objections to the proven sire

While a proven sire is the best insurance that a breeder can have as to how a bull will perform, there are several factors to be considered that are not so favourable to the use of a proven bull. The first, as has already been intimated, is that there is difficulty in properly evaluating the proven bull. A second and more serious one, is that proven bulls are scarce and frequently impossible to find. Then, too, the value of the proven bull is likely to be fully realized by the owner, and the price, therefore, is likely to be too high. Of necessity, the proven bull is considerably advanced in age; and the risk of losing his services because of sterility, death, or injury is great. Many breeders prefer to use younger bulls because there is less danger of their being vicious. The old bull,

Table 16.6: A striking example of what good proven sires

Butterfat production range of Dams (Pounds)	Sires	Sires that		Average production of				Increase (+) or Decrease (-) by Daughters	
		Main-tained or increased production	Dec-reased production	Dams		Daughters			
	No.	No.	No.	Milk Pounds	Butterfat Pounds	Milk Pounds	Butterfat Pounds	Milk Pounds	Butterfat Pounids
250-274	1	1	0	5,341	268	6,540	343	+1,199	+75
275-299	4	4	0	6,967	287	8,436	362	+1,469	+75
300-324	15	15	0	7,072	313	8,012	372	+940	+59
325-349	15	13	2	7,460	339	8,586	393	+1,126	+54
350-374	69	57	12	8,776	359	9,634	400	+858	+41
375-399	85	62	23	9,703	388	10,172	420	+469	+32
400-424	95	70	25	10,355	411	10,809	436	+454	+25
425-449	63	40	23	10,792	437	10,933	452	+141	+15
450-474	37	27	10	11,814	457	12,054	471	+240	+14
475-499	26	13	13	12,328	485	11,941	474	-387	-11
500-524	14	6	8	13,919	511	13,504	506	-415	-5
550-574	2	0	2	15,387	552	12,864	482	-2,523	-70
Total or Average	426	308	118	10,161	407	10,576	433	+415	+26

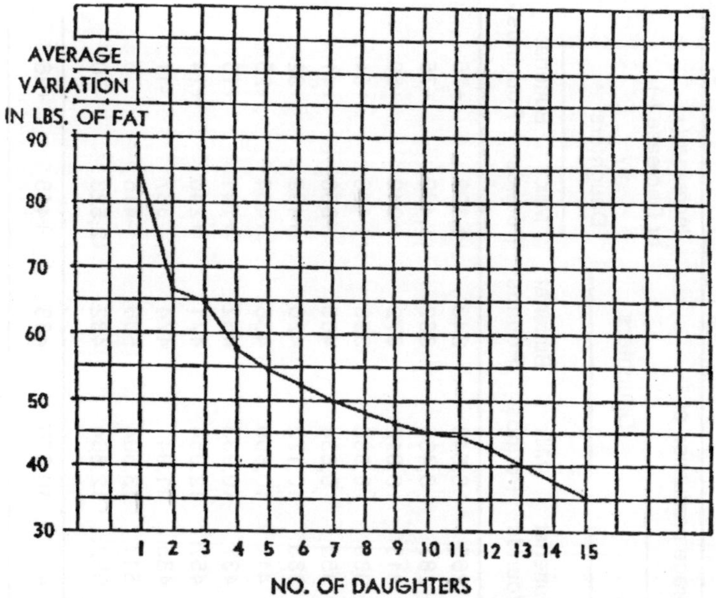

Fig. 16.2: Graphic presentation of the variation (in pounds of butterfat) of each group of daughters of a bull from 1 to 15 - from the average of all daughters.

if he has such tendencies, has had them fully developed when he arrives at the age that he is proven. The latter reason should not be given serious consideration and should not be a deciding factor if the equipment for handling the bull on the farm is adequate.

Bull Association

Bull associations, for some reason, have not been very popular in the United States. Since the first was organized in 1908, the growth in numbers has been slow and disappointing. In Denmark, where probably the most rapid development in dairy cattle has taken place most of the breeders of cattle were members of bull associations and now of artificial breeding associations. In 1936 there were 243 bull associations in the United States. In 1947 this number had dropped to 140, with 23,519 cows. A bull association is an organization formed by breeders of cattle who jointly buy a number of bulls. The association is divided into several blocks with one or more breeders to a block. The association purchases, as a whole, enough bulls so that there is one for each block. After a period of about two years, these bulls are moved; in another two years, they are again moved; and so on, until they have made a circuit or have been put out of service for some reason or other. The advantages of a bull association are self-apparent. First, by pooling the resources of a large number of breeders better bulls can be purchased. Second, it permits buying bulls to promote a definite breeding programme. Third, it reduces the cost of bulls, inasmuch as they are used for a longer period of time than would otherwise be the case. Fourth, and perhaps the most important of all advantages, is that it necessitates the keeping of a bull until he is proven. If a bull is found to be an unusually superior sire, there is usually provision made that his services will be available to all members. Fifth, because of the business organization essential for the promotion of a bull association, it arouses an enthusiasm which is reflected in better business management of the herd in general. Provisions are also made that if a bull should prove to be unsatisfactory, he is immediately sold and replaced by another one. In this way the members of a bull association have the best guarantee possible of having only desirable bulls.

Feeding the Bull

The object in feeding a young dairy bull is to grow him into a healthy, vigorous animal at a rate that will bring him to service at as early a date as possible. A bull calf should be fed in the same way as the heifer calf (see Chapter 19), except that in some cases he should be fed more liberally in order to grow him into size for early service. The amount of feed to be given a mature bull should be gauged by his condition. He should be kept in a vigorous physical condition, but not to fat, as too much fat has a tendency to make him sluggish. The Minnesota Station reported on the amount of feed required to keep service bulls in a satisfactory condition. They called attention to the fact that the amount of nutrients required to keep the bull in the desired condition approximated very closely the nutrients required for maintenance. The daily rations for the bulls are set forth in Table 16.7.

It will be noted that from 4.5 pounds to 5 pounds of grain were allowed daily and that the amount of silage was limited to no more than the amount of hay fed. The mature bull could probably secure the necessary nutrients from roughage, but in so doing, he would develop too large a paunch. While there is no evidence that silage is harmful, it is advisable to limit the amount fed to not over 15 pounds daily.

Table 16.7: Daily Rations Found Adequate for Service Bulls at the University of Minnesota

Cattle	Alfalfa Hay Pounds	Corn Silage Pounds	Grain Pounds
Winter:			
Jerseys	12	8	4.5
Holsteins	18	14	5.0
Ayrshires	16	12	5.0
Summer:			
Jerseys	12	5	5.0
Holsteins	14	13	5.0
Ayrshires	12	12	5.0

The hay preferably should be a good grade of legume, such as alfalfa or the cloves. When the hay consists of a legume, a satisfactory grain mixture consisted of 200 parts of oats, 100 parts of barley, and 100 parts of corn. When the roughage is of the low protein type, such as timothy or prairie hay, 75 pounds of linseed oil meal or some other similar high protein concentrate should be added to each 200 pounds of the aforementioned grain mixture. During the summer it is advisable to furnish the bull with a limited amount of pasture or some soilage crop. While there is no positive evidence that the furnishing of green feed is absolutely necessary, it is possible that the bull may benefit from the vitamins that are present in all green feeds.

For bulls in artificial insemination service, workers at Cornell University are recommending somewhat heavier feeding. They have formulated a tentative feeding standard for bulls in this service in which 40 per cent of the T.D.N. is supplied in grain and 60 per cent in hay. Table 16.8 gives the requirements for bulls ranging from 1,200 to 2,600 pounds.

Table 16.8: Tentative feeding standard for dairy bulls

Body Weight Pounds	Total Digestible Nutrients Required Per Bull Per Day	Pounds of 75 per cent T.D.N. Concentrate to Supply 40 per cent of T.D.N.	Pounds of 50 per cent T.D.N. Hay to Supply 60 per cent T.D.N. Requirements
1,200	10.27	5.5	12.3
1,300	10.93	5.8	13.1
1,400	11.59	6.2	13.9
1,500	12.25	6.5	14.7
1,600	12.91	6.9	15.5
1,700	13.57	7.2	16.3
1,800	14.23	7.6	17.1
1,900	14.89	7.9	17.9
2,000	15.56	8.3	18.7
2,100	16.22	8.6	19.5
2,200	16.88	9.0	20.3
2,300	17.54	9.4	21.0
2,400	18.20	9.7	21.8
2,500	18.86	10.1	22.6
2,600	19.52	10.4	23.4

Housing and Yard

Although it is not necessary to furnish the herd sire with as warm a house as it required for the milking cow, he should be given housing conditions that will protect him from exposure to the elements. The house and the yard for the bull must be considered together, for they should be arranged to facilitate the handling of unruly bulls and to afford opportunity for daily exercise in the yard. The bull may be housed either in a small house by himself or occupy a box stall in a portion of the barn. In either event there should be access directly to a yard through a door that is operated by controls from outside the pen. The box stall or pen should be 12 feet square. The general scheme of a satisfactory arrangement of both the pen and the yard is presented in Figure 16.3.

Attention is directed to the arrangement of the manager in a corner of the pen, to the door operated by cord which opens into the yard, and to the breeding rack with gate arrangements in the yard. The pen is designed so that there will be no need of handling the bull, thereby insuring the maximum of safety. In the care of the pen one of the important considerations is to keep it well bedded during the cold weather to prevent the bull from contracting arthirits, a disease which frequently affects and impairs the use of a bull. While a bull yard is to be preferred over anything else for a place in which the bull may exercise, a fairly satisfactory substitute may be constructed by suspending a stout cable 75 to 100 feet in length, to which the bull may be tied by means

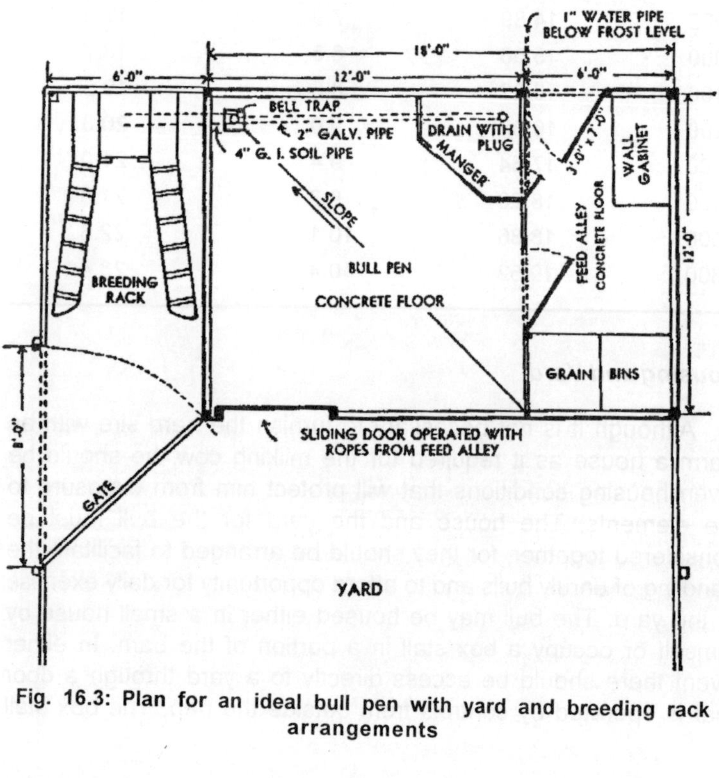

Fig. 16.3: Plan for an ideal bull pen with yard and breeding rack arrangements

of a ring and a swivel joint. By this arrangement he can travel along the entire length of the cable. If one end of the cable is fastened to the barn, it is possible for the bull to go in or out of his pen without being untied.

Cost of Keeping the Herd Sire

The cost of maintaining a herd bull varies with different conditions. The more important items to be considered are the costs of feed, bedding, housing, veterinary service, and labour. In addition to this the interest on investment and depreciation in value must be added.

The feed costs for a service bull, which vary greatly, depend upon the size of the bull and the price of the feeds. The larger bulls consume more feed than smaller ones. This is illustrated in Table 16.9, which compares the amount of feed consumed by a Holstein bull weighing 2,500 pounds and a Jersey bull weighing 1,800 pounds.

Table 16.9: Amount of feed required and cost of keeping a herd sire

	Holstein Bull Weighing 2,500 Lbs.		Jersey Bull Weighing 1,800 Lbs.	
	Amount	Value	Amount	Value
Hay at $15.00 per ton	7,500 lbs.	$ 56.25	5,400 lbs.	$ 40.50
Grain at $25.00	2,000 lbs.	25.00	1,500 lbs.	18.75
Housing, bedding, etc.		22.80		22.80
Labour at 25 cts. per hr		6.75		6.75
Total		$110.75		$ 88.80
Interest on investment, 5% on $100.00		$ 5.00		$ 5.00
Depreciation:				
When used only 2 years		12.50		23.00
When used 4 years		6.25		11.50

The hay consumed by a bull in a year approximates three times his weight, and in addition to the hay 1,500 to 2,000 pounds of grain should be allowed. If silage is fed, three pounds of silage replaces one pound of hay. Thus, three tons of silage would replace one ton of hay.

The costs of housing, bedding, veterinary service, etc. again would vary, and only average figures can be given. According to the United Sates Department of Agriculture, these costs average $22.80 annually. The same source is responsible for the statement that 27 hours of man labour is required annually to care for the bull. The total cost for the Holstein bull referred to above is $110.75 and for the Jersey $88.80 when hay is valued at $15.00 per ton, grain at $25.00 per ton, and labour at 25 cents per hour.

In addition to these costs, charges for interest on the investment and depreciation must also be made. If the bull costs $100.00, there is an annual charge of $5.00 for interest on the investment; and if the bull is used two years and is then sold for beef at three cents a pound, there must be an annual charge of depreciation of $12.50 for the Holstein and $23.00 for the Jersey. If the bull is used four years the annual depreciation charge becomes one-half of that when he is used only two years. It is apparent that the higher the original cost of a bull, the greater will be the annual depreciation charges.

Handling the Bull

The dairy bull is a potential killer, and should be handled with that fact constantly in mind. One should never place himself in a disadvantageous position with a bull, even if the bull is apparently gentle. Many people have been killed or injured when they have gone into the pen or yard with a bull that was thought to be gentle, but that suddenly turned vicious. Before one enters the pen, care should be taken to see that the bull is securely fastened. Bulls a year old or over should never be handled except with a staff, unless there are two or more attendants, each with a rope from the halter, on either side of the bull. A bull should never be teased or played with. He should be handled firmly at all times. Never should he be put in a position where he is forced to test his strength; for on so doing, he will discover his great power, and from that time on will be exceedingly hard to manage. If an especially vicious bull is to be moved from one place to another, extra precautions should be taken. One of the safest ways of handling a bull is to hobble him. This is done by the following method: A band or rope is placed around his chest, with a ring or loop on either side of the body. Through each loop is passed a rope which is fastened to the corresponding forefoot. These ropes extend to the posterior, where each is manipulated by an attendant. When the bull becomes unruly, traction on the rope brings him to his knees. Some people believe this method to be the best way of taming vicious bulls.

Ringing

Regardless of how easily a bull may be handled, he should have a ring inserted in his nose. It is a good plan to insert a ring at an early age (from six to eight months) in order that he may become accustomed to being handled by the ring. At this time a small ring two to two and one-fourth inches in diameter should be inserted; this is replaced by a larger ring at the age of 20 months to two years of age. The ring is inserted in the septum of the nose, in an opening made with a trocar and cannula. When it becomes necessary to replace the smaller ring with a larger one, it is usually not necessary to enlarge the opening in the septum. Occasionally the nose is torn out; then it becomes necessary to insert the rings vertically through the upper portion of the nose, or to use special halters that are made for the handling of vicious bulls.

Trimming the Feet

Because the bull is confined to a relatively small yard, his hoofs grow much more rapidly than they are worn off. Unless they are trimmed, the hoofs become so long that, in addition to being unsightly, they are painful to the animal, producing lameness by creating tension on the muscles and tendons. At least once (better, twice) a year the hoofs should be trimmed. For this the bull is cast or put in stocks. A pair of pinchers may be used in clipping off the toes; this is followed by the use of a rasp to smooth down the surface. If the yard in which the bull exercises is covered with cinders or gravel, the hoofs may be worn down sufficiently to avoid the necessity of trimming.

Dehorning

While heifers should be dehorned when they are two or three days old, it is not advisable to dehorn the bull at this time for two reasons:

(1) If he is to be sold, lack of horns may detract from his sales value.

(2) It is considered a good plan to let the bull develop horns and find out how to use them before dehorning him.

Then when the horns are removed, the bull will be somewhat at a loss as to what to do. This may be one way of taking the meanness out of a vicious bull. It is preferable to saw the horns off when he is about 18 months to two years of age.

Exercising

Unless the bull gets sufficient exercise, he is likely to become important. This is particularly true for older bulls. On the average dairy farm the question of exercising the bull is a problem of no small importance. The first requisite for exercise is a yard of sufficient size. However, even with a bull yard, many bulls refuse to exercise of their own accord. It then becomes necessary to furnish some contrivance to force exercise. Some of the several means that have been resorted to are:

1. Suspending a block of wood by means of a chain from a cross bar. Some bulls take delight in playing with this for hours at a time, thus getting the necessary exercise.
2. Chaining a strong barrel or similar solid object to the ground in the middle of the lot. Most bulls take pleasure in rolling a barrel or other object around the lot, and the chain prevents it from being pushed into the lot corner, from which the bull would be unable to remove it.
3. Training the bull to work in a yoke, thus making use of his power for productive work. Inasmuch as considerable difficulty is experienced in training him and as he is never to be entirely trusted, this way of exercising the herd sire is not very popular.

4. Using the treadmill. Here, too, the bull might produce power for use in grinding feed or pumping water. This means is objected to because considerable labour is involved in bringing the bull to and from the treadmill, and because most bulls soon learn how to rest on the treadmill.
5. Placing two or more bulls in the same lot. If one is a young bull, this is quite satisfactory, as the young bull is quick enough to avoid injury from the older one. Evenly matched old bulls may seriously injure each other. Frequently fights develop which end in the death of one or more of the contestants.
6. Using a sweep. A large timber is pivoted, and a bull is tied to each end. When one bull moves, the other one is forced to move also. For some time, at least, they usually fail to co-operate, and thus each one stimulates the other into action.
7. Using patented bull exercisers. Recently several patented bull exercising contrivances have appeared on the market. These involve the use of motors as a source of traction to keep the bulls moving during the exercising period.

Service Life of a Bull

According to Lush the average reproduction life of dairy bulls in registered herds is 2.2 years. This necessitates an annual replacement of 45 per cent of the dairy bulls. This short service period for bulls is accounted for by the sale of the bull to avoid inbreeding, not because of sterility. Researchers studied 288 bulls and found the average age at which service ceased to be nine years and six months. The details as to the number and per cent total that went out of service for each age class are set forth in Table 16.10. Twenty-one or 7.3 per cent of the 288 bulls were in service at 14 years of age, while 27 or 9.4 per cent went out of service before five years of age.

Age of the Bull and Quality of Offspring

The age of neither the sire nor the dam has any influence upon the quality of the offspring. This is contrary to the belief of some people who hold that the progeny from older parents are superior to those from younger parents. The germ plasm is set aside early in the embryonic life, and there is no evidence that there is any change in the genetic makeup of the germ plasm with the advancing of age; nor is there any reason to expect that there should be any change. Some credence has been given to the assertion that older bulls sire superior offspring. When, as frequently happens, a meritorious bull finds his way into better herds and is mated to superior cows, the offspring from such matings are naturally superior to his previous offspring; this is the only basis for the assertion.

Table 16.10: Ages at which 288 purebred bulls went out of service

Age at last service	No. of bulls	Per cent
Under 5	27	9.38
5 to 6	18	6.25
6 to 7	23	7.99
7 to 8	18	6.25
8 to 9	29	10.07
9 to 10	39	13.54
10 to 11	40	13.89
11 to 12	26	9.03
12 to 13	20	6.94
13 to 14	27	9.38
Over 14	21	7.29
Total	288	

Service

Well-grown bull calves may be ready for light service when ten to twelve months of age. At two years of age, a bull has reached the maximum of his breeding powers; this is maintained until he is about six years of age. After six years of age there is a decline in the breeding powers, so that after eight years of age many bulls are slow and uncertain as breeders. Many bulls however, continue to be excellent breeders up to twelve to sixteen years of age. A bull should not be permitted to serve more than one to two cows a week until he is fifteen months of age. The number of services may then be increased so that at two years of age, five services per week may be permitted. As in most dairies the breeding is confined to a short season, a bull can serve for only 50 to 60 cows. After six years of age, the number of services per week should be reduced with advance in age. A breeding rack should be used when large bulls are bred to young heifers, as otherwise the heifer may suffer injury. When young bulls are mated to large cows, the service may be facilitated by standing the cow in a shallow pit.

Sterility

Sterility in the bull may seriously affect the breeding programme of a herd. It usually requires several months to ascertain whether or not a bull is sterile; and after that some time is needed to acquire another bull. As a result the breeding of some cows may be delayed six months or more. This entails not only a loss in milk production but a disruption of the plans for seasonal freshening of the cows.

There are many causes for sterility and little known about treatment that is effective. In some cases due to inheritance the bulls may be sterile from the beginning or become sterile while still young. Other cases are caused by disease and others by overuse. The part that nutrition plays is not understood. From available experimental data, it would seem that deficiencies in nutrition must be rather extreme to produce sterility.

Low ascorbic acid content of the blood is associated with some cases of sterility but not related to the diet. Sterility due to this cause may be corrected by the subcutaneous administration every three or four days of one gram of ascorbic acid dissolved in 5 cc. of sterile saline solution per 1,000 pounds live weight. Feeding of ascorbic acid is ineffective, since this vitamin is destroyed in the digestive tract. The ascorbic acid solution should be made up fresh before each injection.

Exercise is considered essential for maintenance of good fertility although experimental evidence for this belief is still lacking.

17

Growth and Development

The growth and development of the dairy animals is one of the important considerations in dairying. As a matter of fact, the livestock industry is fundamentally based upon the phenomena involved in growth. The rate of growth and ultimate size affects production, and factors that influence these are of major importance. It will, therefore, be well to consider the fundamentals of the growth phenomena, the requirements of growth, and the factors influencing rate of growth and ultimate size.

Definition

A satisfactory definition of growth is difficult to give, as the growth phenomena are complex. It may be defined for these purposes as a series of physiological changes through which an individual of any species develops from the fertilized egg to maturity.

Historical

Aristotle (384-322 B.C.) was the first to record observations on the growth of animals in a qualitative way. Theophrastus (372-228 B.C.) recorded similar observations on plants. The idea of systematically measuring growth is a relatively new one. In 1834 Quetelet, an astronomer, reported for the first time on a systematic measurement of children. In 1875 Bowditch, a physiologist at Harvard University, reported on the first comprehensive study of growth in children. In 1891 Minot published the first studies on growth in guinea pigs. To Waters of the Missouri Station goes the credit of starting growth studies in cattle. This work, one of the major research projects, was started in 1906 and has continued at that station. From this rather late beginning, a great interest has been manifested in the study of growth. In 1921 Baldwin gave a bibliography of some 900 papers on the subject.

Growth Periods

Growth falls naturally into two major periods, the intrauterine or prenatal period and the postnatal period. Before birth, which marks the division between these two periods, nutrition for the embryo and fetus comes entirely from the dam through the fetal membranes. After birth the nutrient is taken in through the calf's own digestive tract.

The postnatal period lends itself to a further subdivision into two periods - the self-accelerating period and the self-inhibiting period. The self-accelerating period is that period when there is an increase in successive daily gains. This period usually extends to sexual maturity, when the self-inhibiting period begins.

The self-inhibiting period is that period following the self-accelerating period when successive daily gains decrease. This period ends at maturity. In advanced age, there is a shrinkage which is referred to as senility.

Nature of growth

While the exact cause of growth is not as yet well understood, it is known that the secretions of ductless glands are responsible for the growth stimulation. The glands secreting hormones affecting growth are the thymus, pituitary body, thyroid, and pineal. Just what each one of these glands contributes remains to be discovered.

Growth is taken to include any increment in size. This may be accomplished in two ways: by an increase of the number of cells, or by an increase in the size of the cells. The former is the more important, since all individuals start with the one cell and through cell multiplication develop into creatures having millions of cells. Increase of cell size, however, may be a considerable factor, particularly in the fattening process. Researcher found that fat cells might vary from a low as 20 micra in the very thin animal to 200 micra in diameter in the fat animal. The diameters of the muscle cells varied from 20 to 50 micra under the same respective conditions. Researcher found that in rough fed steers the muscle cells averaged 44.8 micra, and in full fed, 62.6 micra. According to researchers, growth is due to a series of chemical reactions. The velocity of growth during a given period is limited to or governed by one chemical reaction. Brody more recently postulated several phases following one another and overlapping; each one is governed and limited by the law of chemical action. He has adapted formulae to growth phenomena which are based upon the laws governing mono-molecular chemical reaction. Researchers studying the course of skeletal growth of cattle and making 20 different measurements, found marked differences in the rates of growth of different parts of the anatomy with advance in age. The changes in form with the advancement of age from the calf to the mature animal are illustrated in Fig. 17.1. Here the younger individuals have been enlarged proportionately for all body measurements so that the younger ones equal the older forms in height at the withers. It will be noted that the calf has relatively much longer legs than the mature animal; he is higher over the rump and has a much shorter body. In general, it may be said that the first growth impulses are toward development of the long bones of the legs, followed by a lengthening and deepening of the body, the latter continuing until final maturity. The last major growth change causes a widening of the entire body.

Figure 17.2 gives the relative per cent of the different measurements of a calf at birth in terms of the mature values. It will be seen that the calf at birth weighs but 6 per cent of the mature weight, while the length of the leg is nearly 70 per cent of the mature value. Eacn individual has an inherited limit to size beyond which it will not develop. However, there are parts of the body that continue to grow throughout life, such as hair, horn, and hoof. The sex organs make their major development just before and during puberty, and the mammary gland develops and involutes with successive gestation and lactation periods.

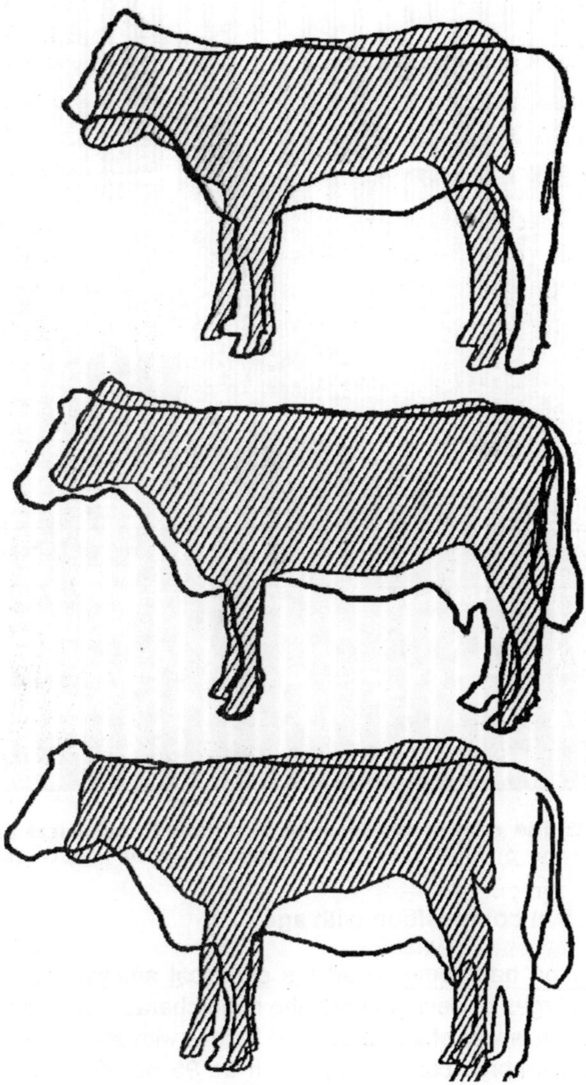

Fig. 17.1: Change in form with maturity. The comparisons are based on enlarging the calf to equal the heifer in height at the withers in the top and the cow in the bottom illustration. In the middle the heifer is compared to the cow.

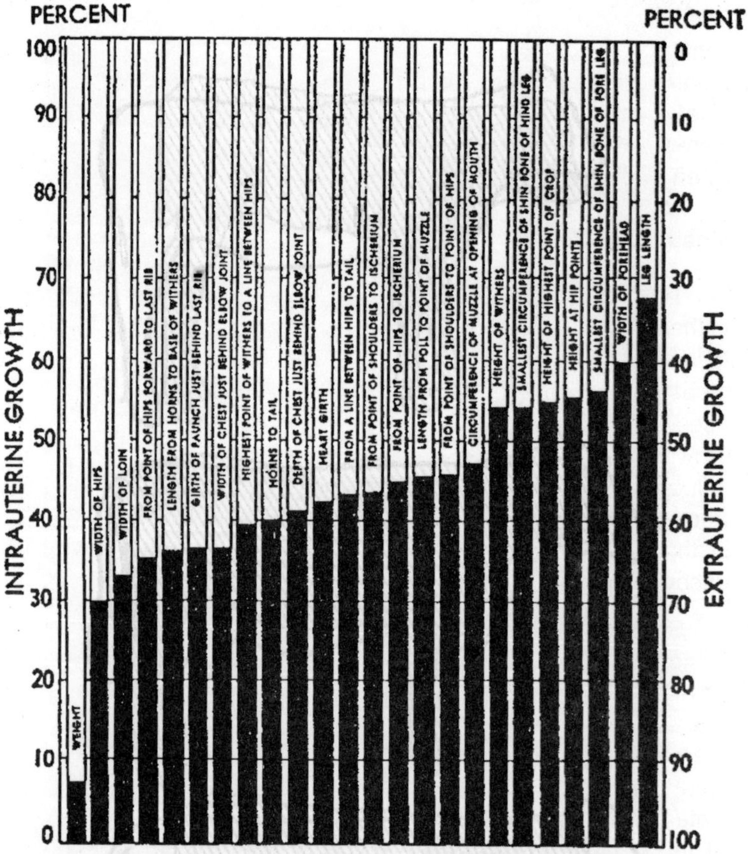

Fig. 17.2: The relative development of different anatomical parts of the bovine of birth expressed in percentage of mature values.

Changes in composition with age

Moulton has summarized the chemical analysis of cattle in various stages of development. the main characteristic change in composition is loss of water from the tissues with age development. The early embryo contains as much as 95 per cent or more of water (on a fat free basis). At birth this has decreased to 75 or 80 per cent, and at 150 days it has decreased to about 73 per cent. From this point the water content from the body decreases until the minimum of 70 to 71 per cent is reached. Nitrogen rises from less than ½ per cent in the early embryo stage to 3 per cent at birth. It then rises rather rapidly to 3.6 per cent at ten months of age and is constant from this point on. Ash rises from .5 of a per cent in the early embryo to 4.3 per cent at birth; it increases to 5 per cent at five months and to 5½ to 6 per cent when mature. (All of the preceding figures are on a fat-free basis.)

Measures of Growth

There is no absolutely satisfactory measure of growth known. In the early embryological stages cell number is the method resorted to in determining development. After that, weight and dimensional measures are the only ones used. Weight is most commonly used and may or may not be truly indicative of the degree of growth, since there are a number of factors other than growth that influence weight. The amounts of water and feed in the digestive tract vary greatly and influence weight. A difference of 50 pounds in the weight of a mature animal because of this factor is not uncommon.

Because there is a great variation in daily weights, it is customary to weigh experimental animals for three consecutive days and use the average of the three weights. There are factors affecting the amount of water in the tissue which may influence the weight without any effect on growth. Fattening produces weight increases by a deposit of fat and a reduction of the amount of water. Starvation produces a loss in weight through a withdrawal of the fat stores. While the latter two affect weights markedly, neither can be said to be strictly growth phenomena. There may be growth without any change in weight. Waters maintained a steer at a constant weight for one year and found that it grew taller at the expense of body depth. For dimensional measurements the height at the withers is most commonly used. Attention is called to the practical difficulties in determining the height at the withers. The posture of the animal at the time the measurement is taken affects very materially that measurement. Usually the height at the withers is measured three times. The animal is moved immediately preceding the taking of the measurement. Dimensional measurements are less sensitive than weights. For cattle a 40 per cent increase in weight is usually accompanied by not more than a 10 per cent increase in the height at the withers. In studying growth in cattle it is customary to take both weight and height at the withers.

Rate of growth

The rate of growth changes with the age of the animal. If the rate of growth is expressed in gains for a definite period of time, such as daily gains or weekly gains, there is an increase until the end of the self-accelerating period, and than a decrease until growth ceases. If the rate of growth for any period is expressed in terms of per cent increase in weight of the animal, the values decrease with age. If the rate is expressed by merely giving the total weight or height of the animal for the different ages, then there is an increase until growth ceases.

Per cent gain in terms of total body weight is a measure of the intensity of the growth impulse. This impulse is the greatest immediately after fertilization, when the weight increase may be as great as 1,000 per cent for one day. At birth about 98 per cent of the growth impulse is lost. That daily gains increase with advance in age up to a maximum with a decrease in growth impulse is accounted for by the great increase in the number of cells. The growth impulse, therefore, does not decrease as rapidly as the number of cells increase until after the self-inhibiting period has been reached. For differences in the rate of growth of prenatal and extrauterine refer to Fig. 17.2.

Normal growth curves

The normal growth figures have value as a guide in determining whether or not animals are doing as well as they should. They are of particular value for the experimentalist who is anxious to know whether a particular ration or type of experiment affects the normal growth of the animal. The normal growth figures for the four dairy breeds as computed by the Missouri Experimental Station are given in Tables 17.1 and 17.2.These figures were gathered from Missuori, Kansas, and Iowa. Attention is directed to the fact that there are great variations from the figures given as normal. Because they represent averages in different sections of the country, perhaps different sets of normal figures should be given. Attention is also directed to the fact that growth in weight continues until past seven or eight years, while maximum height at withers is attained somewhat earlier. Comparing the normal growth figures for bulls with those of females, it will be noted that the bulls make more rapid growth than the heifers.

Heartgirth and Body Weights

There is a sufficiently good correlation between the heartgirth and body weight that this measure may be used for reasonably close estimates of weight of cattle. Estimations made by this method are most accurate for cows but may be used for heifers and claves. The measurement should be taken immediately back of the elbows. The weights for various heartgirth measurement in inches prepared by the Bureau of Dairy Industry, U.S.D. A., are given in Table 17.3.

Limits of Growth

As stated before, each individual inherits a limit beyond which an amount of feed or care will permit it to grow; but whether a limit of growth is reached depends upon a number of environmental factors. A knowledge of these factors is of mere academic interest, but many of them are of great importance in the practical phases of raising dairy cattle. The factors influencing the size of the calf at birth and the effects of breed, gestation, lactation, nutrition, and others upon growth and ultimate size will be considered.

Factors Influencing Size of Calf at Birth

The size of the calf at birth is dependent more on inheritance than on any other factor. In general, the larger the breed the larger will be the calf at birth. This is brought out in the following table, which gives the average weights and height at the withers of calves at birth for the different dairy breeds.

Individual variation is the next biggest factor which affects the birth weight of calves. Jerseys, for instance, may vary from 35 pounds to 90 pounds; and Holsteins vary from 40 to 140 pounds. The age of the dam affects the size. The first calf is usually three or four pounds smaller than the second calf, and the third calf is one or two pounds larger than the second. In extreme old age the calves are generally smaller. Contrary to popular opinion, the condition of the dam has no effect upon the birth weight of the

Table 17.1: Normal growth figures for females*

Age	Ayrshire		Guernseys		Holstein		Jersey	
	Weight	Height at withers	Weight	Height withers	Weight	Height withers	Weight	Height at withers
Months	*Pounds*	*Inches*	*Pounds*	*Inches*	*Pounds*	*Inches*	*Pounds*	*Inches*
1	2	3	4	5	6	7	8	9
Birth	72	27.6	65	26.6	90	29.1	53	25.7
1	89	28.6	77	28.2	112	30.6	67	27.0
2	119	30.2	102	29.8	148	32.3	90	28.9
3	158	31.9	133	31.6	193	34.3	121	30.6
4	198	34.0	173	33.5	243	36.2	158	32.6
5	245	35.5	216	35.3	297	37.7	199	34.5
6	293	37.2	260	36.9	355	39.7	243	36.2
7	344	38.5	305	38.4	410	41.1	286	37.7
8	389	39.9	350	39.9	462	42.3	324	39.0
9	433	40.9	389	40.9	509	43.5	360	40.1
10	469	41.7	427	41.7	552	44.4	393	40.9
11	502	42.5	459	42.6	593	45.3	420	41.7
12	538	43.2	490	43.3	632	46.0	450	42.2

13	577	44.0	524	43.9	671	46.7	479	42.8
14	611	44.8	556	44.6	705	47.3	507	43.3
15	638	45.1	584	45.0	746	47.9	530	43.9
16	669	45.7	605	45.3	782	48.5	558	44.4
17	697	46.2	634	45.9	809	48.9	580	44.7
18	725	46.5	663	46.4	845	49.3	601	45.2
19	758	46.8	686	46.7	878	49.8	622	45.5
20	793	47.4	712	47.0	912	50.2	642	45.9
21	818	47.6	737	47.3	952	50.6	665	46.2
22	844	47.8	763	47.7	986	51.0	684	46.4
23	871	48.1	788	47.9	1,024	51.3	708	46.7
24	902	48.3	818	48.0	1,069	51.7	733	46.9
27	909	48.1	876	48.9	1,151	52.2	816	47.7
30	945	48.3	880	49.3	1,120	52.5	824	47.9
33	965	48.9	905	49.7	1,130	52.7	832	48.0
36	968	48.7	901	49.9	1,165	53.0	855	48.2
39	1,007	49.1	924	50.0	1,176	53.1	899	48.6
42	1,014	49.9	952	49.9	1,202	53.2	895	48.6
45	1,038	50.0	971	50.1	1,197	53.2	898	48.5
48	1,035	50.2	990	50.4	1,232	53.3	897	48.5
51	1,040	49.4	980	50.6	1,261	53.5	927	48.5

1	2	3	4	5	6	7	8	9
54	1,058	50.3	1,024	50.5	1,271	53.6	952	48.6
57	1,073	50.3	1,031	50.5	1,305	53.7	944	48.6
60	1,080	50.4	1,055	50.6	1,330	53.6	937	49.0
63	1,037	49.2	1,043	50.4	1,310	53.5	948	49.0
66	1,055	49.2	1,051	50.0	1,312	53.7	955	48.7
69	1,088	49.3	1,073	49.8	1,343	53.7	966	48.6
72	1,132	49.1	1,093	49.7	1,317	53.7	973	48.4
75	1,067	48.3	1,042	49.3	1,320	53.9	964	48.5
78	1,080	48.9	1,084	49.4	1,357	54.0	998	48.6
81	1,092	49.1	1,071	49.2	1,400	53.8	991	48.4
84	1,122	48.7	1,066	49.3	1,401	53.7	959	48.0
87	1,109	48.8	1,065	49.4	1,402	53.6	952	48.3
90	1,103	48.7	1,053	49.4	1,358	53.7	1,002	48.2
93	1,083	48.5	1,067	48.9	1,335	53.5	984	48.4
96	1,143	49.2	1,070	49.6	1,365	53.2	909	47.7

" Bowling and Putnam (W. Va. Agr. Expt. Sta. Circ. 79) give tables of Aryshire females to 96 months that are slightly lower at birth and slightly higher at older stages.

Table 17.2: Normal growth figures for males*

Age	Ayrshire		Guernseys		Holstein		Jersey	
	Weight	Height at withers	Weight	Height withers	Weight	Height withers	Weight	Height at withers
Months	*Pounds*	*Inches*	*Pounds*	*Inches*	*Pounds*	*Inches*	*Pounds*	*Inches*
1	2	3	4	5	6	7	8	9
Birth	81	27.9	71	27.7	94	29.4	60	26.2
1	101	29.4	87	29.3	125	31.2	78	27.9
2	133	30.9	113	30.6	164	33.2	104	29.7
3	173	32.7	147	32.4	214	34.8	141	31.5
4	217	34.5	190	34.2	269	36.4	184	33.6
5	267	36.1	237	36.1	336	38.8	233	35.5
6	321	37.9	291	37.8	399	40.5	282	37.2
7	378	39.4	345	39.2	456	41.9	326	38.4
8	433	40.7	401	40.3	514	43.1	371	39.5
9	488	41.8	443	41.5	563	44.2	410	40.4
10	536	42.7	494	42.5	620	45.1	452	41.4
11	601	44.1	547	43.3	683	46.4	497	42.7
12			609	44.5	741	47.5	531	43.0
13					796	48.2	566	43.9
14					870	48.8	613	45.0
15					978	49.7	643	45.5

1	2	3	4	5	6	7	8	9
16					1,035	50.5	679	46.1
17					1,090	50.7	726	47.0
18					1,176	52.2	745	47.5
19					1,236	53.3	826	48.4
20					1,286	53.3	856	48.6
21					1,345	54.3	875	48.9
22					1,364	54.3	904	49.3
23					1,410	54.9	931	50.0
24					1,438	55.9	969	50.3

" Bowling and Putnam data (W. Va. Agr. Expt. Sta. Circ. 79.) gives birth wts. of 76 pounds and height at withers of 27.4 inches. At 12 months these figures are 657 and 44.5 respectively.

Table 17.3: Heartgirth measurements for determining body weights of dairy cows

Heart-girth *Inches*	Body weight *Pounds*	Heart girth *Inches*	Body weight *Pounds*	Heart girth *Inches*	Body weight *Pounds*	Heart girth *Inches*	Body weight *Pounds*
1	2	3	4	5	6	7	8
26	80	42.5	248	59.5	622	76.5	1,263
26.5	82	43	257	60	637	77	1,285
27	84	43.5	266	60.5	652	77.5	1,308
27.5	86	44	275	61	668	78	1,331
28	89	44.5	284	61.5	684	78.5	1,354
28.5	92	45	294	62	700	79	1,377
29	95	45.5	304	62.5	716	79.5	1,400
29.5	98	46	314	63	732	80	1,423
30	101	46.5	324	63.5	749	80.5	1,446
30.5	104	47	334	64	766	81	1,469
31	108	47.5	344	64.5	783	81.5	1,492
31.5	113	48	354	65	800	82	1,515
32	118	48.5	364	65.5	817	82.5	1,538
32.5	123	49	374	66	835	83	1,561
33	128	49.5	384	66.5	853	83.5	1,584

1	2	3	4	5	6	7	8
33.5	133	50	394	67	871	84	1,607
34	138	50.5	404	67.5	889	84.5	1,630
34.5	143	51	414	68	908	85	1,653
35	148	51.5	424	68.5	927	85.5	1,676
35.5	153	52	434	69	947	86	1,699
36	158	52.5	445	69.5	967	86.5	1,722
36.5	163	53	456	70	987	87	1,745
37	168	53.5	467	70.5	1,007	87.5	1,768
37.5	174	54	478	71	1,027	88	1,791
38	180	54.5	489	71.5	1,048	88.5	1,814
38.5	186	55	501	72	1,069	89	1,837
39	192	55.5	513	72.5	1,090	89.5	1,860
39.5	200	56	526	73	1,111	90	1,883
40	208	56.5	539	73.5	1,132	90.5	1,906
40.5	216	57	552	74	1,153	91	1,929
41	224	57.5	565	74.5	1,175	91.5	1,952
41.5	232	58	579	75	1,197	92	1,975
42	240	58.5	593	75.5	1,219	....	....
...	...	59	607	76	1,241	....	....

calf unless extreme inanition or nutritional deficiency is manifest. In some cases of vitamin A deficiency the calves may be materially reduced in size at birth.

Table 17.4: Average heights and weights at birth for calves of the different breeds

Breed	Heifers		Bulls	
	Weight	Height	Weight	Height
Ayrshire	72	27.6	81	27.9
Guernsey	65	26.6	71	27.7
Holstein	90	29.1	94	29.4
Jerseys	53	25.7	60	26.2
Shorthorn	73		74	
Brown Swiss	80		85	

Sex of the calf is another factor affecting size at birth. Male calves average from five to ten pounds more at birth than do female calves. The length of the period of gestation also influence birth weights. Prematurely born calves are much smaller than those carried to full term.

Breed as a Factor

Each breed has a characteristic norm for growth and development. From birth to 24 months of age the Holstein (See Tables 17.1 and 17.2) increased 23 inches in height at the withers and gained 948 pounds, as contrasted to an increase of 21.4 inches and a gain of 753 pounds for Guernseys in the same length of time. Referring to the tables, it will be seen that the Jerseys reach maturity earlier than the Holsteins. It is reported that the Jersey has reached skeletal maturity within three to four years, while the Holstein requires four to five years to do this. The maximum weights are reached usually about two years following the cessation of skeletal growth.

Effects of Gestation

Contrary to popular opinion, gestation does not affect the rate of growth to any extent. In 1891 Researcher reported that pregnant guinea pigs gained more rapidly than farrow ones. Researcher found no increase in the nutrient requirements for pregnant cows. That there should be no great demand is evidenced by the small amount of dry matter in the calf at birth. Missouri Station workers have shown that only 26 to 28 per cent of the birth weight of a calf is dry matter. Therefore, there is no more dry matter in a Jersey calf at birth than there is in 100 to 180 pounds of milk. In the case of Holsteins 200 to 275 pounds of milk contain as much dry matter as is found in the calf at birth. It has also been observed that when heifers were dried off immediately after calving, there was no effect upon the growth rate.

Effect of Lactation

As contrasted to the effects of gestation, lactation has a very marked effect upon the rate of growth. In the young dairy animals lactation slows up and sometimes completely stops growth in both height and weight. This is the main reason for desiring size in heifers before the first calving. The reason that lactation stops growth is evident when it is considered that two pounds of daily gain in body weight contain 1.5 pounds of dry matter. Eleven and one-half pounds of milk containing 4 per cent fat also contain 1.5 pounds of dry matter. A heifer producing 40 pounds of 4 per cent fat milk produces 5.2 pounds of dry matter or approximately three times as much dry matter as would be produced in a good daily gain for a growing heifer. It is the demand for the nutrients to make milk that prevents growth.

The age of first calving affects both the rate of growth and the ultimate size obtained. As just noted, lactation demands so much nutrient that the animal is unable to consume sufficient feed to supply the needs of both milk production and body growth. In the dairy animal, with the tendency for milk production so strongly inherent, growth suffers first. Immature animals in milk may be developed into normal size provided they are given long rest periods. It is far better that the heifers be grown to a good size before coming into milk.

Effect of Nutrition

It is well known that body tissues have their origin from the feed consumed. It is therefore only reasonable that the amount of feed and the kind of feed consumed should affect growth. Growth can be speeded up very materially by liberal feeding. There are, however, definite limits to this: first, in the amount of feed that the individual animal can handle, and second, in the amount of growth stimulus that is released by the animal over a given period of time. Growth can be checked very materially by withholding feed. Waters maintained a steer at constant weight for one year. Afterwards this steer was fed liberally, and in one year's time it became normal in size. Apparently different stimuli for growth had accumulated, and when the opportunity came the steer responded in unusually rapid growth. Many people recognize the fact that animals whose growth has been retarded through subnormal nutrition will make much more rapid gains on good feed than will animals of the same size whose ration has been normal.

Effect of Nutrition on Dairy Type and Quality

The general belief that fat heifers develop into poor dairy animals is not substantiated in its entirety by facts. Eckles did find that if heifers were fed light rations during their growing period, they produced slightly more butterfat in the second lactation periods than those that were heavily fed. However, the heavily fed heifer produced more than the lighter fed heifer in the first lactation period. The variability in the production of individuals is great enough to account for the difference in average production of the two groups, and this evidence must not be taken as conclusive.

Factors Influencing Sexual Maturity

Breed is one of the chief factors affecting the age at which an animal comes to sexual maturity. In general, the earliness of sexual maturity is inversely related to the size of the breed, the Jersey reaching sexual maturity the earliest, and the Brown Swiss the latest of the dairy breeds. There are individual variations within the breed that can be accounted for by inheritance. Nutrition is also an important factor; liberal feeding is responsible for earlier sexual maturity. The Missouri Station found that lightly fed Holstein heifers became sexually mature on an average of 273 days of age, while the heavily fed ones did so in 261 days of age. At the Minnesota Station it was noted that animals on a phosphorus deficient ration became sexually mature at a much later date than those having a nutritionally complete ration.

18

Calf Raising

Calf raising is an important problem on the dairy farm. In purebred herds all calves are raised; in others sufficient numbers must be raised to replace cows that go out of the herd. In addition to that, large numbers of calves are raised annually for veal. On an average a cow's production life is about four years. With 25,000,000 cows in the United States according to the 1948 estimate 6,000,000 calves must be raised annually to replace the cows going out of production. Thus, two heifers must be raised annually per eight cows. In order to have two heifers come into production for each eight cows, at least six must be raised for each twenty cows. Since many dairymen sell whole milk and do not attempt to raise calves, others must raise more in order to supply these dairies with milking stock. Approximately 4 per cent of the whole milk produced in the United States is fed to calves. In 1947 this amounted to over 4,500,000,000 pounds. An important consideration in calf raising is that of avoiding the introduction of diseases. By depending upon the purchase of milk cows to replenish those that go out of the herd, there is great danger of introducing one or more of the many infectious diseases with which cattle are afflicted. A good dairyman, therefore, takes the job of raising calves as an important one.

SELECTING CALVES

Since the cost of raising calves to maturity is a considerable item of expense on the dairy farm, only those calves that give indications of growing into profitable cows should be selected. Only by careful selection of calves from high producing dams and families having the desired characteristics can one develop a superior herd. Not always can the mature abilities of a calf be predicted, for the type of the calf is not a reliable indication of the type of cow it will grow into when mature; but when one uses judgment in selection, a much smaller percentage of unsatisfactory mature cows will be raised. Special consideration should be given to the height of production of the dam and her immediate family, and to the strength and vigour of the calves at birth. Weak calves are likely to succumb to the various calf diseases that are encountered. If one has a herd that produces milk of too low a fat percentage, special effort should be made in selecting the calves from the lines that have a high fat content milk. Any other desirable characteristic that one wants in a good cow should be taken into consideration when one selects calves to be raised to maturity.

NUTRIENT REQUIREMENTS

The solution of many of the different problems encountered may be found in the knowledge of the fundamental requirements for growth and development of the calf. The newer knowledge of nutrition has added much to the information of value in practical feeding. Among the more important of these considerations is a knowledge of the digestive tract of the calf, the amount of feed and energy requirements, and the protein, mineral, vitamin, and water requirements.

Digestive Tract

A knowledge of the structure of the digestive tract of the calf will help one to appreciate the necessity for certain types of rations. The digestive tract of the calf differs from that of the cow in its proportionate size and in the different proportions of the stomach compartments (Fig. 18.1) In the mature animal, the rumen occupies 80 per cent of the total capacity of the stomach; the abomasum and omasum each occupy from 7 to 8 per cent. In the young calf, the abomasum and the omasum are two times as large as the rumen and reticulum combined. These proportions change rapidly with the advance in age. In the calf of ten to twelve weeks of age, the omausm and the abomasum are only half the size

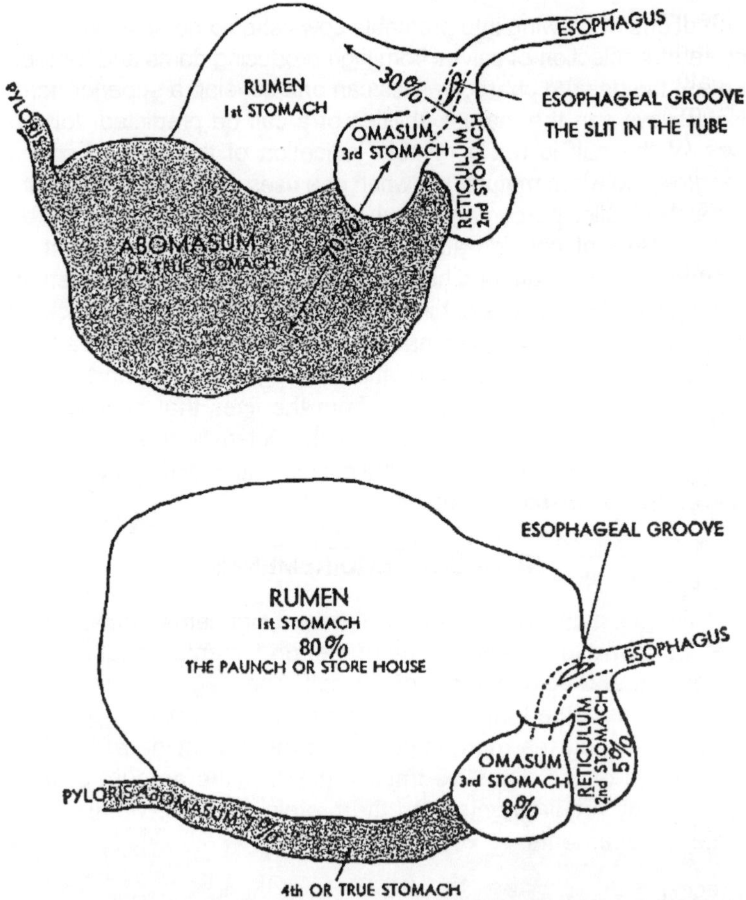

Fig. 18.1: Here are shown the comparative sizes of the various stomach compartments of the calf (above) and the cow (below).

of the rumen and the reticulum. At one year, these proportions have shifted to that of the mature animal. Very little definite information is available as to the exact capacity of the abomasum. This is the true stomach, where the digestion takes place. Milk goes directly into the abomasum under normal conditions. However, if more milk is consumed than the abomasum has capacity for, then it may pass directly into the rumen. As the young calf has no powers for regurgitation, the material may decompose in the rumen and cause digestive disturbances. Some authors claim that the maximum capacity of the abomasum in the young calf is two quarts, and for the whole stomach, less than one gallon. The mature animal of medium size has a total stomach capacity of from 30 to 40 gallons. Large animals may have a capacity as high as 75 gallons. It is therefore apparent that with the development of the calf to maturity the stomach grows more rapidly than the rest of the body.

Amount of Feed and Energy

Because of the small digestive storage facilities, the calf cannot handle much food at a time. It cannot use roughage to any great extent until five or six months of age, and not until ten months of age could even a vigorous calf exist on roughage alone. Energy must come from milk or concentrates. Morrison, an eminent authority on feeding, places the total digestive nutrient requirements at from 1.5 to 2.2 pounds for a calf weighing 100 pounds. For a 1,000 pound calf, the requirements are 11.4 to 12.6 pounds. Therefore, the requirements per pound of live weight are greater for the young calf than for the older one.

Protein Requirements

The protein content of the calf's body increases rapidly up to six months of age through both an increase in the percentage amount in the body and the increase in weight. The relative protein requirements are, therefore, the highest during the first few months of a calf's life. Morrison, after reviewing all experimental work, recommends a nutritive ratio of 1:3:9 to 1:4:5 for calves at 100 pounds of live weight; this gradually widens until at 1,000 pounds the recommended ratio is 1:8:2 to 1:8:4. The quality of the protein is of great importance. There is no better source of protein than milk. When milk substitutes are used, careful attention must be paid to the types of protein as well as to the total amounts. Calves fed whey suffer probably both from an insufficient amount of protein and from an inadequate quality of protein.

Mineral Requirements

Like the protein parts of the body, the skeleton grows relatively most rapidly in the early ages of the calf. The per cent of ash rises rapidly up to 5 months of age. As the major portion of bone consists of calcium and phosphorus salts, the calcium and phosphorus supplies in the diet must be adequate. Milk supplies these important mineral elements in ample amounts. However, after calves are weaned, the ration is frequently inadequate in its calcium and phosphorus content. Iodine is adequate in most normal rations; however, in some iodine deficiency areas, the feeds lack sufficiently in this element to produce deficiency symptoms. If the calves have goiter when they are born, it is an indication that he iodine supply is inadequate. It should be supplied to the cows in the form of iodized salt, which is an adequate source of this mineral element. Iron and copper are both needed for the production of red cells in the blood. Milk under all conditions is deficient in these two elements, and calves fed on milk alone develop anemia. When calves are fed grain and hay in conjunction with milk, there is no danger of insufficient iron and copper.

Magnesium

Milk is relatively low in its magnesium content. Calves that are fed on milk only, sooner or later develop spasms, to which they finally will succumb. The Michigan and Minnesota Stations have recently found that the magnesium content of the blood drops previous to the onset of the spasms. Hay and grain contain adequate magnesium and will prevent the difficulty encountered when milk only is fed. The Wisconsin Station suggests that manganese may be an element needed in the raising of calves, and that milk is deficient in this element. The evidence at this time is not sufficient to warrant drawing definite conclusions.

Sodium Chloride

Sodium chloride, or common table salt, should be furnished calves at all times. It is particularly essential that salt be furnished when the calves begin to eat grain and hay. The failure of supplying salt at this stage frequently results in unthrifty calves.

Vitamin Requirements

As yet the extent to which vitamins are essential in the raising of dairy calves is not definitely known. Some, such as vitamins

B and C, are definitely known not to be required. However, vitamins A and D may be important factors in some of the diseases encountered in dairy calves. The amounts of vitamins A and D in the milk depend upon the amount present in the feed that the cow consumes. Recently it has been shown by the United States Department of Agriculture and the California Station that calves may suffer from a vitamin A deficiency under practical conditions. Researchers fed cows on ripe timothy hay for the entire year, and the calves were either born dead or died on the skim milk diet from such cows. They attributed this difficulty to the vitamin A deficiency in the diet of the cows. Researchers studying the calf diseases on the range, found many claves suffering from what they diagnosed as vitamin A deficiency. They reported that vitamin A deficiency of the diet of the dams is responsible for calves that are weak at birth and that develop severe diarrhea. One of the characteristic symptoms of this deficiency is eye lesions. The Minnesota Station was the first one to produce vitamin A deficiency in calves; but, finding difficulty in preparing a diet sufficiently low in this factor to produce definite symptoms, naturally concluded that under normal conditions vitamin A deficiency would not be expected in dairy calves. Frequent reports of symptoms analogous to vitamin A deficiency would lead one to suspect that this deficiency is far more common throughout the country than has been heretofore suspected.

While the mature bovine synthesizes all of the vitamin B complex and vitamin E the young calf is incapable of doing so and must depend upon body stores at birth and its food for sources of these vitamins. One of the B complex (niacin) is synthesized by the young calf. The rest of the B complex that is needed for the bovine species are synthesized in the rumen by microorganisms present therein. This synthesis does not begin until the rumen becomes functional after consumption of roughage.

While it is possible for a young calf to be deficient in the vitamin B complex it is doubtful that it occurs on farms at least where calves receive colostrum and milk up to four weeks of age. Colostrum is not only rich in vitamin A but also in the B complex as compared to normal milk. Extensive experiments where calves were fed vitamin supplements have shown no lessening in calf digestive upsets nor mortality.

Vitamin A supplement in the form of fish liver oils is beneficial when the diet of the pregnant cows is deficient in carotene and also in some cases of scours. For the most part, however, other causes for scours than vitamin deficiency must be looked for.

Water

Contrary to popular opinion, even when getting large amounts of milk the calf needs water in addition, particularly during warm weather. For successful calf raising, clean water should be available at all times. When calves have not been given water in addition to the milk for a long period of time, they are likely to drink too much when allowed unlimited quantities for the first time.

METHODS OF RAISING CALVES

Calves may be raised by hand or allowed to run with the dams. On the dairy farm practically all calves are raised by hand. Only on race occasions, when a purebred calf is of unusual value, is it permitted to run with a nurse cow. In the feeding of calves on the dairy farm several different problems are encountered because of different conditions. Where butterfat is sold, adequate amounts of skim milk are available, and calf raiding is comparatively easy. Where whole milk is sold, it is necessary to use milk substitutes in order to reduce the expense. In cheese-producing territories whey is sometimes available instead of skim milk, and another feeding problem is created.

Starting the Calf

Regardless of the method used for feeding, the calf is started in the same way. Since it is important that the calf get colostrum, it should be left with the dam preferably for two or three days. If the dam's udder is inflamed, it may be advisable to leave the calf and dam together for a longer period of time. Many dairymen are of the opinion that the calf assists materially in reducing udder inflammation. The importance of colostrum to the young calf has been recognized for a long time, but only recently has the real reason for this need been discovered. Researchers found that calves not receiving colostrum were far more susceptible to infections, particularly of the digestive tract, than those that were fed colostrum. The mortality resulting from these infections was exceedingly high, and B. coli were found in the bodies of the dead calves. Ragsdale and Brody, too, found that calves fed colostrum had a much better chance of survival and suffered less from calf diseases than those not receiving colostrums. Colostrum assists in the prevention of diseases, according to Smith and Little, because of its antibody content. They found at birth the animal had no agglutinins in the blood and within a matter of hours following the ingestion of colostrum agglutinins appeared.

Colostrum differs from normal milk in more than its antibody contents. It has ten or more times as much vitamin A, depending upon the carotene or vitamin A content of the pregnant cow's ration. It contains about twice as much dry matter. Protein content is about 18 per cent compared to 3.5 per cent for normal milk. Most of the protein is in the form of globulin the fraction containing the antibodies. Colostrum contains about five times as much tocopherol as normal milk, about 4 times as much riboflavin, twice as much thiamine, seven times as much choline and about twice as much pentothenic acid. In minerals colostrum also excels normal milk by twice as much calcium, phosphorus, sodium, and chlorine, and three times as much magnesium. It is also richer in potassium, iron, copper, and manganese than normal milk.

When cows are milked before delivery there will be no colostrum following parturition. In such cases other sources of colostrum must be provided or heavy losses in calves may be expected. One satisfactory method is to freeze the first few milkings when prepartum milking is begun, since this will be normal colostrum-provided there has been a sufficiently long dry period. In large herds it will often happen that colostrum, will be available from newly freshened cows.

It is important that the first feed of the newborn calf be colostrum. At this time the intestinal wall is permeable to the globulin antibodies. After the first feed the intestines rapidly become impermeable to this material.

Teaching the Calf to Drink

Teaching the calf to drink out of a bucket is sometimes quite difficult. There are many contrivances on the market that are designed to aid one in teaching a calf how to drink. A number of them are effective, but there is the danger of these appliances becoming contaminated, with the ensuing danger of digestive disturbance in the calf. The natural way for the calf to get milk is by raising his head. The best way to teach a calf to drink is by the following method: First, let him go without food for 24 hours after taking him from the dam. Then insert the fingers of one hand into his mouth and gradually pull his muzzle down into the milk. For a large calf this requires considerable physical strength, but it can be effected by backing him into the corner of a pen and forcing his head down into the milk.

Amount of Milk and Frequency of Feeding

Calves are more often overfed than underfed. Never should more milk be offered a calf per day than 8 per cent of the total weight of the calf. This means that a normal Jersey calf would not get more than five or six pounds of milk per day, and that a Holstein would be limited to a maximum of 8 pounds a day at the start. It is better to feed a calf three times a day than twice a day. The reason for limiting the amount of milk and for advocating more frequent feedings is that the capacity of the abomasum, the true stomach is small, and when it is overloaded, one or both of two things may happen: (1) Part of the milk may pass into the rumen, where putrefaction will occur. (2) Because of a large amount of milk in the abomasum, a large curd is formed which is note completely digested before the next feeding, and putrefaction sets in. Autopsies on calves dying from digestive disturbances invariably reveal large curds in the true stomach and sometimes in the rumen. According to researchers the putrefaction of curds either in the rumen or abomasum is the cause of most digestive disturbances in calves. Feeding smaller amounts of milk at more frequent intervals is the best method of preventing these disturbances. Diluting the milk with warm water at the rate of 1/3 water and 2/3 milk is advocated by some.

Nipple Feeding

Recent studies on the entrance of milk into the stomach of the calf have shown that when milk is swallowed in large gulps such as occurs when drinking from a pail, part of it splashes into the rumen. Since this organ is nonfunctional in the young calf, the undesirability of getting milk therein is readily understood. The position of the head (whether high or low) when feeding from a pail makes no difference in the amounts that splash into the rumen. When calves are fed from nipple pails the amount of milk in each bolus was smaller than in the case of drinking from the pail, and no splashing into the rumen occurred. Many dairymen now feed calves by the use of nipple pails and report less difficulty from common scours.

The author and co-workers fed a limited number of calves by nipple, with milk before them at all times. The milk ranked in temperature from warm to near freezing. The calves consumed from two or three times as much milk per day as is usually considered safe when fed from pails twice daily, without any digestive upsets. The probable reason for freedom from digestive disturbances is the frequency with which they fed and the small quantities taken at each feeding. They consumed milk up to 17 times during a 24-hour period.

Raising Calves on Skim Milk

While whole milk is the best feed, the fat of milk is too valuable to be fed to calves. Where butterfat is sold and skim milk is available, calves should be raised on skim milk, following the original whole milk period. Researcher demonstrated that while calves fed on skim milk did not make quite as large daily gains as those receiving whole milk, they gained more rapidly after weaning and made gains at much lower costs. This is shown in Table 18.1, which contains a summary of work. This work has been corroborated by numerous other trials, in which calves raised on skim milk have been found to look rougher while on the skim milk diet than the calves on whole milk, and to make slightly less gains. They responded better on dry feeds following weaning, and matured as early and to as desirable animals as those raised on whole milk.

Changing from whole milk to skim milk

A healthy, vigorous calf may begin to receive some skim milk when two weeks old. The change from whole milk to skim should be gradual. One pound of skim should be substituted daily for one pound of the whole milk until the complete change in effected. Thus a calf getting ten pounds of whole milk would require ten days to be changed over to skim milk. This change is rather a critical time in the calf's life.

Table 18.1: Skim milk compared with whole milk and running with dam as feed for calves

(There were ten calves in each group. They are fed milk for 140 days, then transferred to a feed lot for 7 months.)

Results for 140 days when on the Milk Diet

	Skim milk	Whole milk	Running with dam
Average gain - lbs	223	287	248
Average daily gains	1.51	1.86	1.77
Cost per 100 lbs. gain	$2.26	$7.60	$4.41
Results for 7 months in the feed lot			
Average gain - lbs	440	405	422
Daily gains	2.10	1.93	2.00
Grain per 100 lbs. gain lbs.	439	470	475

Skim milk differs from whole milk in having the milk fat removed, the amounts of the other constituents thereby being slightly increased. By comparing the analysis of whole milk and skim milk given in the table on the next page, it will be seen that skim milk has slightly more than half of the total digestive nutrient that whole milk has, and that it has a much lower nutritive ratio, there being one pound of protein for each one and one-half pounds of nonprotein nutrients, as contrasted to a ratio of 1:3:9 for the whole milk. When he is changing to skim milk, the calf will be receiving far less energy, but a little more protein than when he is on the whole milk diet. It is, therefore, essential that at this time a grain supplement be furnished to supply the additional needed energy. Corn alone is an adequate supplement; however, any ordinary grain mixture will suffice. Most calves will begin to eat grain at about two weeks of age, and little difficulty should be experienced in getting the calf to take the grain supplement at the time the change from whole milk to skim milk is completed. After the calf is on a skim milk diet, the amounts of milk may be increased, but at no time should the amount of milk fed in one day exceed 10 per cent of the calf's weight. As the amounts of grain and hay consumed increase, it will be necessary to reduce the relative amounts of milk proportionately. At no time is it advisable to feed the calf more than 20 pounds of skim milk a day.

Table 18.2: Average composition of whole milk and skim milk

	Whole milk	Skim milk
Total solids	12.8	9.6
Protein	3.5	3.7
Fat	3.7	0.1
Sugar	4.9	5.0
Mineral	0.7	0.8
Total digestible nutrients	16.2	8.6
Nutritive ratio	1: 3.9	1: 1.5

Raising Calves where Whole Milk is Sold

Where whole milk is sold, the problem of raising calves is different from what it is where there is skim milk available. Seldom are there enough calves, on a farm producing whole milk, to make it worth while to skim a portion of the milk for calf feeding. To solve the problem of raising calves under these conditions numerous experiments have been run at the various experiment stations in the United States. Various proprietary calf meals have also been prepared and are on the market as substitutes for milk. In attempts to develop satisfactory substitutes for skim milk scores of different mixtures have been tried. Cornell University reports excellent results with a calf meal made up into a gruel, replacing the whole milk on the twentieth day. This mixture consists of:

500 lbs. yellow corn meal	200 lbs. soluble blood flour
440 lbs. red dog flour	20 lbs. Calcium carbonate
300 lbs. oat flour	20 lbs. steam bone meal
300 lbs. linseed oil meal	20 lbs. salt

Animals raised on this calf meal have been carried through to the second year of milk production, and according to the report of the authors, no difference can be noted in their size or milk production from those raised on a skim-milk diet. The gruel was made by mixing the calf meal with water at 100°F. in the proportion of one pound of gruel to five pounds of water.

The Oregon Station tried three mixtures for calf meals. One of these consisted of:

Ground oats	150 lbs.
Ground yellow corn	150 lbs.
Wheat bran	150 lbs.
Linseed oil meal	50 lbs.
Soluble blood flour	50 lbs.
Steam bone flour	5 lbs.
Salt	5 lbs.

A second mixture contained 50 pounds of dried skim milk in place of the soluble blood flour, and a third contained 100 pounds of dried skim milk which replaced the blood flour, 30 pounds of ground oats, and 20 pounds of ground yellow corn. The three meals gave satisfactory results, the calves being slightly under the normal growth during the time that they received the calf meals; however, they soon caught up to normalcy. The third formula gave slightly better results than the first two; this is attributed to the high dry-milk content. These calf meals were fed dry, and the calves ate adequate amounts of them for sufficient nutritive intake. Many other stations have developed similar formulae and have reported similar successes. It may be said that if skim milk is available, it is preferable to calf meals for the raising of calves; but if skim milk is not available, the calf meals will prove satisfactory. While no definite experimental work is available on the comparative value of the proprietary calf meals, it may be said that many of them will give satisfactory results.

Raising Calves on Whey

In cheese-producing areas, whey is frequently available and can be used satisfactorily for calf feeding if the proper supplements are made. The Wisconsin Station has obtained good results by changing calves from whole milk to whey in the same way and at the same age as when the change was made from whole milk to skim milk. They increased the whey allowance to 14 pounds when the calf reached six weeks of age. In cheese making most of the protein is taken out of the milk, and therefore the whey contains only 0.8 per cent protein, as contrasted to 3.7 per cent protein in skim milk. It is therefore necessary to feed a high protein grain supplement when whey replaces skim milk in calf feeding. At least 40 per cent of the concentrate should consist of linseed oil meal or soybean oil meal. The Wisconsin Station found a satisfactory mixture to be:

30 lbs. ground corn

30 lbs. standard wheat middlings

40 lbs. linseed oil meal

Since whey is obtained from cheese factories to which a number of farmers contribute milk, it is essential that the whey be pasteurized before it is returned to the farm, in order to guard against transmitting disease.

Raising Calves on Buttermilk

Frequently buttermilk is available at a reasonable price; then it will make an excellent substitute for skim milk. Buttermilk analyzes about the same as skim milk, and whether sweet or sour it can be substituted for equal quantities of skim milk. As it is frequently poorly cared for at the creameries, buttermilk from dirty storage tanks should not be used; it is certain to carry organisms that will produce digestive disturbances. While the cream from which the buttermilk comes is generally pasteurized in all creameries, before bringing the buttermilk to the farm one should make certain that either the cream or the buttermilk has been pasteurized; otherwise infectious diseases may be introduced into the herd.

Dried Skim Milk or Buttermilk and Semisolid Buttermilk

Dried buttermilk or skim milk, when remade by mixing one pound of the dried product with nine pounds of water, makes up a solution of the same composition as liquid skim milk or buttermilk, and can be fed in the same proportions with the same results; or the dried products may be mixed with the grain and fed dry, one pound of the dry product being allowed where ten pounds of liquid skim milk or buttermilk would be used. Semisolid buttermilk is partially dried sour buttermilk prepared especially for livestock feeding. The Minnesota Station found that when this was allowed on the basis of the same dry matter content as in the normal liquid feeding, equally good results were obtained. The only objection to using these products is that frequently they are too costly. Sometimes drying plants have products that grade slightly below the requirement for human food; these products are sold at reduced prices and for calf feeding are equally as satisfactory as the better products.

Hay for Calves

In raising a calf, hay is an essential in the diet. Calves on skim milk have an adequate amount of protein in the diet, and for them high quality grass hays, such as timothy or bluegrass, are preferable to legume hays. Legumes, however, are superior to the grass hay for calves on whey and on some of the calf meals. Legumes are characterized by very high protein and calcium content. The high protein content makes them suitable feed for calves on whey, and the high calcium content makes them a desirable roughage for calves on calf meals, as grains are low in calcium content.

A calf will usually begin to eat hay at about two weeks of age. It should be furnished fresh twice a day. Calves that do not receive hay are likely to suffer from vitamin D deficiency, particularly during the latter part of the winter or early spring, when milks are likely to be deficient in vitamin D and the sunshine is deficient in ultraviolet rays. Hays cured to the green colour have far higher vitamin values than darker coloured or bleached hays and are, therefore, to be preferred for calf feeding. Well-cured hays are also more palatable.

Whole Milk Diet Alone

While milk is considered the most nearly perfect food, it is inadequate for the complete nutrition of the dairy calf. Numerous attempts have been made at raising dairy calves on whole milk with various elemental supplements. Until recently, all such attempts have met with failure. At the Minnesota and Michigan Stations,

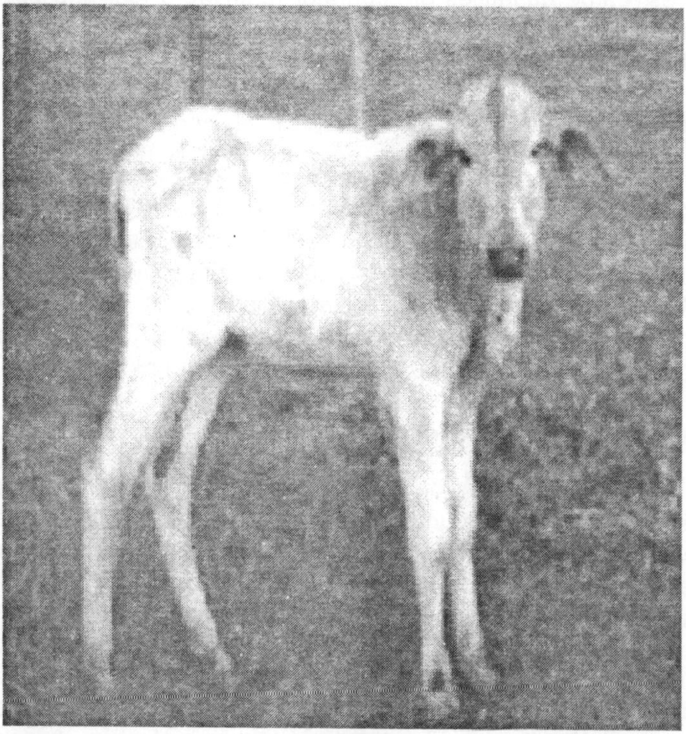

Fig. 18.2: An unthrifty calf. Its condition is due to malnutrition and disease

calves have been raised to maturity on whole milk, with copper, iron, and magnesium supplements, plus cod-liver oil as a source of vitamins A and D. at the Minnesota Station, normal growth and normal reproduction have been experienced on such a diet. Unless copper and iron are added, the animal suffers from anemia and will ultimately succumb to that disease. Additional magnesium is needed in spite of the fact that milk contains fair quantities of that element. For some reason, not as yet entirely clear, the calf on a sole milk diet has a relatively high magnesium requirement.

Effect of Foam in Milk

It is generally assumed that foam, which is common in skim milk, is detrimental to the calves. The South Dakota Station set up an experiment to determine the facts regarding foam fed to calves. Large quantities of separator foam were fed, and in no case was there evidence of any harmful effects from the ingestion of large amounts of it.

Pasteurization of Milk

The question would naturally arise as to whether pasteurization of milk would have any effect upon its nutritive value. The California Station heated milk to 170°F. and could not detect any difference in the nutritive value for calf feeding between milk so heated and raw milk. In the common methods of pasteurization, vitamin C is destroyed. As the calf does not need vitamin C in the food, this would not be expected to impair the nutritive value of milk in any way.

Temperature of milk and cleanliness of utensils

In the early weeks of a calf's life, at least, the temperature of the milk should be around 100°F. when fed. After the calf becomes several months of age, this is not so important. Cleanliness of the utensils with which the milk comes in contact is of utmost importance. Milk is one of the best mediums for bacterial development, and in buckets and other utensils in which small portions of milk are left extensive bacterial development takes place. Many of the types of bacteria so developed when taken into the calf's digestive tract will produce putrefactive changes which, in turn, produce scours. The most serious digestive disturbance can frequently be attributed directly to failure to clean the milk buckets used for calf feeding. These buckets should be cleaned as scrupulously as any utensil with which milk for human food comes in contact.

Calf Pens

The prime requisite of calf pens is that they furnish a light, clean, dry, and draftless place for the calf. One of the chief causes of calf pneumonia is dampness and draftiness, which are also conducive to calf scours. These two diseases cause the heaviest losses among calves. The ideal calf pen is the individual pen with solid partitions between neighbouring pens, 3 feet by 6 feet in dimension. Infectious diseases are communicated by direct contact of calves, and this type of pen prevents such contacts. The solid partition has a tendency to prevent drafts from directly hitting the calf. In the colder climates, it is preferable to have the calf pens located in the cow barn; calves do not generate enough heat to keep a special calf barn warm, and the larger animals will contribute to the warmth. On larger farms, the calf barns are usually furnished with artificial heat. After a calf is six weeks to two months old, he can then be transferred to a larger pen, where a number of calves may be put together.

Bedding

Adequate quantities of clean bedding should be furnished. It has been found, however, that the most satisfactory method is not to clean the pens daily, but to let the litter accumulate, adding bedding in such quantities as are needed to keep the pen dry, and removing the litter only when the accumulation is sufficient to permit the calves to jump out of the pen. The accumulated litter generates heat and makes a much warmer bed for the calf than would be possible if it were removed daily. Some of the most successful dairymen let the litter accumulate for weeks and sometimes months before it is removed.

Calf Ties

After they have been given their feeding of milk, calves are likely to suck one another. In doing this, they swallow considerable hair, which, not being digestible, will form hair balls in the abomasum. Frequently, on slaughter or post mortem examinations, from one up to as many as 20 or 30 hair balls may be found in a calf's stomach. They vary in size from minute ones up to balls two or more inches in diameter. To avoid the ingestion of hair, calves should be tied following the feeding for a period of one-half hour or more. The most satisfactory ties are stanchions that occupy a side of the calf pen. Commercial calf pens have many desirable features of convenience, but homemade ones can be built that serve the purpose adequately.

Pasture

As skim milk is largely water, there is no particular advantage of pasture grass over hay for a calf receiving milk. The calf, too, is very susceptible to injury from exposure to the hot sun and flies. Not until the calf is at least four months of age is it advisable to turn him out on pasture, and then only when shade is afforded.

Silage

While there is no evidence that silage is harmful to a calf receiving milk, there is nothing to indicate that it has any particular value. In the main, silage is not so palatable to a young calf as is hay, and for this reason, it is much better that the calf get its roughage in the form of hay rather than silage.

Spring vs. Fall Calves

From the standpoint of ease of raising the calf, there are advantages for both fall and spring calves. The fall calf must be raised in the barn, and it is more likely to suffer from vitamin deficiency, particularly vitamins A and D, than is the spring calf, as winter milk is normally much lower than spring milk in its content of both these vitamins. The spring calf, however, is more likely to suffer from damage by flies and from digestive disturbances due to bacteria because of the favourable weather conditions for bacterial development. From the standpoint of the economy of raising to maturity, the fall calf has considerable advantage over the spring calf. The fall calf is old enough to make good use of pasture by the next spring, and by the time it is two years of age it thus will have had two pasture seasons. The spring calf is too young to make use of pasture the first season and will have had but one pasture season when two years of age. In addition the fall calf will have been on pasture when its food requirements were the highest- from 18 months to 24 months of age - while the spring calf will have spent the period from 12 to 18 months of age on pasture.

Weaning the Calf

Unless skim milk is unusually plentiful, there is no advantage in feeding it to a calf more than six months old. At that time the normal calf has reached sufficient development to be able to handle enough grain and hay to continue its normal growth. The change from milk to a hay and grain ration only should be made gradually. First the feeding of milk should be limited to once a day, and then the amount of milk should be reduced daily until in ten days it is completely eliminated. At this point if nonlegume hays and low protein concentrates have been fed, it is necessary to add some high protein concentrates to the ration, or to change from a grass hay to a legume hay. One of the most common mistakes made in weaning a calf from skim milk is failure to furnish adequate protein in the ration. If legume hays are fed, then any ordinary grain mixture will suffice. If nonlegume hays are fed, a concentrate mixture containing at least 40 per cent of high protein concentrate, as linseed oil meal or cottonseed meal, is needed to supply the necessary protein requirements. In this case, two pounds of the concentrate should be fed daily.

Production of veal

Vealers consist of a group of immature milk-fed bovine animals usually not over 3 months of age. There are three classes: light weights of 110 pounds or less, medium weights of 110 to 180 pounds, and heavy weights of 180 pounds or more. Each one of these classes is divided into five grades on the basis of quality. One of the requisites of veal is that the flesh must be nearly white in colour. To produce veal of this colour it is essential that no hay or grain be fed; only milk will maintain the desired colour.

Feeding for Veal Production

Nothing but whole milk will produce veal of the highest quality. Numerous trials have shown that it requires about ten pounds of milk to produce one pound of gain. Since the object is to produce as rapid gains as possible, it is necessary to feed the calf as much milk as it will consume. The most satisfactory way is to permit the calf to nurse the dam or some nurse cow. Apparently a calf can consume considerably more milk when it takes the milk directly from the dam than when it is hand fed, without suffering digestive disturbances. While digestive disturbances resulting in scours are detrimental to calves that are to be raised to maturity, they are even more so to the veal calf. The set-backs occasioned from scours will not permit any profit in the production of veal.

Economy of Veal Production

As veal can be produced only on whole milk, there are definite limitations to the advisability of the production of veal. Ten pounds of milk are required on the average to produce one pound of gain; if milk is worth $2.00 a hundred, each pound of gain costs 20 cents. Profits made on the production of veal, if there are any, must be from the initial weight of the calf. The birth weight of the calf is therefore a most important consideration. The most desirable weight of a veal calf is 150 pounds. Table 18.3 shows the amount of milk that is required to raise calves of various birth weight to 150 pounds and the value of the milk consumed when $ 2.00 per hundredweight. A calf weighing 40 pounds at birth will require 1,100 pounds of milk by the time it has reached 150 pounds in weight. With milk at $2.00 per hundredweight the cost of milk is $22.00. With veal at 10 cents per pound the carcass is worth but $15.00. On the other hand, a calf weighing 100 pounds at birth requires but 500 pounds of milk to bring it to the 150 pound weight. The milk there will have cost but $10.00. Heavier calves will require proportionately less milk. Unless the calves are of large sizes to begin with and the milk of low cost or the veal of high value, there is little profit to be made in the production of veal.

Table 18.3: Amounts of milk required to bring calves of various birth weights up to150 lbs.

Birth weight	Amount of milk	Value of milk at $2.00 per Cwt.	Value of veal at 10 Cts.
40	1,100	$22.00	$15.00
60	900	18.00	15.00
80	700	14.00	15.00
90	600	12.00	15.00
100	500	10.00	15.00

CALF DISEASES

Since diseases exact a large toll from dairy herds, one of the first considerations in maintaining a healthy, profitable herd is to select animals that are free from disease. The second problem is to take the proper precaution to prevent diseases, and the third is the care and treatment of animals that have become infected.

Selecting Calves Free from Disease

Insofar as is possible, calves should be selected from cows that are free from diseases which are communicable to the calves. Such diseases as tuberculosis, Bang's disease, and Johne's disease are readily communicable to the calf from the dam, and no calves should be selected from animals infected with these diseases unless the calves are held in isolation for at least 30 days.

Prevention of Diseases

In medicine it is universally recognized that the best treatment for diseases is their prevention. In the raising of calves there are a number of things that may be done to insure a minimum of diseases. Even with reasonable attempts to prevent diseases most herds will experience some infection among the calves, since calves are much more susceptible to disease than older animals. In addition to the majority of the diseases to which older animals are susceptible, there are a number of diseases that are limited to calves. It is only those diseases with which calves are afflicted, and not those afflicting older animals, that will be discussed at this point, together with the methods of prevention and the remedy.

Common Scours

Common scours is the most common ailment of calves. The majority of calves are afflicted with this disease at some time during their lives. The injury done by common scours is impossible to measure. Very seldom does the disease itself end fatally, but it reduces the vitality of the calf to such an extent that susceptibility to other diseases is greatly increased. In addition to this, common scours cause a setback to the calf from which complete recovery is not always effected. Common scours attacks calves at any age. However, calves that did not get colostrum milk are more susceptible at all ages than are those that secured colostrums.

Symptoms

The first symptoms of common scours are general listlessness, dull appearance of the eye, a drooping of the ears, usually increased respiration, and sometimes increased temperature. These are followed by diarrhoea.

Causes

Overfeeding is probably the more frequent causative factor. Sheehy, who has given much attention to this problem, finds that when a calf is overfed, large curds are formed in the stomach that are not completely digested before the next feeding. These curds, therefore, become the subject of putrefactive changes, which, in turn, cause the diarrhea. Too cold milk, also, may initiate digestive disturbances. Probably next to overfeeding is general uncleanliness and contamination of pails, pens, and other equipment with which the calf may come in contact. Alfalfa hay also may sometimes cause looseness of the bowels which is sometimes mistaken for scours.

Treatment

As common scours is due to abnormal conditions of the digestive tract, the first requisite in treatment is to reduce the feed to one-half or less of the normal and to continue the reduced ration until complete recovery is effected. Sheehy also advises diluting the milk with water. A number of other treatments are recommended. A castor oil drench of 3 ounces of castor oil to a pint of milk is recommended by some. This should be administered before any other treatment is given. A number of persons have found that one teaspoonful of formalin given in a pint of milk for two or three consecutive days is effective. Eggs also are often effective in checking the progress of this disease. One or two eggs in a pint of milk should be given at each feed. Various sulpha drugs are now used with good success in the treatment of scours. Sulphanilamide should be given at the rate of one grain per pound of live weight. Next in importance to reducing the feed and administering some therapeutic measure is keeping the calf warm and dry. While common scours is not contagious, it is well to remove affected calves from the healthy ones.

Acute infectious scours

One of the major causes for heavy losses among calves during the first week or ten days of life is acute infectious scours.

Symptoms

Acute infectious scours may be differentiated from the common scours by the more rapid onset, sudden prostration, and extreme weakness. The body temperature is usually greatly elevated and appetite is lacking. The bowel discharges are abnormal. In most cases the feces are yellowish-white and very offensive of odor. In other cases they are bloody, due to damage to the gut wall which causes hemorrhage into its contents. The animal rapidly becomes dehydrated because of the large amounts of fluid discharged into the gut contents. This results in sunken eyes and retracted belly. The respiration is short and rapid and with the progress of the disease the temperature drops. Death ensues as a rule in 24 to 48 hours.

Causes

The organisms responsible for this disease are not well known. For calves that do not receive colostrum, apparently common coliform organisms produce the above symptoms. Infectious scours often attacks calves that receive colostrum and in severe outbreaks attack nearly all calves in a herd even though they have received colostrum. One type apparently gains entrance through the navel cord, since the first evidence is a swelling in the region of the navel. For many cases the causative organism is obscure and all that can be said at the present is that the disease is due to some highly infectious organism.

Prevention

The solution of the infectious scours problem lies in prevention, because once a calf is attacked treatments now known are not very effective. The first and most important factor in its control is proper sanitation. Sick calves must be removed from the healthy ones and the premises thoroughly cleaned and disinfected. The stall in which the cow calves must be cleaned and disinfected. During the summer a clean, grass-covered lot is an excellent place for calving. The calf should receive colostrum for the first day or two, preferably by nursing its dam, and left in an isolated pasture for ten days before being returned to a barn in which there has been infection. Care should be exercised in feeding, as there is some evidence that common scours predispose the calf to attacks of the infectious variety. Dipping the navel cord in tincture of iodine or a 10 per cent solution of silver nitrate immediately after birth is effective in preventing infection from this source.

Treatment

In most case the onset and progress of the disease is so rapid that treatment is of little avail. Administration of four to six ounces of castor oil followed by a standard dose of sulphaguanidine, sulphathalidine, sulphadiazine or sulphamerazine has proven helpful. Intravenous administration of salt solution and glucose is helpful in overcoming the dehydration and furnishing energy.

The administration of antiserums, at one time recommended, has been found wanting. It is possible that future research will develop effective antiserums, since toxic production of the causative organisms seems to be an important factor in producing the symptoms observed.

Pneumonia

Bronchial pneumonia or common pneumonia usually occurs when the calf is in a weakened condition, resulting from scours or some other disease. Common pneumonia is probably the specific cause of most deaths among calves.

Symptoms

The temperature increases to 104° or 106°F. This is followed by a cough, and the respiration becomes increasingly rapid with the advance of the disease until there is "gasping" for breath. The skin, particularly at the nose, becomes dry. In addition, loss of appetite, general listlessness, and weakness occur. A calf that recovers from pneumonia is left in a weakened condition and will seldom attain the vigour that it would have had if it had not been so infected.

Causes

The most common cause of pneumonia is exposure to drafts

and damp, wet quarters. Of course, a predisposing factor, as has been previously mentioned, is a weakened condition of the calf from some other disease.

There is also a highly infectious type of pneumonia that will attack calves even in the most healthy and vigorous state. One form is probably due to a virus, with other bacteria as secondary invaders.

Treatment

Warm, dry quarters is the most important factor in the treatment of this disease. A mild purgative, such as castor oil, should be administered as in the case of common scours; three ounces of castor oil should be given in one pint of milk. The appetite of the calf declines to such an extent that there is no danger of overfeeding.

Goiter

In certain sections of the United States goiter is a common affliction of calves, and the losses caused thereby are heavy.

Symptoms

The chief characteristic of goiter is a swelling of the thyroid gland, located in the throat just below the jaw. There are various degrees of swelling, from one of moderate size to one that is of such size that the calf is choked.

Cause

Goiter in calves is caused by insufficient iodine in the ration of the dam during pregnancy. In many sections there is insufficient iodine in the soil. As a result, plants grown on such soil are deficient in iodine.

Treatment

The calf affected with goiter should be given a small amount of iodine in the milk, but the best way of treating goiter is to prevent its onset by supplying iodine in the ration of the pregnant cow. Under ordinary conditions, the iodized salt on the market furnishes an adequate amount of iodine for the prevention of goiter. If iodized salt is not fed and goiter is encountered, one tablespoonful of potassium iodine solution should be fed daily to pregnant cows. The iodine solution is made up by adding one teaspoonful of potassium iodide or sodium iodide to one gallon of water. One grain of potassium iodide daily is adequate. It may also be furnished in the form of tablets which may be dissolved in drinking water.

Ringworm

Calves are very susceptible to ringworm, and it is not uncommon to see whole calf herds so affected.

Symptoms

Ringworm causes the hair to fall out in spots of various sizes. It may attack any part of the body but is more frequently found first around the neck, head, and shoulders. Ringworm, is very irritating, and the calf constantly wants to rub the affected, parts against fences or walls of the pen. The disease usually disappears during the summer when the calves are on pasture.

Causes

Ringworm is caused by a fungus which attacks the epidermic layers of the skin. The disease is very contagious, its spread being effected by direct contact with an infected animal or from objects that have been contaminated by the infected animals.

Treatment

First the infected spots should be washed with soap and water and the crusts removed, and then tincture of iodine or nitrate of mercury ointment should be applied daily until cure is effected. All pens should be thoroughly disinfected with ordinary disinfectants, and the fences or pen walls should be whitewashed, to destroy the spores scattered by the infected animal. Also, the infected animals should be removed from the noninfected ones to prevent the further spread of infection.

It has recently been shown that a solution of Phemoral (1:1000) when properly applied to the ringworm scabs is very effective. The

Phemoral is applied by a wad of cotton soaked in the solution and should be administered three times at weekly intervals.

Warts

Warts may affect calves on any part of the body, but they appear most frequently about the eyes, the neck, and shoulders. They cause no particular damage but are unsightly. There are two types of warts: one that forms a cauliflower-like tumor, and one that forms a dense club like growth. It is the latter that is the more common and unsightly. Warts range in size up to a weight of 14 pounds.

Cause

Warts are caused by a filterable virus.

Treatment

The most satisfactory way of treating warts is by surgery. They may be twisted off if small, clipped off with a pair of scissors, or ligated by means of a rubber band or a horse hair tied tightly around the base of the wart. The latter strangulates them and they will ultimately slough off. After removal, the roots should be cauterized with a caustic or glacial acetic acid.

19

Raising the Heifer from Weaning to Calving Time

IMPORTANCE OF RAPID DEVELOPMENT

As a heifer following weaning is comparatively easy to raise, this particular period in the animal's life is given less attention than any other period. There are, however, some very important economic problems to consider in feeding and caring for heifers of this age. The important fact to keep in mind is that a maximum development and earliest maturity consistent with cost is to be desired. It has been shown previously that earliness of maturity is, to a considerable extent, dependent upon the rate of growth. The nutrient requirements for maintenance are proportional to the weight of the animal. Assuming a constant rate of growth up to 1,000 pounds of live weight, when one animal, because of liberal feeding, attained that weight in 600 days while another animal, because of a lower plane of nutrition, required 900 days, 50 per cent more nutrients was required for the maintenance of the second animal than for the first. As the average weight for the period in either case is 550 pounds, if the calf weighs 100 pounds at the beginning, 550 pounds of live weight must be maintained for 300 days longer in the case of poor feeding than in the case of liberal feeding. The maintenance requirement for this weight is approximately four pounds of total digestible nutrients per day. The slower grown heifer would, therefore, require 1,200 pounds more total digestible nutrients to bring it to the 1,000 pounds live weight than would the more rapidly grown one. Unless the cost of the ration for the slower growth is less than two-thirds of the cost of the faster growing ration, the faster growing ration brings the animal to 1,000 pounds weight at lower cost.

A second point in favour of rapid growth and development is that the earlier maturing heifer will bring earlier returns on the investment. A third point in favour of rapid and full development is the fact that a higher production may be expected from the well-developed heifer at the time of the first calving.

Feeding the Calf from Six Months to One Year

Since the calf is weaned at six months, this is a critical period in its development. Because there is reduced food intake, the change from skim milk to a dry feed usually checks growth temporarily. At this point the amount of grain allowed should be increased, and particular attention should be paid to the protein content of the ration. A normal Holstein weighs approximately 400 pounds at weaning time. According to Morrison's Feeding Standard, such an animal requires .8 to .9 pound of protein and 6.5 to 6.6 pounds of total digestible nutrients daily. If the animal is furnished a low protein roughage ration, there is a great shortage in protein unless a high protein concentrate is added. An illustration will indicate the importance of sufficient protein in the ration at this time. A 400 pound calf will consume approximately ten pounds of hay daily. Ten pounds of timothy hay contains .29 pound of protein, which is .6 of a pound short of the requirement. It would require two pounds of linseed oil meal a day to supply the additional protein requirement. Ten pounds of alfalfa, on the other hand, contains more than enough protein for normal growth, and the concentrate that is added may be of any kind. More frequently than not, heifers at this age are suffering from insufficient protein in the ration.

Roughage

From the previous discussion it is apparent that a legume hay is the best roughage for the heifer from six months to one year of age. This can be fed *ad libitum*, and if it is of good quality, the animal may take more than 2½ pounds per 100 pounds of live weight. On most farms silage is available, and while there is no particular reason for feeding silage to calves of this age, there is no evidence that it is harmful. If silage is fed, it may replace one-half of the hay ration, three pounds of silage replacing one pound of hay. In so doing, however, if the concentrate is corn or barley or similar low protein grains, there is a danger of getting insufficient protein. If grass hays are fed, such as prairie, timothy, and sudan grass, a high protein concentrate must be furnished.

Hay Alone

Roughage has been tried in numerous experiments for calves of this age, and all have resulted in failure to secure normal growth. The reason is probably that the rumen of calves is relatively small up to approximately one year of age, and the calf is, therefore, unable to consume enough feed.

Concentrates

The heifer at this age should have at least two pounds of concentrates daily if the roughage is of high quality, and more grain if it is of low quality. If the roughage is a legume, any kind of grain will suffice. Corn only, corn and barley, and barley only have been used in different trials with excellent success. In most cases, however, the regular herd ration is satisfactory. When the roughage is of the low protein variety, the grain mixture must have at least 25 per cent of digestible protein. If the roughage consists of a mixture of one-half legume and the other half nonlegume, a grain mixture of two parts oats, one part barley, and one part corn, furnishes adequate protein.

Pasture

Pasture grass, when immature, has adequate protein content to supply the needs of calves from six months to a year of age. However, it is still too bulky to produce normal growth in heifers of this age, and a concentrate should be added; this should be the same as when alfalfa hay is fed. If the grasses are mature, the protein content becomes inadequate, and the grain supplement should be changed to approximately that recommended for the grass hays.

Minerals

When the calf receives skim milk, adequate phosphorus and calcium for normal growth are supplied. When legume roughages are fed, the calcium supply is adequate, but under certain soil conditions there may be a deficiency of phosphorus. When the grass hays are fed, there may be a deficiency of calcium. It is, therefore, to be advised that bone meal be supplied to calves on such rations. If it is not needed, there is enough experimental evidence to show that an excess will do no harm, and the costs are negligible. Ordinary salt should always be available. Often calves, especially when on pasture, are forgotten and not supplied with salt.

Raising Yearling Heifers

The age from one year to just before calving is probably the easiest time to care for and feed dairy cattle. The digestive tract of the year old heifer has assumed mature proportions and she can handle any feed in the same proportion that the mature animal can. The care of heifers naturally divides itself into two sets of problems: first, those concerned with winter feeding; and second, those concerned with summer feeding.

Winter Feeding

The different problems of winter feeding center around the kind of roughage used. For normal growth a yearling heifer needs an equivalent of 1.2 per cent of its body weight in total digestible nutrients and from .1 to .13 per cent in digestible protein. The kind and amount of concentrate supplement to be fed depends upon the kind and quality of roughage supplied.

1. If legume roughages are of excellent quality and early cut, and the heifer consumes two and one-half to three pounds per 100 pounds of live weight, satisfactory growth can be secured on roughage alone. If, however, the roughage is unpalatable, so that an insufficient nutrient intake results, corn is an adequate supplement. Any other grain cheaper than corn may be substituted.
2. When legume hay and low protein hays mixed are fed,

if these hays are palatable and consumed at the rate of two and one-half to three pounds per 100 pounds of live weight, normal growth is secured. This type of roughage, however, is seldom palatable enough for the heifer to consume the requisite amounts. Usually it is necessary to furnish one to two pounds of concentrate daily in order to secure normal growth on this type of roughage. One-third of the concentrate should be of the high protein type.

3. When legume hay and corn silage are fed as roughage in the proportion of one part hay to three parts silage, the situation is identical to that with mixed hay as the only roughage.

4. Corn or sorghum silage as the only source of roughage makes it necessary to furnish both additional energy and protein in the form of concentrate supplement. Silage is too bulky for the normal heifer to consume enough to furnish the necessary energy. Nonlegume silage is also greatly deficient in protein. At least two to three pounds of concentrates must be fed daily; one-half of these should be of the high protein group, such as linseed oil meal, cottonseed meal, soybean meal, or gluten meal.

5. When the roughage consists of the low protein kinds, such as timothy or prairie hay, or any sorghum fodder, high protein concentrates must be added. Satisfactory growth has been secured when silage was consumed at the rate of three pounds per 100 pounds of live weight plus two to two and one-half pounds of either linseed oil meal, cottonseed meal, or gluten meal. Five pounds of bran proved too bulky as a supplement to corn silage.

Whether roughages of the high protein types are adequate without concentrate supplements depends upon the quality and palatability of the hays and the condition of the heifers. Early cut, leafy, and well-cured roughages are usually palatable enough that the heifer takes in adequate nutrients. When good roughage at moderate costs is available and concentrates are high priced, it is probably better to feed roughage alone even at the expense of a slightly reduced rate of growth.

Concentrates alone

Concentrates may be the sole source of nutrients for growing heifers if vitamins A and D and calcium are supplements. Vitamins A and D may be furnished in cod-liver oil, and calcium in the form of calcium carbonate. Unless these supplements are furnished with the grain, serious difficulties are encountered that usually terminate fatally. Feeders of baby beefs encounter these difficulties where grain is offered freely. Frequently when calves have free access to grain they do not eat hay, and hay is the chief source of calcium and vitamins A and D.

Summer feeding

Good pasture furnishes adequate nutrients for the growth of yearling heifers. Unless there is a shortage of pasture, it does not pay to feed concentrates to heifers on pasture. When heifers in ordinary condition are let on pasture they continue to gain at normal or above normal rates. When heifers in poor condition are let on pasture they will gain at faster than normal rates. Heifers that are somewhat below normal, when let out on pasture, frequently have caught up to normal by the end of the pasture season. Those that are much below normal, however, will not make sufficient gains on pasture to make up for the deficiency. Animals that are extremely fat when put on pasture do not as a rule make normal gains.

Housing for yearling heifers

The type of housing that will furnish adequate protection for yearling heifers differs with the severity of the climate. It is not necessary to furnish as warm quarters for heifers as for the milking cows. Many believe that all the protection necessary for heifers is a roof with sided that will "break" the wind, even in severe Northern winters. But if the heifers are subjected to severe cold, much more feed is needed to supply the energy for additional production of heat, and this additional energy must come from added concentrates; therefore this type of protection becomes economically unsound under most conditions.

In the colder climates, if the cow barn has enough room, a large pen in a corner of the barn in which the heifers may run loose is very satisfactory. From 35 to 45 square feet should be allowed per head. Many find it advantageous not to clean out the pen for weeks at a time but to keep the pen dry by the daily addition of bedding. If the cow barn does not permit the building of this pen, a cheaply constructed shed built with matched boards is adequate. Here, too, the heifers may run loose and the litter may accumulate to form a warm bed. Under this plan there is no need for concrete or other types of floors. The dirt serves as a good drain for excess liquid. The only inside equipment needed is a hayrack with a, manger and a watering trough.

For warmer climates, a satisfactory shelter is a partially open shed. This should be closed on all but part of the south side. When stalls and stanchions are available in the regular barn, the heifers may be quartered there. Some difficulty, however, will be experienced in keeping them clean.

Age at which to breed heifers

The age at which heifers should be bred depends to a certain extent upon the stage of development, which varies with the breed and individual animal. It has been pointed out previously that growth is retarded by lactation, if not entirely checked. The following may be taken as the age to breed normally developed animals of the different breeds:

Brown Swiss	21 months
Holsteins	18 months
Ayrshires	17 months
Guernseys	16 months
Jerseys	15 months

Heifers that are larger than normal for the age may be bred earlier. Those that are smaller should be bred correspondingly later.

Gestation period

The average gestation period for the cow is 280 days, with

a variation from 265 to 295 days. Wing reports an almost equal number of births for each day from the 274th to the 287th day. Although some claim a slightly longer gestation for male calves than for females, wing found no difference.

Cost of raising heifers

The cost of raising dairy heifers varies greatly, depending upon the price of feeds and the methods of raising. Feed makes up more than one-half of the cost. Some other items are the expenses of labour, housing, bedding and veterinary service. To this must also be added the initial value of the calf.

While the amount of feed required to raise a calf to two years of age varies with the size of the animal and the method of raising, these variations are not as great as the variations in cost. The Table 19.1 gives the average amounts of feed and labour used in the raising of 889 heifers to two years of age.

Table 19.1: The average amount of feed, pasture, and labour required to raise 889 dairy heifers to 2 years of age

Whole milk	826 pounds
Skim milk	1,323 pounds
Concentrates	643 pounds
Hay	2,125 pounds
Silage	1,848 pounds
Fodder	217 pounds
Straw	16 pounds
Pasture	332 days
Labour	65 hours

Table 19.2 compares the relative amounts of feed and labour used by Holsteins and Jerseys. These figures are not to be taken as absolute values but as guides in considering the cost of raising dairy heifers. By using the prevailing prices for the various feeds the feed cost can easily be calculated. For most sections it is found that when all the costs are considered, grade dairy heifers sell for less than the cost of raising.

Table 19.2: Comparative amounts of feed, pasture, and labour used in raising Holstein and Jersey heifers to 2 years of age

	Jersey		Holstein	
	Purebred	Grade	Purebred	Grade
Whole milk (lbs.)	932	794	1,976	596
Skim milk (lbs.)	1,384	1,382	634	871
Grain (lbs.)	900	527	736	585
Hay (lbs.)	2,055	2,120	1,866	1,767
Silage (lbs.)	1,621	2,004	3,142	2,153
Fodder (lbs.)	44	86		178
Pasture (days)	310	335	325	348
Labour (hours)	73	69	55	51

Feed Before Calving

Eckles and others have shown conclusively that the level of milk production following calving is dependent upon the condition of the cow at calving time. Beginning about three months before calving time, the heifer should have additional concentrates in order to put on more flesh. The main objective is to put on fat; in order to do this, a mixture of one part corn, one part barley, and two parts oats forms a very satisfactory grain mixture. This should be allowed at the rate of five or six pounds daily if the animal was in medium condition to being with. The amounts to be fed should be governed more by the condition of the animal than by any arbitrary rules.

20

Factors Influencing the Quantity and Quality of Milk

It is well known that milk from different cows and breeds may vary widely in chemical composition and in amounts produced. That milk from the same cow is subject to variation in chemical composition and amounts produced is not so generally recognized. Some of the variations from day to day are called "normal variations," and no causative factors have been ascribed to them. Other variations in both quantity and quality are due to large numbers of factors. It is the object of this discussion to consider the factors that affect the quantity and quality of milk. among the factors that affect amounts of milk and the composition of milk may be listed:

1. Heredity
2. Stage and period of lactation
3. Time and frequency of milking
4. Condition of the cow
5. Climate
6. Environment
7. Feed
8. Disease

Normal Variations

That there are daily variations in both quantity and quality of milk that cannot be attributed to a definite cause, is well known. It is not uncommon for fat percentage to vary from day to day as much as 30 per cent, and for milk production to vary as much as 20 per cent. Usually a low fat percentage accompanies a low milk production when daily variations are considered. This is accounted for by the probability that a low milk production is due to a failure of the letting-down of all the milk, the latter part of which is high in fat content. Thus, the high fat milk will be retained and let-down on the following day to give a relatively large amount of milk with a high fat content.

The other constituents of milk also may vary from day to day, although the magnitude of their variations is not so great as that of the milk fat and amount of milk. In the order of the degree of variation, proteins are first, lactose is next, and the salts are the least variable.

HEREDITY

Hereditary Factors

The variations of both quantity and quality of milk produced by the representatives of the different breeds are given in the table on the next page.

It will be observed that there is an inverse ratio between the quantity of milk and the fat percentage. The variations within the breeds are considerable. While the Jerseys average 5.36 per cent of fat, there are individual Jerseys producing milk with less than 4 per cent of fat, and also those that exceed 7 per cent. Variations for the other breeds are proportionately great. The amounts of milk vary to a much greater extent than does the fat percentage and, therefore, it is more important to know the milk production of a cow than the fat percentage of her milk in order to evaluate her.

Persistency, which is an inherited character, affects materially the total milk produced for the lactation period. Cows with the same initial production may vary as much as 50 per cent in the production for the year because of a difference in persistency.

Table 20.1: Composition of milk by breeds

Breed	Total Solids Per Cent	Fat Per Cent	Protein Per Cent
Jersey	14.80	5.36	3.80
Guernsey	14.50	4.98	3.75
Brown Swiss	13.00	4.00	3.50
Ayrshire	13.00	4.00	3.50
Holstein	12.30	3.42	3.30

Breeds and individual cows differ widely in the capacity for secretion of the yellow pigment, carotene, into the milk. The Guernseys are noted for their ability to produce yellow coloured milk and butter from feeds rich in carotene. The Jerseys rank second and the Holsteins last in this regard.

The fat particles in milk vary from 1 to 10 microns in diameter. The fat particles in Guernsey milk are the largest, while the Holstein and Ayrshires have the smallest fat particles. The size of the fat particle in general varies with the fat percentage of the milk, the higher fat milk having the larger fat particles. A quart of milk has from five to ten trillion fat particles.

STAGE OF LACTATION

Stage of lactation

The stage of lactation affects both the yield and the composition of milk and milk fat. A normal lactation curve, together with the fat percentage curve, is given in Fig. 20.1 It will be noted that after the first 50 days of lactation, there is a decline in daily milk production until the end of the lactation period. The curve for fat percentage is somewhat inverse to the curve for daily milk yields, as about the time that daily milk yields begin to fall, the fat percentage begins to rise. The tendency is, therefore, for the daily fat production to be more constant than either the fat percentage or the daily milk yields. With the advance of lactation, there is also a decrease in the size of the fat particles in the milk. The daily total number of fat particles produced has a tendency, therefore, to be even more constant than the daily fat production.

Persistency curves for three generation groups

A. Daughters from Group C sired by Majesty's gamboges Origa

B. Daughters from Group A sired by Pogis 99th of Hood farm 31st

C. Dams of Group A

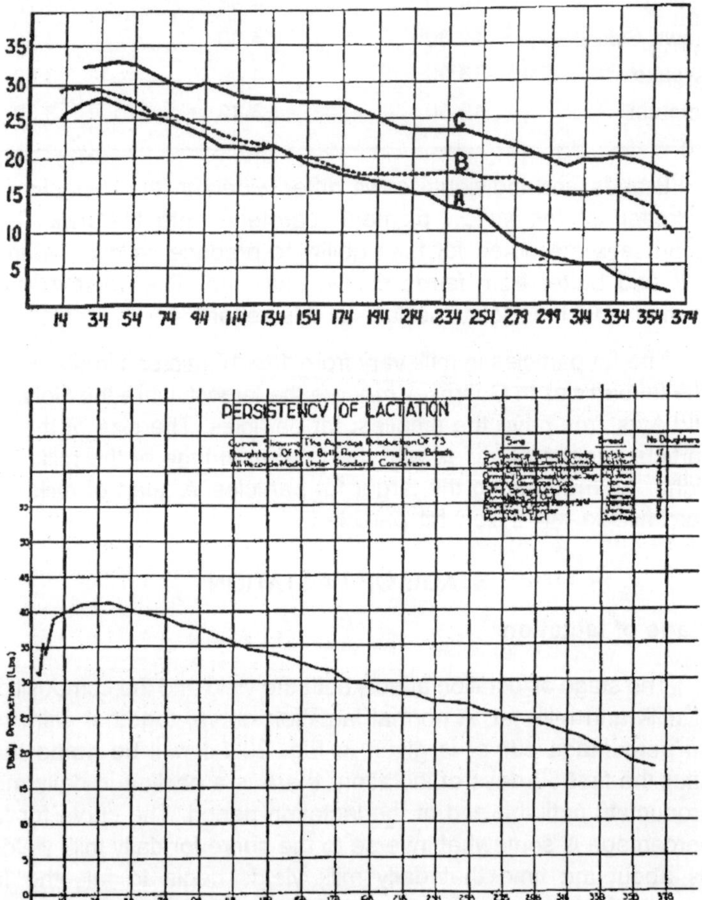

Fig. 20.1: Persistency curves. (Upper) The persistency curves for three generation groups of Jerseys, showing marked variations between the different groups. (Lower) Composite lactation curve of 73 cows from 3 different breeds owned by the University of Minnesota.

Researchers observed that the fat particles of milk in the twelfth month of lactation were about one-half the size of the particles during the first month of lactation.

The other constituents of milk also change in amounts as lactation advances. Colostrums milk, which is discussed under a separate heading, changes to normal milk in about ten days and then remains of relatively constant composition to about the 90th day of lactation. From this point the milk proteins increase in percentage amounts until the end of the lactation period. The increase in the percentage of protein with the advance of lactation is greater than the percentage increase of fat. Eckles and Shaw reported an increase of 30 per cent for protein of the advanced lactation milk over the average, while fat showed only a 20 per cent increase. Milk sugar remains practically constant for the entire lactation period, except in the colostrum milk, as also do the mineral constituents.

The chemical composition of the fat also changes with the advance of lactation. There is a decrease in the Reichert-Meissl number which indicates the lower fatty acids. Saponification values also fall for the same reason. The iodine values increase as the lactation advances.

Bitter Milk

Frequently during advanced lactation, the milk becomes bitter after standing for a short time. This is due to the action of an enzyme (lipase) which is secreted with the milk and splits the fat into free fatty acids and glycerin. The free fatty acids, which taste rancid, unite which the cations of the milk to form soap. The soap contributes to the "bitter" taste, and in the case of cream it makes for difficulty in churning - in some cases completely prevents the formation of butter.

Effect of Parturition upon the Composition and Properties of Cows' Milk

If the cow has been given a rest period before calving, the milk following calving differs markedly in its chemical and physical properties from normal milk. If the cow is milked up to parturition, the milk following parturition differs less from normal milk. However, if the cow is milked up to parturition, there is an increase in the heat coagulable proteins, which were found to reach their maximum in the first milking following parturition. Researchers studied the chemical composition of milks before and after parturition, when cows were milked up to parturition. They found that with the exception of the heat coagulable proteins the milk under these conditions was normal for all constituents. If the cow is given a rest period before calving, then normal colostrum milk is produced following parturition. The chemical composition of colostrum milk is compared with that of normal milk in Table 20.2. It will be seen that the colostrum, milk differs from normal milk primarily in its protein and lactose content. The lactose content of colostrum milk is lower than that of normal milk, and the protein is mainly globulin with a relatively small amount of casein, as contrasted to the reverse proportion for normal milk. In addition to these, colostrum milk contains so-called colostrum corpuscles, which are cell-like particles believed to be partial degenerative products of white blood cells (leucocytes).

Table 20.2: Comparison of colostrums and normal milk

Constituents	Colostrum Per cent	Normal milk Per cent
Total solids	28.30	12.86
Ash	1.58	0.72
Fat.	.15 to 12.0	4.0
Lactose	2.50	4.8
Casein	4.76	2.8
Albumin	1.50	0.54
Globulin	15.06	
Total protein	21.32	3.8

Colostrum milk also has been shown to contain a concentration of vitamin A, which may reach a figure as high as 20 times that of normal milk. This, together with the antibodies which colostrum milk contains, is held to be responsible for the beneficial effects observed in feeding colostrum milk to new born calves. When cows are milked up to parturition, colostrum does not contain the concentration of either the vitamin or the antibodies.

MILKINGS

Number of Milkings Per Day

A number of experiments have been conducted to ascertain the effect of milking more than twice daily upon a total milk production. All workers have reported increased production for the three-times-a-day milking over the twice-a-day milking; likewise, milking four times a day has been responsible for further increases in milk production. The magnitude of the increase in milk production by increased frequency of milking varies with the different reports. It is apparently dependent upon the individuality of the cows, some cows showing much greater increases than others with increased frequency of milking. As little as one per cent increase for three times milking over two times milking and as high as 25 per cent increase have been reported. For four times milking as high as 33 per cent increase over three times milking has been reported. Most of the trials comparing different frequencies of daily milking have been for but short periods of time.

Researcher carried two groups of cows through entire lactation periods. After milking one group twice daily and the other group three times daily, he found much greater increases for the three-times-a-day milking over the entire period than would be expected from the observed increases of short period trials. The results of Researcher's work are illustrated in Fig. 20.2, where it will be seen that cows milked three times daily are much more persistent than those milked twice a day.

Researcher also reported a trial where a cow was milked but once a day and her production compared with that when she was milked two times daily. He found that when milked but once a day, the cow produced but 5,292 pounds of milk and 207 pounds of fat, as contrasted to 12,078 pounds of milk and 434 pounds of fat when milked twice daily. The significant observation of Researcher's work is that persistency is greatly reduced with the reduced frequency of milking, and that milking a cow but once a day has a tendency to dry her off.

Whether milking more than twice daily will be economically sound depends upon the increased amount of milk that can be obtained from more frequent milking and the value of the milk, as

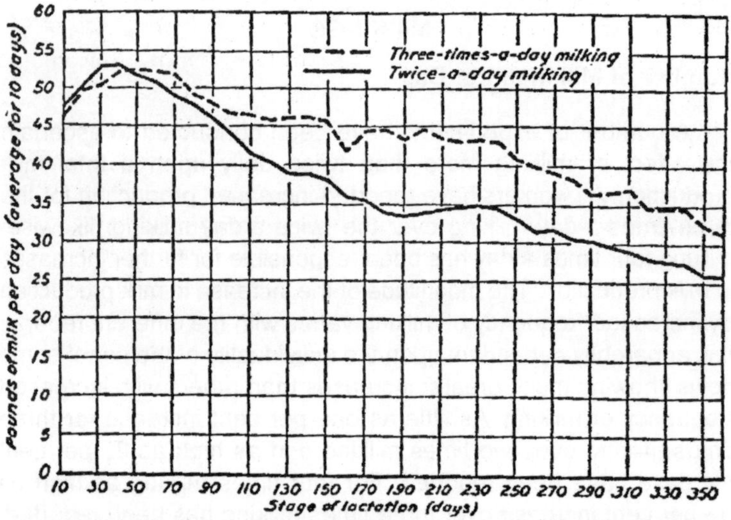

Fig. 20.2: Effect of the frequency of milking upon persistency. The cows milked three times a day are more persistent than those milked twice a day.

the cost of milking three times daily is 50 per cent higher than the cost of milking but twice daily. It is doubtful whether milking more than twice daily will pay when the product is sold for butter or cheese making.

The Interval Between Milkings

The length of the interval between milkings affects both the quantity and the quality of the milk. According to MacIntosh, when the interval between night and morning milking is 14 hours, the morning's milk will be amount 40 to 50 per cent higher in quantity than the evening's milk; the fat percentage of the morning's milk will be about 1 per cent of fat lower than the evening's milk. If the intervals between morning and evening milkings are equal or 12 hours apart, there is a tendency for the morning milk to be lower in fat content and slightly higher in total quantity of milk. That the evening's milk is higher in fat is usually explained by the fact that the cow has exercised more during the daytime than at night and that the exercise is responsible for letting-down more fat.

Effect of First and Last Drawn Milk

With the progress of a milking, each successive portion of milk has an increased fat content. The variation in fat content of successively drawn milk depends upon the activity of the cow and the manipulation of the udder prior to milking. In Jerseys, if the cow has been standing for two or more hours before milking, the first drawn milk may contain as little as 1 per cent fat and the last drawn milk may contain as much as 12 per cent fat. If the cow is walked or the udder massaged immediately before milking, the spread between the fat content of the first and last drawn milk is greatly reduced. Following the manipulation of the udder, Turner found that the first drawn milk contained 6.3 percent fat and the last drawn 8.2 per cent fat. Incomplete milking results in a lower fat content of the milk due to the leaving of the highest fat milk in the udder. Discarding the foremilk is sometimes practised to increase the fat content of milk from "low testing" cows.

The other constituents of milk on a fat-free basis do not vary with the progress of milking.

Variation of Different Quarters

Both the amounts and quality of the milk drawn from each quarter vary. On the average the forequarters produce 40 per cent and the rear quarters 60 per cent of the milk. The forequarters may in some cases produce more than the rear quarters. The right and left quarters also vary. Very seldom do two quarters produce the same amount of milk, the variations being up to more than 100 per cent. The fat percentage of the milk from the different quarters varies less, and also independent of the variations in milk yields. The average deviation of one quarter from the other three quarters would be about ±.2 per cent. The relative proportion for the quarters may change from one lactation to another.

The order in which the quarters are milked affects both the amount of milk and its fat content. Both the amount of milk and the fat percentage decrease with the order in which the teats are milked. No appreciable differences have been observed for the other milk constituents when the order of milking the different quarters is varied.

CONDITION OF THE COW

Influence of the Condition of the Cow at Calving Time

Researcher studying the effects of various conditions of the cow at calving upon the yield following calving, observed that the condition of the cow at calving time had a marked influence upon subsequent milk yields and upon the fat content of the milk. A cow is good condition when calving would start with as much as 25 per cent higher daily milk yields than the one in poorer condition, and the relative spread would be maintained for the entire lactation period. It is well known among people caring for official test cows, that cows in very fat condition at calving time produce milk of much higher fat content for a considerable time after calving. This phenomenon was taken advantage of in the production of seven-day official test records, when it was possible to increase the fat percentage of the milk as much as 30 per cent.

Length of Dry Period

The length of the dry period cannot be entirely dissociated from the condition of calving time, as, in the main, a better condition is obtained with the increased length of the dry period. There are, however, effects upon the production of the subsequent lactation period that are attributable to the rest period. During the dry period the mammary gland is prepared for the next lactation, and only a rest period will permit full development.

A rest period preceding the second calving has a greater effect upon the next lactation than do the rest periods of subsequent lactations. This is accounted for by the fact that during the first lactation period there has been little chance for growth. When lactation is stopped, the heifer grows rapidly and becomes capable of higher production for the next lactation period.

The udder of the first-calf heifer also needs the rest period for further development, which is reflected in higher production for the next lactation period. The average increases in production for second calvers and older cows for dry periods of varying length are presented in Table 20.3.

Table 20.3: Increased production due to dry periods of various lengths

Days dry period	2nd calf heifers Per cent	Older cows Per cent
5	5.0	2.6
15	14.1	7.6
25	21.8	11.8
35	28.0	14.5
45	33.2	18.5
55	37.6	21.1
65	41.3	23.3
75	44.3	25.2
85	46.8	26.7
95	48.9	28.1
105	50.6	29.3
115	52.2	30.2

Effect of Gestation

It is well known that the latter months of gestation have an inhibitory effect upon the production of milk. This inhibitory effect begins about the fifth month of gestation and continues with an increasing rate of inhibition until parturition. The inhibitory effect of advancing gestation varies with individual cows; some decline in milk yields more rapidly than others. Cows with low persistency would naturally be less affected by the inhibitory force.

Researcher reported a 19 per cent decrease in a year's milk production for a group of cows bred to calve within 12 months as compared to the same group when bred to calves more than 15 months' interval.

Two reasons are given for the decline of milk yields with the advance of pregnancy. One is that the added nutrient requirements for the growing fetus compete with the nutrients to be used for milk production. The other is that with the advance of pregnancy there is secreted a hormone which inhibits milk production. The latter is the more probable cause for the major part of the decrease, but the nutrient requirement for the growing fetus is also a factor. Since the dry matter content of the fetus is small, relatively small amounts of nutrients are required for its building; but there remains the question of maintaining the fetus. The amount of nutrients required for maintenance of the fetus is not known but would probably approximate, proportionately to size, the requirements for the growing animal.

Table 20.4: The effect of the length of the service period upon the production for the lactation period, breeding 85 days after calving being the standard to which the increases or decreases are compared

Days Following Calving When Bred	Increase in Milk Production for the Lactation Period for First-Calf Heifers Per cent	Older Cows Per cent	Increase in Length of the Lactation Period Per cent
30	-18.4	-21.3	-15.1
50	-10.6	-11.9	-9.6
70	-4.2	-4.6	-4.1
85	0	0	0
90	1.1	1.1	1.4
110	5.8	6.3	6.8
130	10.1	10.7	12.3
150	11.4	14.8	17.8
170	17.9	18.3	23.3
190	21.4	21.7	28.8
210	24.5	24.5	34.2
230	27.4	27.2	39.7
250	30.0	29.5	45.2
270	32.4	31.8	50.6
290	34.8	33.5	56.2
310	37.0	35.3	61.7
330	38.9	36.8	67.1
350	40.6	38.1	72.6
370	42.5	39.5	78.1
390	43.9	40.8	83.6

Table 20.4 presents the effect of the interval between calving and breeding upon the milk and butterfat production for the lactation period. These figures are based upon the increase or decrease in production from a service period of 85 days following calving that can be expected for service periods of varying lengths of time. A service period of 85 days would make the second calving in 365 days. The variations in the length of the lactation period due to different lengths of the service period is also presented. It will be noted that a small difference in the effect of length of service periods is found for first-calf heifers and other cows. For service periods of less than 85 days there is a larger per cent decrease in production than the decrease in the length of the lactation period. For service periods longer than 85 days the per cent increase in the length of the lactation period is greater than the increase in production due to the delayed breeding.

Effect of Estrus

No general rule can be laid down as to how the estrus affects milk yields or its quality. In the majority of cases the estrus is accompanied by a decrease in milk yield and an increase in fat percentage. Individual cows, however, may vary in opposite directions or show no variation.copeland found that out of 211 Jersey cows 75 increased and 131 decreased milk production, with an average decrease for all of .63 pounds daily. While daily variations from normal due to estrus occurred up to over ten pounds, 75 per cent varied less than two pounds.

Butterfat percentage averaged .13 more for the days in estrus than for the normal, with 126 showing increases and 81 decreases. The average variation in butterfat percentage was 0.43, with the extreme variation 2.00.

Effect of Age

A large number of studies have been directed toward showing the effect of advancing age upon the amount and quality of the milk produced. In general there is considerable individual variation, but a heifer calving at two years of age can be expected to produce about 70 to 77 per cent of the amount she will produce when mature; with the second calf at three years of age, 80 to

87 per cent; with the third calf at four years of age, 90 to 95 per cent; with the fourth calf at 5 years of age, 98 per cent; and at seven years of age, 100 per cent. The fat percentage varies but slightly with age, due to a tendency to lower slightly after the first lactation period. Commencing with ten years of age, there is a tendency for both milk yields and fat percentage of the milk to decline. In extreme old age milk yields may be as low as 50 per cent of the maximum mature capacity.

Table 20.5 presents the age correction factors used by different breed associations for converting immature records to a mature basis. The figures of the Holstein and Jersey breeds are arrived at from studies of the Advanced Registry records, while the figures for the other breeds are more or less arbitrarily arrived at.

Table 20.5: Age correction factors used by various breed associations in computing immature records to the mature equivalent

Age at calving		Holstein	Jersey	Guernsey	Ayrshire
Years	Months				
Under 2 yrs.		1.50	1.45		
2	0	1.43	1.36	1.249	1.33
2	6	1.33	1.28	1.194	
3	0	1.25	1.20	1.162	1.22
3	6	1.19	1.14	1.100	
4	0	1.14	1.08	1.068	1.12
4	6	1.10	1.04	1.029	
5	0	1.06	1.02	1.00	1.00
5	6	1.04			
6	0	1.03	1.00		
6	6	1.02	1.00		
7	0	1.01	1.00		
7-6 to	9.6	1.00	1.00		
10		1.01	1.02		
11		1.03	1.02		
12 and over		1.05	1.05		

Relation of Size and Production

A number of students have shown that a direct relationship exists between the milk and fat yields and the size of the cow. Researcher reports an increase of 20 pounds of butterfat annually for each 100 pounds increase in body weight. A study of 220,000 records by the Bureau of Dairying reveals a correlation of size with increased milk and fat yields, and also a larger income above feed cost. Researcher recently showed that on the average the larger cows, while producing more than the smaller ones, are less efficient. It is apparent that size is not the most important consideration for economical production.

EFFECT OF SEASONS

Seasonal Variations

For a long time it has been recognized that there is a seasonal effect upon both the quantity and quality of cows' milk. Fat percentage is the lowest beginning with August; from this time there is an increase until January, when again there is a gradual decline until August. The amount of milk declines from the high point in January to the low of July and August. The seasonal variation in both milk and fat percentage is inversely proportional to the temperature. Several studies have shown that temperature variations may effect a greater variation in the fat percentage of milk than advancing lactation. For Jerseys and Guernseys the fat per cent of milk may be as much as 1.1 lower in the hot summer than in the winter. For the lower testing breeds the difference is 0.6.

When the temperature becomes too high, the amount of milk is reduced more than the amount of fat, resulting in an increased fat percentage. Cows kept at 85°F. or over in a closed room at the California Station reached what is known as the critical temperature, when the above phenomenon was observed.

High humidity accompanied by high temperatures accentuates the depressing effects. With increasing humidity there is a decrease in the evaporation from the body, and thus the cooling effect of evaporating moisture is lost. That a much higher temperature in the open than 85°F. does not effect an increase in fat percentage is due to the cooling effect evaporation of moisture has upon the body.

Season of Calving

As there is a seasonal effect upon both the quantity and quality of milk produced, the total milk and fat production for a lactation period is affected by the season in which a cow calves.

Researcher divided the records of 10,870 cows into four groups corresponding to the seasons in which they freshened and found the following average productions:

Season	Milk production Pounds	Butterfat production Pounds
Spring	5,842	236
Summer	5,941	236
Fall	6,689	268
Winter	6,439	258

Cows calving in the fall produced the most milk and butterfat, those calving in the winter ranked second. Owing to the lower fat percentage of milk during the summer, although the cows calving during the summer months produced slightly more milk than those calving during the spring, there was no increase in butterfat.

There are two reasons for the higher production of milk and butterfat of fall and winter calving: First, the seasonal effect on fat percentage is such that the height of the milk production due to fall and winter calving will have the higher tests. Second, cows freshening in the fall and winter will still have sufficient capacity for milk production to respond by increased production when put on the spring pastures, while cows calving in the spring and summer are so advanced in lactation that they have lost most of the capacity for increased production and cannot respond to the stimulus of fresh pasture.

FEED

The Effect of Inanition

Inanition or underfeeding has been shown to have a marked effect upon both the quantity and the quality of milk produced.

The most marked effect of inanition is the decline in the amount of milk produced. This decline continues as the period of inanition progresses. Accompanying the decline of milk yields are increases in the percentages of fat, protein, ash, and total solids. The percentage of lactose and the specific gravity decrease. When the lactometer reading is the only test performed, the decrease in specific gravity leads to the suspicion that the milk has been watered.

Effects of Feed

Both the quantity and quality of milk may be affected by the feed a cow receives. Until recently it has not been generally agreed upon that feed affects the quality of milk to any great extent; recent work, however, tends to show that there may be marked effects of some feeds upon the composition of milk. In addition to affecting the quantity of milk, the feed may affect the fat percentage and the character of the fat, and it may add compounds to the milk or fat which may affect both its nutrient value and its flavour.

Effects of Feed upon Milk Fat

It is still controversial as to whether it is possible to increase the fat percentage of milk by feeding. Several short-time experiments have shown that the addition to the ration of fats such as linseed oil, cottonseed oil, tallow, butterfat, lard, soybean oil, coconut oil, and others causes a marked increase in the fat percentage of the milk. Others, comparing high fat content feeds with low fat feeds for the entire lactation period, were not able to observe any differences in the fat percentage of the milk that could be ascribed to the fat intake.

Feeding cod-liver oil to milking cows has been shown by a number of investigators to cause a marked lowering of the fat percentage of the milk without affecting the amounts of the milk yield. This is said to be due to the specific effect some of the fatty acids of the oil have upon the epithelial cells of the mammary gland. Other fish oils are reported to have the same effect as cod-liver oil.

A minimum amount of fat in the ration seems necessary for milk production. A diet devoid of fat but adequate in all other respects resulted in much lowered milk and fat yields. The exact minimum level of fat in the ration that is necessary for normal milk production has not been established.

Effect upon the Quality of Fat

Numerous experiments have been conducted to ascertain the effect of various feeds upon the quality of the milk fat. It has been demonstrated that the composition of milk fat can be markedly changed by a number of different types of feed. In the main, the fatty portion of the feed is responsible for the effect upon the composition of the milk fat. Cottonseed oil produces a very hard fat, while linseed oil produces a soft fat. Linseed oil, having a high linoleic and linolinic acid content, produces butter with relatively high amounts of these two fatty acids, which are mainly responsible for the softened condition of the butter produced when flax, oil meal, and the oil is fed. Due to an increase of the lower fatty acids, such as butyric, caproic, and caprylic acids, pasture grass produces soft butter. The hays and legumes, being as a rule low in their contents of fats, have a tendency to produce hard butterfat. Corn has a tendency to produce fat of a moderate hardness, while barley and other cereals are more neutral in their effects upon the milk fat.

Effect of Feed upon other Milk Constituents

No evidence has been presented that has shown feed to have any effect upon the lactose or protein content of milk. There is, however, some evidence to show that the amount of certain other constituents of milk is dependent upon the extent that these are present in the feed; among these are vitamins A, D, and E, certain flavouring compounds, mineral elements and, drugs, and other organic compounds.

Vitamins

Vitamins C_1 (ascorbic acid) and at least B and flavin of the Vitamin B complex may be synthesized in the bovine; and as a result these vitamins are always present in milk and vary but little due to variations in the feed. Vitamins A, and D, however, are not synthesized by the bovine, and the amounts present in the milk are dependent upon the amounts present in the feed, and, in the case of vitamin D, also upon exposure to sunlight.

Carotene, the chief plant precursor of vitamin A, is a yellow pigment which can be split in the animal body to form vitamin A, which is colourless. Cows may secrete the carotene into the milk, producing a yellow fat, or they may split the carotene and secrete the colourless vitamin A into the milk. Although there is no known difference between individual cows in utilizing the vitamin A of the feed for total vitamin A potency of the milk, there are marked individual and breed differences in the amounts of carotene converted into the colourless vitamin A. The Guernsey is noted for the secretion of the carotene into the milk; the Holstein converts most of the carotene into the colourless vitamin A; and the Jersey is intermediate. Sometimes feeds are so deficient in vitamin A or vitamin A precursors that the milk produced is deficient in vitamin A to the extent that calves cannot be raised upon it. Matured timothy hay has been shown to produce milk upon which calves could not be reared because of its deficiency in vitamin A.

Vitamin D is present in milk proportionately to the amounts fed in the feed, except when the cows are exposed to direct sunlight during the spring, summer, and early fall, when vitamin D may be formed in the animal body from the ultraviolet rays of the sun. Commercially, the production of vitamin D milk during the winter is affected by the feeding of irradiated yeast.

Minerals

The amounts of the most prominent minerals in milk, the salts of phosphorus, calcium, magnesium, sodium, potassium and chlorine, cannot be changed by the amounts in the feed. Copper, silver, and zinc, which are always present in milk in very minute quantities, are likewise unaffected by the quantity in the feed. Iodine and iron are the only two natural mineral constituents of milk the amounts of which are influenced by the quantity in the feed. Of these iodine may be influenced to the greater extent and iron but slightly. The ingestion of iodine in any form will increase the iodine content of milk. In the low iodine regions some dairymen feed iodine in various forms in order to increase the iodine content of the milk produced. From 3 to 20 per cent of the iodine ingested may be recovered in the milk - more of a recovery taking place during the winter than during the summer. To increase the iron content of milk, large quantities of inorganic iron must be fed; and then the increased amount in the milk is small.

Arsenic, mercury, lead, bromine, and boric acid, not normally present in milk, when fed, will pass into the milk. When heavy does are administered, sufficient quantities of these elements may pass into the milk to make the milk toxic to humans.

Drugs Passing into Milk

There are a number of drugs and anesthetics used in the treatment of cows that will pass into the milk. Alcohol may be found in the milk 30 minutes after its administration, and disappears in four to seven hours. As much as 0.4 per cent of alcohol in milk has been reported. Ether and chloroform behave similarly to alcohol, as does turpentine. The active substance of rhubarb passes into milk to produce a yellow colouring of the milk. The active substance of aloes (a bitter plant) passes into the milk in such quantities as to alter both the colour and the taste.

The white snakeroot contains a poisonous compound known as tremotol which passes into the milk. Ordinarily cows do not eat the white snakeroot, but in cases of severe drought and feed shortage, cows have eaten it in sufficient quantities to make the milk toxic to humans, producing what is known as milk sickness. Milk sickness has proved fatal in a few cases.

Flavour-producing Constituents of Feed

Most of the normal flavouring constituents of milk have their origin in the feed. There are, however, many feeds that produce very undesirable milk or milk fat flavours. Among the more common feeds that impart undesirable flavours to milk, if fed shortly before milking, are silage, large amounts of alfalfa hay, turnips, rutabagas, rape, cabbage, green rye, and pasture grasses.

Many weeds consumed when pasture grasses become scarce or because they are admixed with the grasses produce undesirable flavours of varying intensities. The more common of the undesirable flavour-producing weeds are wild onions, French weed, ragweed, mustard, sagebrush, and dandelions.

Of the essences, absinthe, fennel, and artichoke produce strong flavours in milk. The oral administration of cumin, anise, gentian, and juniper has no effect upon the flavour of milk produced.

In the main, the compounds producing off flavours in milk are volatile and may be removed from the milk by feeding the flavour-producing feeds immediately after milking or by removing the cows from the feed for varying lengths of time before milking. These compounds are eliminated from the blood by either the lungs or kidneys, or both. They pass into the milk from the blood, forming an equilibrium between these two fluids. As the quantities of the compound are reduced in the blood through elimination, these compounds pass from the milk back into the blood until finally the milk is entirely freed of them.

Effect of Drugs upon the Amount of Milk Secreted

A number of drugs have been studied for their stimulating effect upon milk secretion. While the results of the different workers do not agree, in the main, very few, if any, compounds are known to have galactogogic effects. Alcohol, ginger, rhubarb, aloes, pituitrin, pilocarpine, calomel, atropine, and a number of other drugs have been shown to have no galactogogic effects. Pituritrin administered subcutaneously or intravenously causes an increase in the amount of milk and milk fat produced at the following milking. This is due to the contractile effect of the pituitrin upon the glands, which results in the forcing out of all the milk and fat in the alveoli, and not to any stimulus for increased secretion of milk. The active principle of ergot causes a marked decrease in the amount of milk produced, probably due to the constricting action of ergot upon the blood capillaries. Pumpkin seeds, hedge oranges, acorns, and oak leaves have been reported by dairymen to cause a drying up of cows. There is, however, no experimental evidence to support this contention.

Thyroprotein

Thyroprotein is a term applied to proteins, usually casein, so treated with iodine that they develop thyroid hormone activity. When fed to milking cows both milk and fat percentage will be increased. A sufficient amount of the thyroprotein must be administered or no effect will be observed. Small amounts will depress the thyroid activity in proportion to the amounts that get into the system. About 15 grams of the standard thyroprotein must be administered daily, usually incorporated in the feed.

The question as to the practicability of feeding thyroprotein is not settled. While milk and fat production is significantly increased, the feed requirements are also greatly increased because of the greatly increased activity in metabolism. Heart and respiration rates are greatly increased and questions are raised as to the effect upon the health of the animals and upon reproduction. Indications are that good milkers past the peak of the lactation respond best to the administration of this drug and that poor producers give the least response.

EFFECT OF DISEASE

Udder diseases (principally mastitis), digestive disturbances, and other diseases are responsible for a decrease in milk yield and affect the quality of the milk in various ways.

Mastitis

The composition of the milk may be changed in various degrees by mastitis infection, depending upon the severity of the infection. The reduction in milk of the affected quarter is likewise dependent upon the severity of the attack. The sugar content decreases from a very slight amount in a light attack to practically nothing in a very severe attack. Sodium chloride increases until it approximates the concentration in the blood. The character of the proteins changes with a decrease in casein and an increase in the heat coagulable proteins. The pH changes from approximately 6.5 to 7.4 in the extreme case, and the cellular materials, principally leucocytes, increase from a few thousand in normal milk to millions per cc. in extreme mastitis milk. The fat content usually declines.

Digestive Disturbances

Any marked digestive disturbance, such as going "off feed" or diarrhea, is followed by a marked decline in milk yield. The fat percentage of the milk usually increases, but in some cases it may decline. The flavour of the milk is also usually affected; putrefactive decomposition compounds are resorbed from the digestive tract by the blood and are diffused into the milk.

Other Diseases

Any disease which is severe enough to produce an increase in the body temperature or to reduce the appetite for feed is accompanied by a decline in milk yield. Usually the fat percentage of the milk increases, but sometimes the reverse may be the case.

Practical Aspects of Feed Effects upon Milk

The deleterious effects of many feeds upon flavour of milk is well known, and dairymen refrain from using such feeds or feed them immediately after milking or allow sufficient time between feeding and milking for the undesirable flavour to have passed off. That there are substances that may be fed to produce desired flavours in milk seems most likely. Determining such substances seems to offer a fruitful field in research. It is also possible that certain food substances may be found that may counteract the undesirable milk flavours produced by some feeds.

21

Management of Dairy Cows

Importance

Everything that pertains to the feeding, care, and breeding of dairy cattle can properly be classified as coming under the term "management." It has previously been pointed out that for a cow to be an economical producer of milk, she must have the right inheritance; however, given a cow with the inheritance for the capacity to produce large amounts of milk, economical production is not necessarily assured. The cow must be properly fed and cared for in order to bring out the potentialities that she has inherited. It is the purpose of this chapter to consider the more important managerial factors that relate to bringing out the inherited potentialities for milk production.

Normal Physical and Physiological Activities

A knowledge of the normal activities of dairy cattle is of value in the management of the herd, and it may aid in arranging work to fit the activities of the cow and help to determine whether a cow is normal. The amount of information available on this subject is limited, the New Hampshire Station furnishing the most extended work on dairy cows. They report that cows in the barn during winter spend about equal amounts of time in standing and in lying down; there is, however, a tendency for cows in advanced pregnancy to spend more time in lying down than in standing. Individual variations ran from as high as 76 per cent to as low as 35 per cent of the time spent in standing. Cows got up and down on an average of 14 times during the 24 hours.

Variations in the number of urinations and defecations per day between dry cows and milking cows were observed. Dry cows average 6.1 urinations to 7.9 for milking cows. For daily defecations, dry cows averaged 13.7 times as compared with 15.7 for cows in milk.

No difference was found between dry cows and those in milk as to the amount of time spent in eating and in ruminating. Cows fed hay, silage, and grain in proportion to milk yields spent approximately three hours in eating and eight hours in ruminating. Since roughage consumption is proportional to the size of the cow and grain consumption is proportional to the amount of milk produced, and since it requires longer to eat a given weight of roughage than of grain and grain is not ruminated the reason for high producing cows requiring no more time for eating and rumination than dry cows do is easily perceived.

The large amount of work done by a cow in eating and masticating feed is indicated by the average daily number of jaw movements:

Eating grain and silage	4,700
Eating hay	10,530
Ruminating	26,400
Total daily jaw movement	41,630

A difference was observed in the number of jaw movements per minute when hay, grain, and silage were eaten. A still different rate was observed for ruminating. The average jaw movements per minute for hay are 78, for grain and silage 94, and for ruminating 55.

Great variations are found in the pulse and respiration rates. Judkins observed the average pulse and respiration rates for different breeds to be as follows:

Breed	Rate per minute		Ratio R to P
	Pulse	Respiration	
Ayrshire	69.6	28.6	1 : 2.4
Guernsey	59.8	18.6	1 : 3.2
Holstein	68.6	28.6	1 : 2.8
Jersey	62.7	21.7	1 : 3.2

The respiration rates varied from 11 to 64 per minute, and the pulse rates from 38 to 96 per minute. Both pulse and respiration rates increased when cows were milking heavily.

The Behaviour of the Cow

Ever since dairying became a specialty people have recognized that some individuals are able to obtain better performance from cows than others. More recent work has shown that cows that are well adjusted to their environment will let down their milk more completely and probably also will eat better than those that are not so adjusted. One of the major jobs of the dairy herd manager is to see that the members of the herd are content and well adjusted. In order to attain this end most effectively one needs to know some of the fundamentals about the pattern of behaviour of the cow. The two basic features are: (1) cows have a well-established herd order and (2) they are quick to make associations of pleasant or unpleasant experiences with places, objects, and persons.

Herd Rule

In every herd there is a well-established social order in which there is one cow that rules over all the rest, followed successively by the other members of the herd with the last cow in the social order being bossed by all the others. The position in the social order is established by physical combat. Once a cow has succeeded to the top position she retains it for life unless an ambitious individual is brought into the herd from the outside. The younger members developing in a herd accept the supremacy of the leader of that herd. Studies by the author reveal that sometimes members in the middle of the social order of larger herds may be unhappy. They manifest their discontentment by irritating members in the lower social order. It is presumed that these unhappy individuals are aggressive and aspire to a higher rank but do not possess the physical strength to gain it and, consequently, suffer from frustration. These individuals, incidentally, are the more difficult to handle from the managerial standpoint.

Associations

The fact that cows readily make associations with pleasant and unpleasant experiences in relation to the human element is very important from the caretakers and particularly the milkers relationship. Often veterinarians are forced to inflict pain in carrying on their work with cattle. One such experience is sufficient for the animal to associate that painful experience with the veterinarian and his subsequent presence will cause nervousness and excitement. Milk production has been noted to fall markedly due to the presence of the herd veterinarian at milking time.

It is of utmost importance that the caretaker of cows so handle them that they like his presence. Only when there are pleasant associations will cows be relaxed and at ease in the presence of particular individuals. Where cattle are well treated by all humans they like their presence and even in the case of strangers show no fears. In the case of unkind treatment cows will make effort to escape or at least will not be approachable by strangers.

Regularity

While there is no definite experimental evidence to establish the value of regularity in milking, feeding, and caring for the dairy cow, there is enough evidence to warrant the statement that regularity is an important factor in getting the most out of the dairy herd. It has previously been shown that lengthening the periods between milking increases the milk production, but that the increase is not in proportion to the length of the interval. The cow is a creature of habit. If the time for milking or feeding is delayed, she is likely to become nervously excited, and this results in reduced milk production. At definite routine in milking, feeding, and caring for cows should be established. If the cow is to be fed before milking, the practice should be followed regularly. It has frequently been observed that if a cow which has been accustomed to being fed before milking is milked before feeding, she fails to completely let down the milk.

Quietness

The chasing of cows by dogs so excites the cows that decreased milk production results. Even the presence of too many people will result in decreased production. For this reason experienced herdsmen in charge of cows on official tests, where a maximum production is sought regardless of cost, sometimes lock the barn in the interim between milkings to prevent anyone from disturbing the cows. Under these conditions the visits of strangers are seldom permitted, because of the probable effect on production.

CARE OF HEALTH AND APPEARANCE

Grooming

Grooming has usually been considered as having a beneficial effect upon the general health of the cow, as effect which would be reflected in increased production. Recently carefully controlled experiments failed to reveal any increased production of milking cows due to vigorous grooming with a stiff brush. The chief advantage of grooming is that dirt is removed from the skin and hair-not that production is increased. Most benefits from grooming will come in the production of cleaner milk.

Exercise

It is usually believed that exercise is essential for the health of dairy cattle. Recently it has been found that exercise is not essential for the health of milking cows. Cows maintained in stanchions or box stalls have been found to have suffered no ill effects from the confinement. The milking cow performs a large amount of work in the mastication and metabolization of the feed that she necessarily must handle; this activity seems to furnish adequate exercise. Young stock and dry cows, on the other hand, seem to be benefited more by moderate exercise. In the colder climates letting the milking cows out into a yard for exercise during the winter probably does more harm than good.

Trimming Hoofs

When cows are confined to barns during the winter months and when they are pastured on soils that are lacking in abrasive material, the hoofs grow faster than they are worn off, resulting in the development of long toes that ultimately produce discomfort to the cow both in standing and in walking. In extreme cases lameness leading to a crippled condition may be experienced. The hoofs should be trimmed by chiseling off the fore part of the toe and rasping off the excessive growth underneath. Extreme care must be exercised in the trimming to avoid injury to the quick. Injury to this tissue may lead to infection and lameness of long duration.

Training Horns

For some breeds when animals are to be shown, it is not only essential that the horns be retained, but also that they conform to the standards for the breed. Frequently the direction of the natural growth of the horn is not that which is most desired. It is then necessary to force the horn to grow in the desired direction. The time when the direction of the growth can most easily be changed is before the horn core is securely fastened to the skull. Therefore, the training of horns should begin about the time they are two inches in length.

The direction of the growth of a horn may be changed by the application of pressure. If the horn tends to grow upward, the direction may be changed downward by fastening weights to the horn tips until the growth is in the desired direction. If the horns have a tendency to grow outward when it is desired that they should curve inward, the desired curvature may be effected by applying tension between the two horns by means of horn trainers fastened to the horn tips. Care should be taken not to put too much tension on the horns, as it will produce not only discomfort to the animal but also too abrupt curvature of the horns. In the case of the Ayrshire it is desirable that the horn turn upward. This may be effected by directing the force upward by means of weights hung on cords that have been attached to the horns and then run over pulleys.

The direction of the growth of the horn may also be changed by scraping it on the side toward which the direction of growth is desired.

Horns are frequently too large and thereby detract from the general refined appearance of the animal. In order to correct this, they may be trimmed by rasping off a portion of the outer covering known as the horn shell. Care should be taken not to take too much off or the outer shell may become so weakened that it will break off from the bony horn core. Frequently animals that have been shorn lose the outer horn shell because of its weakened condition from excessive rasping or scraping. Following the rasping, the horn should be sandpapered with find sandpaper or emery cloth until a smooth surface is secured. Then a horn polish may be applied and the horn polished with a cloth. For show purposes the hoofs may be trimmed and polished in a similar manner.

Dehorning

It is generally agreed that unless it is necessary to retain the horns on dairy cattle for show ring purposes or for the probable enhancement of the value of an animal are horned, injuries are often experienced. In addition, the more timid individuals of the herd are constantly harassed by the more aggressive members. The best method of dehorning is the application of caustic potash when the animal is but two or three days of age. However, horns may be removed from older animals without much danger and with practically no effect upon the milk yields of even heavy producing cows. A number of observations have shown that milking cows drop in milk yield for but a few days following dehorning. Horns may be removed either by the use of clippers or by sawing. Sawing is generally to be preferred, for when clippers are used there is the danger of crushing the bony horn core, which may result in excessive bleeding or infection. In dehorning, care should be taken to cut the horn low enough to leave a fringe of hair and skin on the removed portion of the horn. Unless this is done, the horn is likely to grow out again. The early spring is the best time for dehorning. It should not be done during fly season, because of the danger of infection resulting from flies settling on the injured area. Also, when the cattle have been fed sweet clover either as hay or silage, dehorning should be avoided. Frequently the sweet clover hay or silage develops a substance which prevents clotting of the blood, and if the animals are then dehorned, they may bleed to death.

TREATMENT OF COMMON VICES

Cows may develop several vices that are annoying. The more common ones are kicking during milking, sucking either themselves or other cows, fence breaking, and becoming vicious. Most of these vices can be avoided if the tendency is discovered in time and proper treatment applied. After any one of these has become a habit, it becomes exceedingly hard, if not impossible, to break.

Kicking

The habit of kicking during milking is most frequently developed as the result of wrong treatment when the heifer is first milked. At first the cow kicks either because of pair or fear. If she is maltreated at this time, kicking becomes an act of resentment and rapidly develops into a habit that cannot be broken. Frequently cows kick only when milked by certain milkers. When kicking during milking has been established as a firm habit, there is nothing that can be done to break it. The treatment then lies in tying the hind legs in order to protect the milker. The most effective and convenient method is the use of antikicking chains. These consist of two hooklike pieces of iron connected with a chain. A hook is placed above each hock with the chain passing in front of the legs. When the chains are not available, the hind legs may be tied together either with straps or with rope.

Sucking

The habit of sucking is also practically impossible to break. Cows have been tied up in stanchions for more than a year without any chance of sucking either themselves or other cows without being broken of the habit. The treatment lies in methods of prevention. The sucking cow may be prevented from sucking by the use of anyone of three contrivances:

(1) a contrivance such as a chain or two bull rings placed in the nose in such a way that it hangs over the muzzle, preventing her from getting hold of the teat;

(2) a bridle equipped with a quarter-inch gas pipe drilled full of holes used as a bit, which does not permit sucking;

(3) a halter with a muzzle strap containing sharp points that are two or more inches in length.

The self-sucking cow may be prevented from sucking by making it impossible for her to turn her head back to the rear flank. This may be accomplished by fixing a surcingle around her chest, fastening one end of a short stick to the surcingle, and then passing the stick between the front legs and fastening the other end of it to a close fitting halter. Although not proved, some believe that feeding skim milk to cows in conducive to forming the sucking habit.

Fence breaking

The habit of fence breaking or fence crawling is usually developed when cows are kept within poor fences. When once developed, this habit can be broken only by the use of good fencing. A cow may be prevented from crawling through fences by a yoke placed around the neck. Fence breakers frequently teach other cows in the herd the same habit. For this reason it is advisable to dispose of them unless they are valuable producers.

Viciousness

Not infrequently cows become vicious to the extent that they will attack children and sometimes adults. In the early stages of the development of this habit it may sometimes be broken by a few sharp blows over the nose. This is more effective if done by the person attacked at the time of the attack.

CARE IN BREEDING AND CALVING

Gestation period and estrus cycle

The average gestation period for the cow is 281 days, with about equal chances of calving on any day from the 275th to 287th day. There is a question as to how many days short of the 281 that a calving can be considered normal, and when it should be considered an abortion. Gestation periods as long as 300 days have been reported.

The normal estrus cycle in the cow is 21 days. Variations of five days from the average is not uncommon. The first oestrus cycle usually occurs one week following calving. Disease and malnutrition may be the causes of complete suppression of the oestrum. In extreme nutritional deficiency such as a lack of phosphorus or a vitamin deficiency, oestrum does not occur until the deficiency is corrected and the body stores recuperated.

When to Breed Cows

According to the data, breeding a cow so as to conceive on the 75th to the 110th day following calving results in the greatest average daily milk production for the lactation period. Breeding on the 85th day results in calvings 12 months apart. Breeding earlier than the 75th day results in a greater reduction of milk yield than in the time between calvings. Breeding for conception on the 30th day following calving causes a reduction in the milk yield of 18.4 per cent for heifers and 21.3 per cent for older cows, while the time is shortened by only 15.1 per cent. When more than 110 days intervene between calving and conception, the per cent increase in the length of time between calvings becomes greater than the increased milk yield, resulting in lower average daily yields (Table 21.1).

By breeding cows on the first heat period following the 75th day after calving it is possible to secure pregnancies for all but a small per cent of a normal breeding herd by the 110th day following calving.

Breeding Efficiency

The number of services required per pregnancy is partly dependent upon the amount of sterility present in the herd, and for any one herd it would vary considerably from year to year. The data presented in the previous table, secured from the University of Minnesota herd over a period of 29 years, is probably representative of what may be expected in a herd over a period of years. It will be noted that there is one chance out of 2.3 that conception will occur to the first service. With each additional service, the chance of conception becomes less.

Table 21.1: Relation of the number of service periods to conception

No. of service	No. of cows	No. of conceptions	%age of conceptions	Chance of conceptions
First	1,280	547	42.7	1 : 2.3
Second	729	258	35.3	1 : 2.8
Third	466	146	31.3	1 : 3.2
Fourth	306	79	25.8	1 : 3.9
Fifth	210	55	26.1	1 : 3.8
Sixth	142	29	20.4	1 : 4.9
Seventh	104	17	15.8	1 : 6.1
Eighth	78	9	12.0	1 : 8.7
Ninth	63	6	9.5	1 : 10.5
Tenth	52	4	8.0	1 : 13.0
Eleventh to twentieth	168	4	2.3	1 : 42.0
Twentieth to fortieth	100	0	0	0

Sterility

One of the very serious problems that a breeder encounters in building up a herd is that of sterility. The percentage of sterility for each age group as observed in the University of Minnesota dairy herd over a period of 29 years is shown by the following table. It will be noted that the highest proportion of sterility up to nine years of age occurs in the two year old group. After ten years of age, the percentage of sterility increases rapidly with increate in age.

While not all the causes of sterility are known, a number of factors are known to cause or contribute to sterility either temporarily or permanently. Heredity is undoubtedly one of the major factors contributing to the sterility of the two year old group, and it is not inconceivable that sometimes temporary sterility may be due to hereditary factors. From the preceding table, it is seen that age is a factor. Nutrition is also a factor. Badly undernourished cows do not come into estrus. Animals on a phosphorus deficient ration frequently do not show normal oestrus until the phosphorus level of the body has been restored.

Table 21.2: Relation of age and sterility in dairy cows

Age years	Total cows	No. sterile	Per cent sterile	Ratio of sterile to total
2	311	23	7.4	1:14
3	217	8	3.6	1:28
4	139	5	2.8	1:36
5	127	8	6.3	1:16
6	87	5	5.7	1:18
7	69	3	4.3	1:23
8	56	2	3.6	1:28
9	51	4	7.8	1:13
10	41	2	5.0	1:20
11	34	4	11.7	1:9
12	25	3	12.0	1:9
13	19	4	21.0	1:5
14	12	2	17.0	1:6
15	9	3	33.3	1:3
16	5	1	20.0	1:5
17	2	1	50.0	1:1

The part that nutrition plays in sterility is not fully understood. Cows in severe inanition states do not show esturs and, whether or not there is ovulation, from a practical standpoint breeding efficiency is impaired. Phosphorus deficient cows may ovulate with regularity yet estrus is absent and practical sterility results. Vitamin E has been shown not to be a factor in bovine fertility as rations free of vitamin E showed no impairment of estrus or lowered conception rates.

One of the major causes of sterility is diseases of the reproductive tract. Brucellosis, trichomoniasis, accidents to the genital tract during parturition and many other disease factors are responsible for much temporary and permanent sterility.

The Rest Period

It has previously been shown that by giving a cow a rest period lactation will be increased in the following lactation period. There are probably two reasons why a rest period results in greater production during the subsequent lactation period. The more important is undoubtedly the building up of body reserve to be used in the production of milk following calving. The other reason is the effect of the rest period upon the recuperation of the mammary gland tissue.

The manager of a dairy herd is confronted with the problem of deciding the length of the rest period that will give the best results. The objectives may be either to have the cow produce the largest amount of milk regardless of cost or to produce economically. The data given by Sanders, presented in Table 20.3, showed that up to a certain rest period, of at least 115 days, there is an increase in total production for each increment in the length of the rest period. Therefore, in order to prepare a cow for maximum production regardless of cost, the longer the rest period the greater the production that can be expected.

For the most economical production other factors than those that affect maximum production must be considered. While the production of the subsequent lactation period continues to increase with the increases in length of the dry period, the rate of increase decreases with each successive lengthening of the dry period. This, with the fact that lengthening the dry period shortens the current lactation period, makes it obvious that there is a limit to the length of a dry period that will be the most economical. A difference is noted for heifers and older cows in the effect of the length of the dry period upon subsequent production. It is apparent that longer dry periods are to be advised for heifers than for older cows; this is due, no doubt, to the need for further growth and development of the heifers. According to the data given by Sanders, a dry period of 45 days for heifers increased the subsequent production by 33.2 per cent, while for older cows an increase of only 18.5 per cent was experienced over no dry period. For 115-day dry periods the respective increases over no dry period were 52.2 per cent and 30.2 per cent. With a 45-day dry period as the base, an extension of 75 days increased the production 8.1 per cent for heifers and 3.8 per cent for cows. Extending the dry period to115 days increased production 14.2 per cent and 6.0 per cent respectively.

Under average conditions optimum results are secured with a dry period of 40 to 45 days for older cows and 70 to 75 days for younger cows. There are, however, conditions which will alter the length of the dry period. Cows in poor condition need longer dry periods for building up the necessary body stores, and underdeveloped heifers need more than the normal length of dry periods for the needed additional growth and development.

Care of the Dry Cow

Since the main object of the dry period, aside from the possible recuperative effect upon the mammary gland, is to build up body reserve for the next lactation period, the cow should be fed liberally with well selected feeds. As the body stores are made up mainly of fat and mineral matter and contain only relatively small amounts of protein, the feeds furnished during the dry period should supply adequate minerals and energy with enough protein to satisfy the maintenance requirements. The guide to a satisfactory ration will be the condition of the cow. If an excellent quality of legume hay is fed, it alone may be adequate provided the cow is in fair condition at the beginning. Good pasture is always adequate. When the cow is in poor condition to begin with, it is essential to feed some concentrate. The cheapest concentrate, selected on an energy basis, is the one to be chosen. If the cow is in very poor condition, six to eight pounds of concentrate may be fed daily. In localities where the soil is deficient in phosphorus or where a poor grade of nonlegume hay is fed, bone meal should be furnished as a source of calcium and phosphorus.

During the winter in colder climates, expect for the severest days, the dry cow should be let out daily for exercise. During the warmer months she may be left in the pasture continuously. While mechanical abortions are comparatively infrequent in cattle, the cow in advanced pregnancy should not be chased by dogs, hurried on ice or slippery pavements, or handled roughly.

Care at Calving

The welfare of both the cow and the calf is frequently dependent upon the care given during calving time. Neglect and improper attention at this time may result in the loss of both the cow and the calf, or may cause a weakened condition of both that results in the ultimate loss of the calf and decreased milk production for the cow. The cow is subject to several hazards at this time, including difficult calving, congestion of the udder, retrained afterbirth, digestive disturbances, and milk fever, any of which may result in disaster and which may be avoided by careful attention.

The approach of calving is ascertained from the breeding date and the appearance of the cow. As calving time nears, the external genitalia become enlarged, the ligaments on either side of the tail head become relaxed and sunken, and the udder becomes more congested. When these signs are observed, the cow should be carefully watched. She should be placed in a maternity pen in the barn or in a small clean pasture lot if the weather is favourable. The maternity pen should be disinfected with lysol solution and bedded with clean straw or shavings. A laxative feed should be fed; three or four pounds of a mixture of barn, ground oats, and linseed oil meal is excellent. At the first signs of labour, the cow should be carefully watched for any needed assistance, but should not be disturbed, as any excitement interferes with the natural process. If no progress is made after two hours of labour, an examination should be made to determine whether the calf is in normal presentation of forefeet and head foremost. If the presentation is abnormal - that is, if other parts of the calf's body are foremost - assistance is needed, and a veterinarian should be called, as should be done for all other difficulties in calving.

The newborn calf sometimes has a membrane over the nostrils; this must be removed or suffocation will result. If the calf is of normal strength and the cow is normal, it is best to leave the cow and the calf alone in the box stall or small pasture lot. Only when the calf is weak or the cow shows inattention toward the calf should assistance be rendered. If the cow fails to lick the calf, it should be dried by vigorous rubbing with straw or cloth. When the calf is too weal to nurse, it should be assisted to secure colostrum milk as soon as possible after birth, preferably within one-half hour. Colostrum milk, in addition to furnishing food, is laxative and contains antibodies which make the calf more resistant to later infection.

Unless the cow is infected with some contagious disease, it is well to leave the calf with the cow for the first two or three days after calving.

Loss of Weight due to Calving

If the cow has been properly fed, there is a progressive increase in body weight up to calving and then a sudden decline. The increase in weight during pregnancy is due to three factors: growth of the fetus and fetal membranes, body growth, and storage of mainly adipose tissue. The greatest increases in weight occur with the first calf heifers, with progressive decreases for each successive gestation until maturity. The decrease in weight at calving time is due to the loss of the calf, placenta, and amniotic fluid. After calving, there is a still further decrease in weight for an average of 45 days, due to insufficient feed intake to supply maintenance and milk production requirements. Milk is then produced in part from body stores.

Nebraska Station workers studied weight gains during pregnancy and losses due to calving for 656 gestations. They found weight losses varying from 78 to 151 pounds. For the first gestation the loss in weight represented 11.8 to 12.9 per cent of the cow's weight, while for older cows the loss varied from 8.1 to 12.0 per cent. The placenta and amniotic fluid weights varied greatly, the lowest being 22 pounds and the largest 58 pounds. In terms of body weight, this represented 1.9 to 5.1 per cent.

Feeding After Calving

As soon after calving as the cow will drink, she should be supplied fresh water. It is desirable that the water be lukewarm; it is essential that ice cold water be warmed. As much hay as the cow will consume should be allowed, and the laxative grain mixture should be continued for at least two days. The amount of feed consumed for the first few days is not important; if the cow is in good condition when calving, the body reserve will supply the body needs. The important problem is to maintain a good condition of the digestive system by avoiding overfeeding. After the second or third day following calving, if normal progress has been made, the calf may be removed and the cow retuned to the herd. The amounts of concentrate should then be gradually increased with the aim of reaching full feed in three weeks- except for very high producers, which may not reach full feed in less than six weeks' time.

Difficulties Encountered Following Parturition

Following parturition, the cow is subject to a number of afflictions that, unless immediate and competent attention is given, may result in disaster. These afflictions may be divided into those that affect the generative organs and those concerned with the mammary glands.

Due to the strain of calving and the engorged condition of the genital tract, the vagina and uterus may become bruised or torn, leading to infection; this condition requires the attention of a veterinarian. These and other factors may be responsible for eversion of the uterus and retained afterbirth. In eversion of the uterus the organ fails to contract, inverts, and protrudes. By the skilled attention of a veterinarian, the uterus may be returned and held in place by appropriate means until it is completely contracted.

Retained Afterbirth

Normally the afterbirth should come away within four to six hours following parturition. Following abortion, and for other reasons not known following apparently normal calving, the afterbirth fails to come away naturally. The afterbirth is attached to the uterus walls by from 50 to 100 cotyledons through which the nourishment passes from the blood to the fetus. Normally these attachments are such that they break from the uterine contractions following parturition, but sometimes they grow firmer and the afterbirth is not expelled.

If it is not normally expelled, the afterbirth may be removed by pinching off the attachment of the cotyledons. This should never be attempted by anyone except a skilled person. Unless carefully done, injury will be caused that will result in permanent sterility.

As soon as it becomes evident that the afterbirth will not be expelled naturally, it should be removed. Unless this is done decomposition sets in and the toxic decomposition products are absorbed into the system, causing loss of appetite and marked decline in both weight and milk yields. The decomposing retained afterbirth may also be a contributory factor to sterility.

Congested Udder

High producing cows usually suffer from a congestion of the udder immediately following calving; this congestion lasts for varying lengths of time. In some cases the congestion may be due in part to an infection. In the majority of cases, however, it is a natural sequence to the rapid development of the gland and is caused by the accumulation of tissue fluid (or lymph) in the gland tissues.

The degree of congestion is influenced by a number of factors. Exposure to drafts and chills intensifies the congestion and may lead to infection (discussed under "Udder Diseases"). The higher producing cows are more subject to congestion of the udder than are lower producers. Cows in high condition also suffer from greater congestion than do those in poorer condition. The claim by some that certain feeds are specifically conducive to udder congestion is not warranted by fact.

In extreme cases of congestion milking becomes very difficult because of the shortened teats and the slowness with which the milk is let down. When this is the case, it may be advisable to leave the calf with the cow until the congestion has somewhat receded. Some believe the massaging of the udder by the calf is helpful in reducing the congestion. Additional vigorous massaging by the hands will help to start the flow of the lymph out of the tissue and reduce the congestion.

As the result of several recent studies, prepartum milking has been demonstrated to be the most satisfactory solution of the congested udder problem. Milking should be started as soon as signs of congestion develop. With the beginning of milking not only is further progress of congestion stopped but the swelling that is present will gradually disappear. Work thus far indicates that prepartum milking will not depress milk flow following parturition.

In prepartum milking there will be no colostrum following freshening and provisions for this substance for the newborn calf must be made in other ways. The first two or three milkings (prepartum) will result in normal colostrum, which may be preserved for the calf by freezing.

Prepartum milking not only prevents undue swelling of the udder and thus makes milking easier after calving, but also is a factor in preventing a breaking away of the udder. The excessive swellings that sometimes occur puts more weight and stress on the suspensory mechanism than it is able to withstand and a breakdown results. Mastitis may be lessened to some extent by prepartum milking because the excessively large swollen udder is more subject to injury and thus predisposed to infection.

Milk Fever or Parturient Paresis

Milk fever is a diseases usually limited to high producing cows. While it may occur at any time during the lactation period it rarely occurs except following calving. The first symptom of this disease is staggering, with particular lack of control of the hind legs. The disease advances with progressive increases in paralysis and ends in prostration and complete coma; and unless relief is administered, it terminates in death. When complete coma has appeared, the cow lies with her head turned back against her chest. The eyes have become glassy and she will not respond to pin pricks. The temperature becomes lower rather than higher as is indicated by the name.

Milk fever is caused by a lowering of the calcium slats of the blood. Reducing the calcium slats of the blood by intravenous injection of sodium citrate brings about symptoms analogous to milk fever. Intravenous injection of calcium chloride brings about rapid recovery. The lowering of the blood calcium to produce milk fever can be explained by the fact that whole milk containing about 20 times the concentration of calcium that blood does is rapidly being produced and the calcium is being withdrawn from the blood, the mechanism for releasing calcium from the body stores replenishing the blood is not functioning. This explains why leaving most of the milk in the udder when milking for the first days following calving helps prevent milk fever.

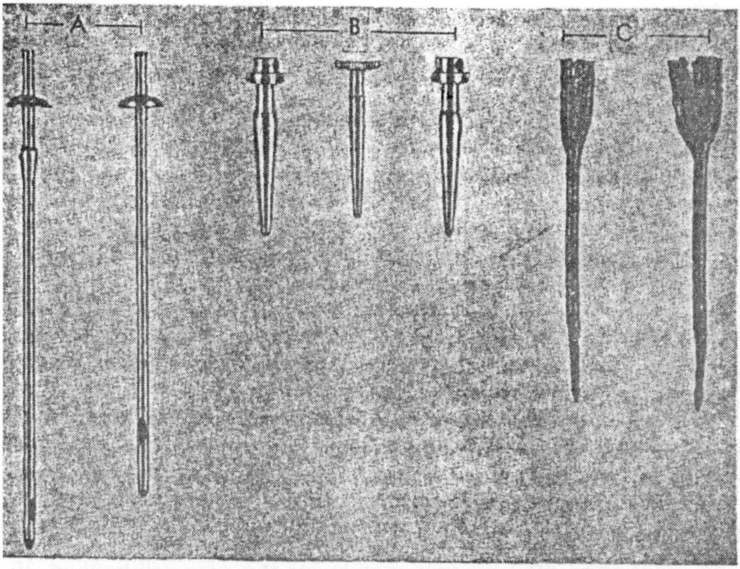

Fig. 21.1: Milk tubes, teat plugs, and teat dilators: A, two types of milk tubes - self-retaining on the left; B, three types of teat plugs; C, wax teat dilators.

Milk fever may be cured by either the intravenous or the subcutaneous injection of calcium gluconate or by insufflation of the udder with air. By injecting calcium gluconate (200 cc. of a saturated solution) the calcium of the blood is restored, and recovery is sudden. Insufflating the udder with air to a pressure that stops milk secretion, stops the drainage of calcium from the blood and permits gradual building up of the blood calcium from the body stores.

For air insufflation of the udder, a teat canula or milk tube (Fig. 21.1) is inserted in the teat and air is pumped into the quarter, first passing through a cotton filter. Each quarter is inflated with a pressure equal to that which the maximum milk pressure exerts in a well-distended udder. Extreme precautions must be taken to prevent infection. The ends of the teat must be washed in an antiseptic solution, and the teat canula or milk tube must be sterilized by boiling. With the best care possible, infection frequently follows this treatment. For this reason the safest treatment for milk fever is the intravenous injection of calcium gluconate.

CARE IN MILKING

The object in milking is to perform the act in such a manner as to obtain all of the milk in the udder. As has been shown previously, when the milkings are incomplete there is a tendency to dry-off the cow. The letting-down of milk is a reflex act (involuntary) essential to a complete milking. The stimulus causing the reflex is sensory. Immediately after calving the sight of the calf and later the manipulation of the udder and teats are stimuli causing the letting-down of milk. Unpleasant sensations produce counter stimuli which result in an effect that is usually referred to as "holding up the milk" but that, more properly, is failure to let down the milk.

The first essential in milking is to prevent undue excitement and to make the act as pleasant for the cow as possible. Loud talking or uncommon noises about the barn at milking time, mistreating the cow, or any other uncommon activity at milking time must be eliminated for effective milking. Excitements of the kind mentioned may be responsible for the cow withholding 20 per cent or more of the milk, as well as for lengthening the time required for milking.

The second essential for good milking is rapidity. Apparently there is a time limit to the stimulus for letting down milk. If all the milk is not withdrawn by the time the letting down action has expired, a complete milking cannot be effected. Probably one of the chief differences between a good milker and a poor milker is the difference in the rapidity with which they milk.

Methods

There are several different methods used in hand milking, differing chiefly in the manner in which the teats are grasped. The most common and preferred method is the full hand grasp with the thumb and index finger encircling the teat at the base, closing off the teat system with pressure when the milk is to be expressed. Forcing the milk out is then effected by applying pressure on the teat by closing the finger tips against the palm of the hand. A modification of this method consists in bending the thumb so that the knuckle is against the teat, closure of the teat canal being effected by the index finger pressing the teat against the thumb. The milk is then forced out by applying pressure as in the former method. A third method, sometimes called the strip method, consists in grasping the teat at the base between the thumb and forefinger. By pressure the teat canal is closed, and by sliding the pressure toward the end of the teat the milk is expressed.

Some people moisten the hands in milking. This practice is to be condemned not only because it is unsanitary and results in contamination of the milk but also because the moistened teats will become sore when they are exposed to the cold.

The order of milking the teats is not important. It is most common however, to first drain the milk accumulated in the cisterns of the front teats, then to do the same for the rear teats, and then to return to the front teats, when the major portion of the milk should be completely let down.

Drawing out the last milk is known as stripping. Care should be taken to strip as rapidly as possible in order to avoid making the cow a stripper. If the stripping action is prolonged, the cow soon adjusts herself to the situation and the milk is let down slowly over a long period. When this habit is formed, it is difficult to break.

Milking the Heifer

The way in which a heifer is trained will largely determine how she will react to milking when mature. If at the beginning a heifer develops an unfavourable attitude toward milking, she is likely to continue this attitude and become a "kicker" or a cow that holds up her milk.

For breaking in a heifer, the training should start several weeks before calving. She should first be placed in a stall with the rest of the milking cows to become accustomed to the surroundings. She should be brushed daily and treated gently, preferably by the person who will milk her following calving, in order that her confidence may be gained. When milking is started, special effort should be made to make the act as pleasant as possible. Severe remonstrations for kicking or misbehaviour result in an attitude of antagonism that may become permanent. When this becomes the case, the suggestion of milking becomes a stimulus for fight; this is not conducive to good behaviour during milking and reacts against stimuli for the rapid letting down of milk.

Milking before Calving

While there is no evidence that milking a cow before calving has any detrimental effect upon the subsequent milk production, there is no evidence that it is at all necessary. Recent work has shown that the accumulated milk in the udder will produce only a maximum pressure equivalent to 40 mm. of mercury when secretion ceases; thus, by refraining from milking, no more than pressure equivalent to 40 mm. of mercury will be developed, and there is no evidence that such a pressure is harmful. Milking before calving removes the colostrum milk and deprives the calf of this essential first food.

Milking after Calving

It is usually not necessary to milk the cow until 12 hours after calving. For the first two days, as a precaution against milk fever, it is well not to remove all the milk.

Hard Milkers

Frequently the sphincter muscles encircling the streak canal are overdeveloped or lack elasticity; this condition results in hard milkers. Not only does it require more energy to milk these cows but also more time. In some cases the sphincter muscles may be expanded to some extent by strong milkers. Inserting "teat expanders" (Fig. 21.1) in the form of rubber or metal plugs into the streak canal in the interim between milkings will also help. However, fully overcoming hard milking requires a delicate surgical operation in which the sphincter muscles are partly cut. If too many of the sphincter muscle fibers are cut, the teat may leak milk.

Sometimes one or more teats become hard to milk because of a wart-like growth from the walls of the teat system. This growth is known as a spider. The only remedy for this condition is a surgical operation by an experienced veterinarian. Unless carefully done such an operation is apt to cause mastitis.

Drying-off Cows

Frequently a real problem is encountered in drying-off high producing dairy cows for the necessary 6 weeks' rest period. It has usually been advised that cows should be dried-off by lengthening the intervals between milking and then removing only a portion of the milk in order to partly relieve the pressure in the udder. It is usually advised to begin by milking but once a day, then once every two days, and lengthening the interval until the time that they are completely dried-off. To reduce the stimulus for milk secretion, the grain allowance is markedly reduced during the drying-off process. This has a tendency to defeat the purpose of the drying period, which is to build up the body reserve for the next lactation. Another objection to drying-off cows by lengthening the intervals between milkings and to remove only a part of the milk is that the milk produced under such conditions is not normal. When milk is left in the udder for more than the normal length of time, its composition is changed and it takes on some of the characteristics of colostrum milk.

A more desirable way of drying-off cows is to stop milking completely whenever the rest period is to begin, regardless of the amount of milk produced. After the last milking it is desirable to carefully wash and dry the teats and then dip them in collodion to seal the ends of the teats. This will prevent entrance of organisms into the teat through the streak canal. It has been shown that when the milk is not removed, a maximum pressure is soon developed at which milk secretion ceases and resorption of the milk begins. Carefully controlled experiments have shown that drying-off cows by this method has no detrimental effect upon the milk produced or upon the bacteria content of the milk in the subsequent lactation.

Leaking Teats

There are two conditions producing leaking teats. In one the sphincter muscles are too weak to effect a closure of the streak canal against the pressure of the milk in the udder. In the other there is either a natural fistula to the teat cistern or one caused by a teat wound extending into the teat cistern. There is no known method by which the sphincter muscles may be strengthened. The only practical solution to the problem of leaky teats due to weak sphincter muscles is to seal the ends of the teats after each milking by dipping them in collodion.

The fistula, whether it is natural or produced by a wound, may be closed by cauterizing it either with a hot iron or by other surgical means. The cauterization must be done when the cow is dry.

Sore Teats

Sore teats may be caused by exposure to the cold, particularly when wet; by injury, such as wire cuts or bruises; and by a number of infections, of which cowpox is the most common. Whatever the cause, sore teats are a source of extreme annoyance during milking and result in losses from spilled milk and incomplete letting down of the milk.

In all cases of sore teats the pain due to milking may be ameliorated by bathing the teat in a warm salt solution (one teaspoonful of salt to one quart of water) to soften the sores, and then applying vaseline. In the case of severe wounds and bruises, the wound should first be cleansed with a disinfectant solution, and then medicated vaseline should be applied. In severe cases the milk should be withdrawn by means of a milk tube.

Warts sometimes cause sore teats or discomfort to the milker. Warts are usually temporary. Vaseline or olive oil applied daily will prevent their spreading and speed up their disappearance. Large warts may be removed by clipping them off and then touching the wound with a stick of caustic potash or a 5 per cent solution of silver nitrate.

Use of a Milk Tube

In case of severe teat injury the best means of withdrawing the milk is by using a milk tube. The tube should be inserted in the injured teat when the other teats are milked, as a more complete drainage of the milk is effected at this time than when inserted following the milking of the normal quarters. In using a milk tube, extreme care must be taken to guard against infection. The tube must be sterilized by boiling and the end of the teat must be carefully cleansed with a disinfecting solution such as Lysol before the tube is inserted.

Why cows leave the herd

Cows are disposed of for the following reasons:

1. Surplus stock
2. Poor producers
3. Old age
4. Accidents
5. Deaths
6. Disease
7. Sterility

No adequate study has been made to show what proportion of the cows disposed of annually falls into each of the categories listed. For any one herd the distribution would vary greatly, depending upon the incidence of disease and the amount of surplus stock. Scattered cow testing associations' reports indicate that from 15 to 20 per cent of the cows disposed of are sold because of low milk yields. Sterility and disease constitute the cause of disposal of more than 60 per cent of the number. Misner estimated that less than one-third of the disposed animals were sold for productive purposes in a region of relatively great demand for cows.

The length of productive life of cows

There is a scarcity of authentic material on the length of time cows are productive. That there is great variation among cows as to the age at which production ceases and they are eliminated from the herd, is well known. Cows have been known to produce and reproduce when 20 or more years of age, although this is rare. It is a commonly accepted belief that cows are productive for 5 years, although individual studies vary from 3.6 to7.5 years. Actual studies revealed the following ages of productivity of cows:

Delaware County, N.Y.	3.6 years
Chester County, Pa	4.34 years
Lenawee County, Mich	4.52 years
Mason City, Iowa	4.5 years

In addition, Researcher reports one heifer replacement for 5.5 cows as adequate and Researcher 6 years as the average productive life of cows. Estimates by farmers run as high as 7.5 years by 131 farmers in New York.

PROTECTION AGAINST FLIES

Damage

The damage done to cattle by flies is not known. Some people believe that the generally supposed damage of flies to milk production is overestimated. Flies, however, are responsible for great economical losses due to preventing cattle from grazing, the spreading of disease, the damage caused to hides and flesh, annoyance during milking, and the great sums of money expended in combating them in the form of sprays, screens, flytraps, and other devices. The more important flies attacking cattle are stable flies, horn flies, house flies, warble flies or cattle grubs, horse flies, and screw worm flies.

Stable Fly

The stable fly resembles the house fly in appearance. It differs from the house fly in that it has piercing mouth parts that penetrate the skin and with which it sucks blood. The annoyance to cattle is due to the pain caused by piercing the skin. Eggs of the stable fly, which develop into adult flies in about two weeks, are laid in manure and decaying straw.

Horn Fly

The horn fly is smaller than the stable fly. It gets its name from the fact that it roosts at the base of the horns. This fly has a painful "bite", sucking blood as does the stable fly. The horn fly may be recognized by its habit of spreading the wings when feeding. It breeds in fresh manure, and requires ten days to develop from the egg to the adult fly.

House Fly

The house fly does not bite the cows but annoys them by crawling over their skin, and it is a general nuisance in the barn and milk house. It breeds in manure and in moist decaying matter of all kinds.

Warble Fly

The warble fly or heel fly or cattle grub is found in all parts of the United States. While this fly does not bite, it is one of the most annoying to cattle. It deposits its eggs on the hair of the legs, on the body, and one species on the heels, and when in the act of depositing eggs, it causes fear in the animal that often results in a stampede. The eggs hatch and the larvae burrow through the skin and tissues to find their way upto under the skin of the back, where they pupate. Damage to the animal is caused when the larvae burrow through the skin and tissue and when the pupae dig holes in the skin along the back from which they exit in early spring. Aside from the adult stage, the whole life cycle is spent on the animal. Control lies in the destruction of the larvae.

Since the warble fly will travel considerable distances, control of this pest must be an area undertaking. The pest can be controlled by distruction of the larvae before they emerge. One method applicable to small herds is to squeeze the larvae out and destroy them. The more common method is to destroy them *in situ* in one of several ways. Dusting about one and one-half ounces of a mixture of one part derris powder containing 5 per cent rotenone and nine parts wettable sulphur along the back and then brushing vigorously against the hair with a stiff bristled brush is effective. Another satisfactory method is to make up a solution of ten ounces derris powder and four ounces neutral soap with one gallon of water and apply along the back with a stiff bristled brush. For large-scale operations spraying with a sprayer that will develop 200 or more pounds of pressure is preferred. The spray is made up of five pounds derris powder and ten pounds wettable sulphur in 100 gallons of water. About one-half gallon will be required per head.

Fly Control

Flies may be controlled by destroying the breeding places, by use of various repellants, and killing the adult fly. In recent years a number of insecticides have been developed that are effective in killing flies when they contact a sprayed surface. Among this list are DDT, TDE, toxaphene, benzene, hexachloride, chloridane, and methoxychlor. DDT (dichloro-diphenyl-trichloroethane) has been used the most extensively for the spraying of barns, milk houses, and cattle. It has been very effective in controlling the fly nuisance when properly used except in some cases where it has been reported that the flies have developed a tolerance for the drug to the extent that 50 or more times the amount of the material is required to be effective.

Recently because of the possible injury to human health DDT and others of the chlorinated hydrocarbons except methoxychlor have been removed from the list of recommended insecticides to be used as sprays for milking cows or for barns or milk houses. It has been shown that when DDT is ingested it will be absorbed into the system and will be deposited in the body fat and in the milk. Because of the deposit in the body fat the drug will be found in the milk for up to 60 days after the last ingestion of the substance. Spraying young stock and bulls with DDT is not contraindicated because there is no evidence that the ingestion of DDT in amounts as would be gotten from this source is injurious. Likewise manure piles and other places where flies may breed may also be sprayed with DDT provided that milking cows are kept away.

Methoxychlor is now the only one of this group of insecticides that is recommended for spraying dairy barns, milk houses, and milking cows. This substance is held to be noninjurious to humans in the amounts that could possibly get into the milk.

Spraying of Barns

Methoxychlor should be used for the spraying of the barn and milk room. This drug is obtainable in 50 per cent wettable powder and should be made up to a .5 per cent solution with water. DDT may be used as a spray for other places where flies gather but where cows in milk do not contact. DDT for this purpose should likewise be made up to a 2.5 per cent solution either in oil or in water. One gallon of either DDT or methoxychlor solution will cover about 300 square feet of surface. Spraying should be repeated each two months during the fly season. To be most effective all surfaces where flies alight should be sprayed. This includes walls, ceiling, supports, screens, stanchions, and the outside where flies usually roost around doors and windows.

Spraying Cattle

Both DDT and methoxychlor are very effective in the control of the house fly and the horn fly and less effective for the biting stable fly when applied to the animal. They are not effective in the control of deerflies and are of no value against warble flies and bot flies. Only methoxychlor should be used on milking cows, while DDT may be used on bulls and young stock. Only wettable powder made up with water should be used for cattle sprays. A .5 per cent solution of methoxychlor and a 2 per cent solution of DDT should be used. About two quarts are required per cow per spray. Either spray must be applied every three weeks during the fly season.

Older methods of using fly traps, electric killing devices, and fly repellants do not seem to have a place in the fly control programme that is not taken care of more effectively by the use of DDT. Repellants do not reduce the fly population but merely protect the animals by keeping the flies off. Oil base repellants have been shown to increase the body temperature of the animal and to cause skin burns.

Lice

There are three species of lice that commonly affect cattle, causing damage through irritation of the animal. Two species are blood sucking (the short-nosed cattle louse, Hamotopimus eurysternus, and the long-nosed louse, Linognathus vituli) and the third is a biting louse) Trichodeates scalaris or red louse). Due to the itching caused by the lice, affected cattle rub themselves against any available object or lick themselves, either of which will cause loss of hair, leaving denuded areas. Cattle engaging in excessive rubbing or licking should be investigated for possible infestation of lice. The neck, the back of the head, and the back are the most probable places to look for lice. Lice reproduce by laying eggs called nits. The nits hatch in about ten days.

Lice are controlled by the adequate use of DDT. Before the cattle are stabled and while the weather is still warm, all parts of the body should be thoroughly wetted with a 0.25 per cent DDT or methoxychlor spray made up of from wettable powder. One such treatment is usually sufficient, since there will be sufficient residual DDT or methoxychlor on the hair to kill lice that hatch from eggs on the body at the time of the spray. During the winter in cold climates lice may be effectively treated by dusting with a 5 to 10 per cent DDT or methoxychlor dust.

22

The Milking Machine and Milking

The largest single labour item in the care of dairy cows is that required for milking. Estimates of the per cent of time required for milking vary from 53.6 per cent of all labour requirements for the milking cow to 41 per cent of the total labour requirements for the whole herd. While the time required to milk a cow varies with the milker, the amount of time needed depends upon the amount of milk a cow yields and the ease with which she milks; on the average, seven minutes are required per milking, or 14 minutes per day. This means that approximately 75 hours are spent annually in milking each cow. Because the labour requirement is so large, and because milking requires daily and exact attention, hired labour is difficult to secure; therefore a great deal of interest has been manifested in the mechanical milker.

The history of the development of the milking machine, the different types of machines, the comparison of hand and machine milking, the economical phases of machine milking, and the care of the milking machine are subjects with which the student of dairying should be familiar.

History of the milking machine

Attempts at making milking machines began in the United States as early as 1819. All of the earlier types were failures; this fact did much to establish the early prejudices against milking machines. The earliest types used tubes inserted in the teats. These were followed by pressure devices to squeeze out the milk, and they in turn were followed by suction machines of various types.

The milk tube milking machines were soon discarded because of the injuries to the teats and the spread of disease. It is possible to draw the milk from the udder by means of the milking tube, but in inexperienced hands the end of the teat is frequently injured; and unless the tube is sterilized before each insertion, mastitis infections are generally spread.

Although a large number of patents have been granted on the pressure types of milking machines, none of them are now in use. In reviewing the development of milking machines, Erf describes machines of this group using rollers, pads, plates, belts, and mechanical fingers. All were based upon the principle of hand milking: that is, applying pressure to the teat, beginning at the upper portion and working downward. The force for applying the pressure was furnished by means of belts, shafts, and in some cases, by pneumatic devices. All of these types proved unsatisfactory because the amount of labour involved in their operation was large and also because they were inflexible and annoying to the cows. Most of the machines had to be securely strapped around the body of the cow. With some types the power was furnished by hand, and more work was expended in turning the machine than would have been expended in hand milking.

The first suction machine, patented in 1860, was operated by continuous suction. While this type of machine was much more satisfactory than any of the previous types, it found disfavour principally because of the injury it caused to the teats. The continuous vacuum on the teats caused a severe congestion.

In 1895 the Thistle milking machine, which proved to be a distinct advance in the evolution of milking machines, was developed. This machine is usually credited with being the first to use intermittent suction or pulsation, which is the basic principle of all modern machines. The Thistle machine was crude and complicated as compared with the modern machines. The pulsations were created

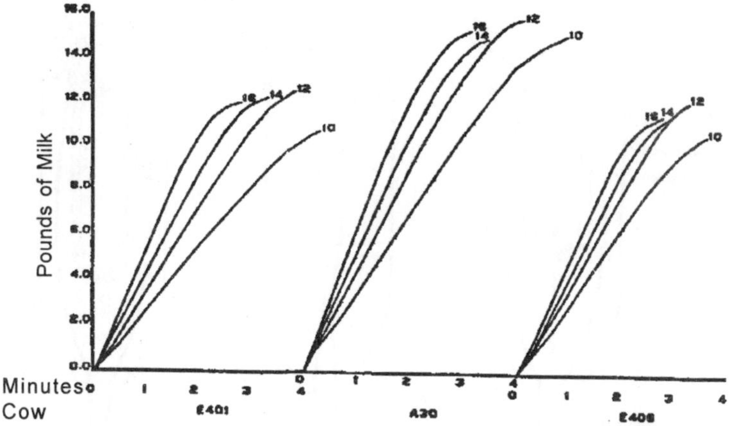

Fig. 22.1: Here is shown the effect of varying the negative pressure (vacuum) from 10 to 16 inches of mercury upon the rate of milk withdrawal in three cows.

at the vacuum pump, and by the time they reached the teat cups they were not sharp and well defined. A large vacuum pump and a large amount of power were needed, since all the air in the entire vacuum system had to be expelled with each pulsation.

The next important advance in the development of the milking machine occurred in 1902 when Lawrence and Kennedy of Glasgow, Scotland, developed the first mechanical milker with the pulsator on the lid of the milker and the pressure created by vacuum. This principle permits the maintaining of a continuous vacuum in the vacuum system and the giving of sharp and distinct pulsations at the teat cup. All modern machines embrace this principle, although different mechanical means are used by different manufacturers.

Types of modern milking machines

Although all modern milking machines use negative pressure fro extraction of the milk there are differences in the mechanical means used. Mechanical milkers fall into two groups:

(1) single action and

(2) double action.

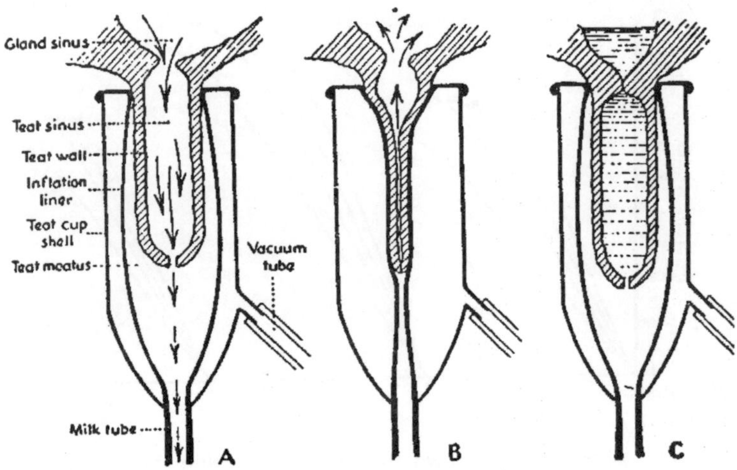

Fig.22.2: The action of the mechanical milker is shown in the above diagrams.

Single action

The machines falling in the single action class have teat cups without rubber inflations, and depend upon the negative pressure being applied from a piston pump or the like in which that pressure is created by the outward stroke and release is afforded by the return stroke. The pulsation rates are, therefore, established by the speed of the pump. The level of negative pressure increases from the beginning of the stroke till the end, when partial release is afforded. If there is complete release of negative pressure, the teat cups will not remain attached.

The negative pressure is confined to the milk tubes, teat cups, and head. On the outward stroke, the milk gathers in the head set over a pail and on the backward or release stroke the milk is dropped into the container. Some of the machines are constructed so the head will fit over a milk can. In spite of the partial or nearly complete release for one-half of the cycle the teats become congested from these machines.

Double Action

The double action machine is characterized by a teat cup having a rubber inflation or lining on the inside. This type of machine requires a constant negative pressure coming from what is known as a vacuum tank. The vacuum tank may supply the negative pressure to where it is needed through a pipeline, or both the motor and the vacuum tank may be portable. These machines are equipped with pulsators, devices that make or break the negative pressure. These pulsators may be adjustable or regulated electrically at a constant rate. The negative pressure from its source usually is connected to the pulsator which is customarily placed on top of the milking machine pail.

From the pulsator the negative force is directed two ways, one into the milk pail and the other to the outside of the teat cups. The full negative pressure always goes to the outside in the teat cups. In many cases the force going to the pail is reduced by what is known as a check valve. The amount of reduced force through the action of the check valve varies but usually is about equal to two inches of mercury pressure. On such a machine operating with 14 inches of mercury negative pressure in the pipeline will deliver not over 12 inches to the teats. Those machines that do not have check valves can deliver the full force of the pipeline negative pressure to the teats.

The negative pressure in the pail is applied through the milk tube to the teats on the inside of the rubber inflations. This force is constantly applied. The teats, however, the alternately protected against the congesting effect of this force by the collapse of the inflations due to release of the negative pressure in the outside shell. Upon release in the shell, the rubber inflations collapse with sufficient force to produce a substantial massaging action.

The double action machines are subdivided into the suspended or short tube and the floor or long tube types. The suspended machines, as the name indicates, are suspended from a surcingle and has short milk tubes, each tube from the teat cup being connected to the head of the machine. The floor type of machine usually has the milk tubes and vacuum tubes from each teat cup enter a claw to which there is a single vacuum tubes and from which the milk is taken to the pail in one milk tube.

The Releaser System

The releaser system employs the regular milking machine principle for milking, but instead of the milking machine pail begin used, the milk is drawn through sanitary piping into the milk room. Vacuum is employed in the transport of the milk into one of two containers. When one container is filled, or when one or more cows have been milked, the vacuum is released from the filled or partially filled container to permit emptying its contents, and the other container is evacuated. This is accomplished by the so-called releaser device.

The releaser system was developed in New Zealand and Australia, where it is extensively used. In this country a modification of the releaser system is used in the so-called "milking parlour." Here the milk is drawn directly from the cow into a glass container suspended from a scale and located above the stall. The milk is drawn from the glass container into the milk room by the releaser method. The releaser system has reached its highest development in the Roto-lactor owned by the Walker Gordon Company of New Jersey. The Roto-lactor consists of a revolving table containing 50 stanchions and one releaser unit for each stanchion. The table makes one revolution in 12½ minutes; during this time a cow is milked. Many special features are incorporated in the Roto-lactor system. Every machine is washed and sterilized by automatic arrangements following the milking of each cow. Special alleyway arrangements are used in taking cows to and from the Roto-lactor to minimize labour requirements and confusion. The cows are washed as they enter the machine and dried before the milking machine is attached.

Cows are not stripped following milking by the releaser type; toward the end of the milking the udders are massaged to facilitate getting all the milk in the udder.

Comparison of Hand and Machine Milking

A number of experiments have been conducted to test the relative efficiency of hand and machine milking. Only the more recent work is worthy of note as only such would include studies of the modern perfected milking machine. The Iowa Station compared hand milking with the milking of one of the modern machines by alternating the two for a period of 51 weeks. The average daily milk yield of 20.22 pounds for the machine and 20.18 pounds for the hand milking shows no significant difference for the two methods. This is in accord with previous studies using the same method of approach.

Recently researches reported on comparisons of hand and machine milking for a group of seven cows that were milked by machine the first, second, and fourth lactation periods, and by hand the third lactation period. He observed that cows milked by machine were not quite so persistent as those milked by hand. The differences were not great and have no bearing upon the advisability of using machines.

It may be concluded that machine milking is probably not quite so efficient in getting the most milk as the best hand milking, but it is better than the average hand milking. It has been universally recognized that cows like machine milking as well as or better than hand milking. Most of the harmful effects of machine milking appear to be due to leaving the machine on the cow too long.

Stripping by Machine

The question as to whether one should strip by hand following the mechanical milk has and still is subject to a good deal of debate. There is no argument about the desirability of removing all of the milk, for reasons that have been fully discussed in a pervious chapter. The question then is one of whether all of the milk can be removed by the machine or whether it is more practical to do so by hand stripping. At the Minnesota Station it has been established that all milk that has been let down can be removed by the proper manipulation of the teat cups and massaging of the udder.

Any milk in the teat cistern must be removed to the action of the mechanical milker. The problem is that of getting the milk into the teat cisterns. As milking progresses, the lower part of the udder becomes soft and flabby due to the release of the pressure caused by the let-down milk. As a result these soft tissues are gradually drawn into the teat cup first to slow down the flow and finally to completely block the passageway for the milk from the gland cistern to the teat cistern. By drawing the teat cups downward to reopen the passageway and, simultaneously, with the freehand, massaging each quarter to facilitate drainage of the (sp) tortonous ducts, every bit of the milk that has been let down can be withdrawn by the machine.

While all of the milk can be removed in all cases by proper manipulation of the teat cup assembly, there are cases in which special skills are required to accomplish this fact. Sometimes growths occur in the walls of the teat cistern that will necessitate drawing the teat cups down so far before passage for the milk is opened that they are apt to drop off. Different anatomical anomalies of teats and lower udder also contribute to difficulties in stripping by the machine. The number of cases that present serious difficulty is few and perhaps the best solution for the out-of-the-ordinary difficult ones is hand stripping.

There are three reasons why cows should be stripped by the machine rather than by hand.

1. Time and effort is saved. One extra trip to the cow at each milking is saved.
2. The cows are kept in better milking habits. Hand stripping, particularly if prolonged has a tendency to make strippers out of cows. Many cows will develop the habit of not letting down all of the milk to the machine and require a second let-down to the stimulus of hand stripping.
3. Most of the visible particle contamination in milk comes from the practice of hand stripping.

The question of how much milk may be left in a quarter without damaging effects is still not settled. It is not feasible to spend enough time to get the very last milk out. Milk continues to drain from the network of ducts for some time after milking is completed. The all important point is to so carry on the milking that the milk is forced out of the alveoli. From the evidence now available, leaving a few ounces in a quarter provided the alveoli are emptied is not deleterious.

Principles of Milking

Milking is accomplished only by the proper application of force in which the sphincter muscles surrounding the teat meatus are stretched to make an opening for the milk to be discharged. In hand milking the upper part of the teat cistern is closed tightly by the hand to prevent the milk from flowing back into the udder cistern and pressure is applied to the milk-filled lower part of the teat. The increased pressure inside of the teat stretches the sphincter muscles and the teat meatus is forced open. Measures by the author of the pressures exerted in hand milking varied from 20 to 35 inches mercury pressure with each squeeze by seven different hand milkers. In general the faster milkers applied the greater force, although this was not always true. In some cases failure to close the upper part of the teat cistern soon enough or to close them completely caused some of the teat contents to flow back into the gland cistern and a proportionately small stream was evacuated with each squeeze.

In machine milking the pressure on the inside of the teat is left unchanged. The pressure inside the teat cup is lowered by the machine so that the normal pressure inside the teat in relation to the outside pressure becomes great enough to force the meatus open and allow the milk to flow out. In the double action machine the milk is not squeezed out, as is claimed by some. The milk flows out of the teat only when the inflations are distended by the application of negative pressure in the outer teat cup. Upon collapse of the inflation milk stops flowing.

The relation of negative pressure levels and speed of milking

Other things being equal the greater the negative force the faster the milk will be withdrawn. There is a great difference among cows in the amount of force required to milk at a satisfactory rate. In so far as the force required in the speed of milking, it is due to the strength of the muscles surrounding the meatus. Injury which produces sear tissue around the meatus usually increases the force that is required to withdraw the milk speedily. There are other factors than hardness of milking that impedes the rate of milk withdrawal and that are not improved by increasing the amount of force. One is the failure of the cow to let down her milk as fast as it can be taken away and the other and more common are the obstructions (either natural or developed) in the upper teat cistern that will not permit the milk to enter the teat as fast as it can be withdrawn.

The best level of negative pressure to be used is still not settled. It is obvious that in herds where most of the cows are hard milkers a higher negative pressure should be used than where the cows are easy milkers. There is this interesting automatic feature about mechanical milking that for easy-milking cows a much smaller portion of the total potential negative force is delivered to the teat than for hard-milking cows. The reason for this automatic regulation is due to the fact that the greater the flow of milk in the milk tube, the greater will be the resistance to the negative force reaching the teat. For easy-milking cows the author has found as little as fie inches of mercury negative pressure on the teats with 13 inches N.P. in the pail. When the milk ceases to flow, the full force in the pail will be directed to the teat.

Injury from Mechanical Milkers

A great deal has been said about the injury to the teats and udder caused by mechanical milkers. Misuse can cause severe damage but by proper use less force need be exerted on the teat by the mechanical milker than by hand milking. Studies by the author have revealed that, when milk flows out of the meatus, no force is exerted on the inside of the teat. With the double action machine left on for five minutes no detectible congestion or swelling of the teat was observed except in the very end. With the single action machine left on for five minutes there was a noticeable increase in both the length and thickness of the teats.

When milk does not flow through the meatus, the negative pressure extends inside the teats with damaging effects. The inside lining becomes congested and the upper part of the teat and sometimes the lower part of the udder are drawn into the teat cups where a shearing action takes place with each pulsation. These injuries invite infection and produce growths that interfere with milking. If the mechanical milker is not attached until the milk is let down and removed soon after the milk stops flowing, no harmful effects are to be found from its use. The greatest damage comes from leaving the mechanical milker on too long.

Pulsation Rates

There is a general idea that increasing the pulsation rates

speeds up milk withdrawal. In trials where pulsation rates ranged from 20 to 120 per minute and the level of the negative force was kept constant, no difference in the rate of milk removal was observed. This is what was to be expected because milk is removed only during that half of the cycle when the inflations are distended. By increasing the rates the number of cycles per minute is increased but milk is withdrawn just one-half of the time.

Just what is the optimum pulsation rate is not known. When pulsation rates were slow, below 40 per minute, there was evidence of pain and some congestion to the teats. With the faster pulsation rates, danger from congestion is avoided but the amount of power to maintain the proper negative pressure levels is increased. Usually when the pulsation rates are substantially increased, the negative pressure drops particularly after a machine is attached and some time is required before it again reaches the desired level with the result that the rate of milking is reduced.

Effect of the Milking Machine upon the Quality of Milk

The bacterial and sediment content of milk drawn by the milking machine is dependent upon the care used in cleaning and operating the machine. If the machine is sterilized and handled in such a way as to prevent contamination during the milking process, milk can be produced as clean as with the best hand milking. Many certified dairies, where low bacterial and sediment content of milk is paramount, use milking machines. If the machine is not properly cleaned and sterilized between each milking, and if, through careless and slovenly methods of handling, the teat cups become contaminated in operating, the machine may be the cause of increased bacterial and sediment content of the milk. In most trials under ordinary farm conditions machine produced milk has been found higher in bacterial content than milk produced by hand milking.

The Milking Machine and Udder Diseases

The milking machine sometimes is accused of being responsible for injuries to the udder and the spreading of mastitis. While this is true in some cases, nearly all workers studying the efficiency of milking machines report no injuries or infections that can be attributed to the use of mechanical milkers. There is every reason to believe that the milking machine may spread mastitis in the same way and to the same extent that hand milking will. When cows are not stripped following machine milking or when the udders and milk are not carefully examined for abnormalities, udder troubles may become more pronounced with machine milking than with hand milking. If examinations for abnormalities are not made, the disease may become quite advanced before it is discovered, and more time will be given for the infection of noninfected cows. Also, treatment of the infected cows will be delayed, and their chances for recovery lessened.

Leaving the milking machine on the cow too long and using too great a vacuum are, predisposing factors for mastitis. Either one of these practices may injure the delicate membranes lining the teat cisterns and increase the chances of infection at the point of injury, from which infection may spread to the deeper parts of the udder.

Economy of Milking Machines

Whether or not milking by machine is to be advised depends upon whether one or more of the following three points are to be met:

1. To reduce the cost of milking.
2. To overcome the difficulty of securing competent hand milkers.
3. To obviate dislike for hand milking.

The cost of labour and the size of the herd are the chief factors which determine whether the use of milking machines will lower the cost of milking. The use of milking machines will reduce the time required for milking by more than 50 per cent. The Iowa Station reported a saving of 52.1 per cent in the actual time required for milking. The Illinois Station, from a study of hand milking on 34 farms and machine milking on 32 farms, found an average of 133.9 hours of labour for care and milking per cow per annum when milked by hand and of 81.5 hours for cows milked by machine, or a saving of 52.4 hours of labour per cow per year. With the saving of time required in milking it would appear that the milking machine is a time and money saver for any sized herd. This is not true, since there are certain costs in connection with the milking machine that are constant, increasing but slightly with the increase in herd size. The chief items are depreciation at the rate of 10 per cent per annum, interest on investment, and repairs and replacements. To these must be added the cost of power and the extra labour involved in cleaning the machine. At the Iowa Station in 1929 these items amounted to a total of $172.61 for 22 cows. On the average farm with 25 cows, Illinois found that labour represented 76.5 per cent, power 13.2 per cent, and charges against the machine 10.3 per cent of the total costs of milking by machine. When the labour rate varied from 12 to 30 cents per hour, the annual saving per cow for herds with less than 25 cows ranged from $0.46 to $9.55, and for herds above 25 cows, from $2.76 to $12.37.

On farms where plenty of labour is available that would not otherwise be utilized from an economical standpoint, the labour should be used in hand milking, even at low returns per hour. Where additional labour must be employed, the milking machine begins to be a profitable investment with herds of 12 cows, with increasing savings for larger herds. When hand milking is very much disliked and it is difficult to secure competent hand milkers, the purchase and use of milking machines for smaller than 12-cow herds may be advisable.

Care of the milking machine

Like any other mechanical device, the milking machine will do good work only when properly cared for. Two mistakes are frequently made in running milking machines: the pulsator is not properly adjusted, and the vacuum is not properly maintained. If the pulsator rate is either too slow or too fast, the maximum efficiency of the machine cannot be attained. At regular intervals the rate of pulsation should be checked and adjusted if necessary. While the vacuum is usually prevented from becoming too great by the proper safety valve furnished by the manufacturer, the operator is frequently responsible for too little vacuum, with resulting inefficiency of the machine. Leakage in the line, in the rubber tubes, or in the pail from improper fitting of the cover may be sufficient to lower the vacuum below the point for maximum efficiency.

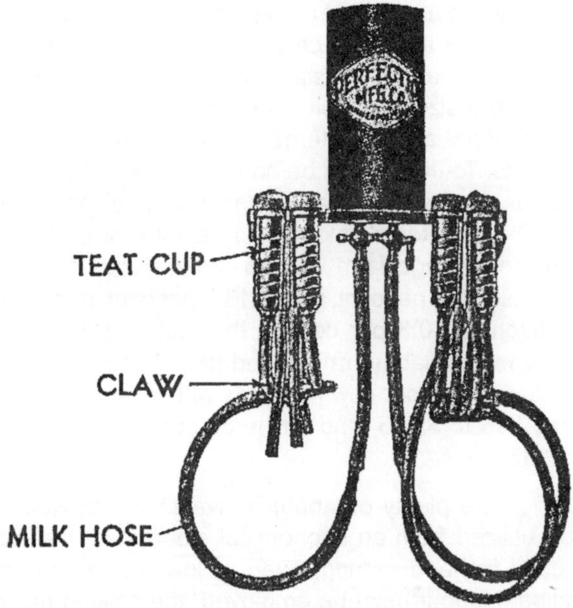

Fig. 22.3: Milking machine sterilizing rack. The sterilizing solution is run out of the container to fill all the parts with which the milk comes in contact during the milking.

The milking machine frequently suffers from lack of care, particularly in the oiling of the few movable parts in the vacuum pump and pulsator. The pail and teat pumps are frequently dropped and become dented so as to permit leakage of air and resultant loss of vacuum. The rubber inflations may not be properly adjusted, or they may become cracked. Cracked or improperly adjusted inflations may leak air and draw milk into the chamber between the inflation and the teat cup shell; this results in poor milking, and sometimes in milk getting down into the pulsator. All faulty inflations and other parts should be replaced.

Replacing inflations constitutes the greatest repair expense for milking machines. It is, therefore, good economy to give special attention to those considerations that will increase the length of life of the inflations. Fat and dirt cause rapid deterioration of rubber, and their prompt and thorough removal will do much to lengthen the life of the inflations. Also undue stretching of the inflations should be avoided.

Cleaning the milking machine

It is possible to produce as clean milk with as low bacterial content by machine as by the best of hand milking; but in order to do so, special effort must be made to thoroughly clean and sterilize the parts of the machine with which the milk comes in contact. The milking machine pail may be cleaned and sterilized like any other pail by first scrubbing it thoroughly, and then scalding it with boiling water or steam. The rubber parts, however, do not permit this treatment because they are inaccessible and also because the heat will injure the rubber. It is therefore necessary to use some chemical sterilizer. For a chemical sterilizer to be effective, all of the milk must be removed.

Immediately after milking, before any of the milk has dried on the machine parts and while the machine is still on the vacuum, several gallons of cool or lukewarm water should be drawn through each unit. This is done most effectively by dousing the teat cups up and down in the water to permit water and air to be drawn through alternately. This procedure is followed by drawing through, in the same manner, one or more gallons of a hot solution of washing powder. Use two heaping table-spoonfuls of any good washing powder to a gallon of water. The teat cup liners should be brushed, especially the portion extending outside the teat cup shell.

After the milk has been removed, the tubes and teat cups with the liners may be immersed in the chemical sterilizing solution, or they may be placed in the "sterilizing rack." (Fig. 22.3) The sterilizing rack is a device so constructed that the teat cup assembly with the milk tube is automatically filled with the sterilizing solution. In either case the equipment should be left in the sterilizing solution until just prior to the next milking, when it should be rinsed with clean water.

The sterilizing rack has several advantages over the immersion method of sterilizing. The outside shell of the teat cups is not exposed to the action of the solution, and since the contents of the tubes and teat cup assemblies are discarded after each usage, fresh sterilizing solution is used for each time of sterilization. In continued use of the solution, followed when the equipment is immersed, the solution becomes contaminated and weakened.

The sterilizing solution may be made up according to directions from a large number of sterilizers on the market, or it may be made at home. Some recent work indicates that a lye solution not only is an effective disinfectant but also is an excellent cleansing agent that prolongs the life of rubber. A stock solution of lye is made by dissolving a 14-ounce can of lye in a gallon of water. One-half pint of the stock solution is used to one gallons of water in making up the solution for use in sterilizing.

A homemade hypochloride stock solution may be made as follows: Dissolve one pound of sal soda in one gallon of water,

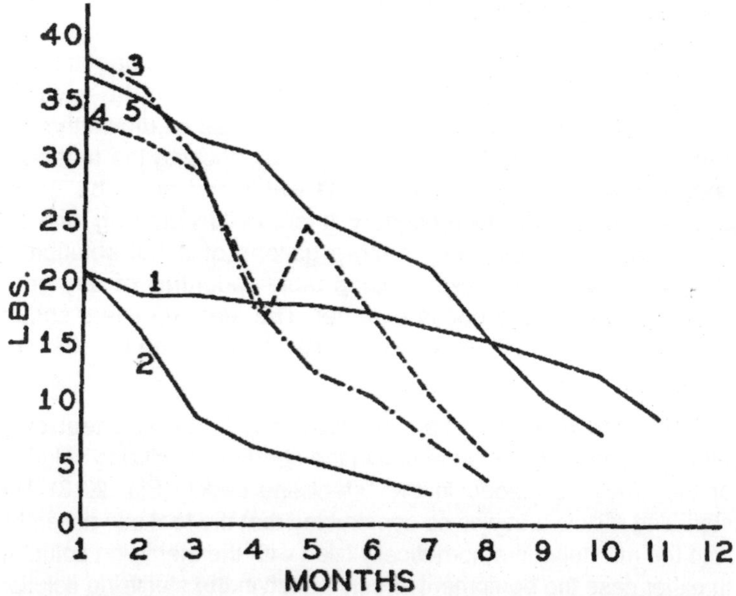

Fig.22.4: Incomplete evacuation of the udder causes rapid drops in milk flow. Lactation curves are shown for five consecutive lactations of a cow that let down her milk well on the first lactation resulting in good persistency. During the second, third, and fourth lactations she developed the habit of letting down the milk completely on infrequent intervals resulting in steep slopes of the lactation curves. For two weeks in the fifth month of the fourth lactation the udder was emptied after each milking by the injection of oxytocin. Note a more than 50 per cent rise in milk production. During the fifth lactation she was milked by a milker she responded to with complete let-down of milk resulting in a 61.2 per cent increase in milk for 305 days.

then add one 14-ounce can of chlorinated lime, and stir or shake vigorously; let this mixture set until the sediment has settled to the bottom; then syphon off the clear supernatant liquid into a dark coloured glass bottle, and stopper the bottle tightly. One quart of this stock solution will make 20 gallons of sterilizing solution.

The vacuum line should be flushed out occasionally. Moisture from the milk condenses in the pipes, and sometimes milk may be sucked over, resulting in high bacterial contamination.

Proper Milking

To get all of the milk out of the udder at each milking is the one fundamental objective in milking. Failure to do so is an important cause for premature drying up of cows. Some cows are unknown reasons are not able to let down all of the milk but retain constant quantities to leave a "meaty" udder after milking. One such cow was found to retain eight pounds of milk, the amount ascertained by injection of oxytoxin after each milking. This cow dried up in a few months. Others are erratic in their response to milking, letting down their milk completely at infrequent intervals. In these types there is usually not a good milker-cow relationship. One such cow for instance produced 4,413 pounds of milk in 305 days in the best of three lactations when milked by the regular herd milkers. In all three lactations there was a great variation from milking to milking with a steep slope in the lactation curve. When milked by a milker she liked, the milking to milking variations became small and she produced 7,114 pounds milk in 305 days with other conditions similar to her previous lactations. This is an increase of 61.2 per cent over her best previous performance and which increase is due to the milker who was able to get all of the milk out of the udder.

There are many other reasons why cows are not completely milked out. Undue excitement at milking time, improper stimulation for the let-down of milk, too long an interval between stimulation for let-down and beginning of milking, too slow milking and incomplete withdrawal of the milk that has been let down are all important contributory factors to poor milking. In addition to these there is the consideration of injury to the teat and udder from improper use of the milking force and which injuries are prominent predisposing factors to mastitis. Five rules have been formulated as guides for proper milking as follows:

Rule 1

Avoid excitement of cows either before or during milking. Excitement blocks the response of hormone secretion to the milking stimulus. For the best response the cow must be relaxed and enjoy being milked.

Rule 2

Stimulate let-down about one or two minutes before milking is to begin. The most effective stimulus is a vigorous massage of the teats and lower part of the udder by a cloth taken out of water as hot as the hands will stand-about 125°F. This stimulates both the warmth and touch preceptors in the skin of the teat. Use of a strip cup acts as additional stimulus and opens up the teat meatus. Do not commence milking until the milk has been let down as evidenced by the distention of the teats and lower part of the udder.

Rule 3

In hand milking use the full grasp of the teat. Point compression such as digging in with the finger tips or use of the thumb knuckle is likely to injure the sensitive lining on the inside of the teat as well as produce pain to the cow.

In machine milking operate the milker according to the directions of the manufacturer and see that it is in good working order. Poor mechanical condition of milking machines is responsible for much poor milking. Defects that are often found are vacuum pump in bad repair, vacuum gauge out of order, dirt in the pipeline, leaks in air tubes or stall cocks, and broken or distorted inflations.

Rule 4

Begin stripping as soon as the teat cups crawl upward. This is done by pulling the teat cups downward as far as is possible with dropping off with one hand and successively massaging each quarter with the other hand. Very few cows cannot be completely

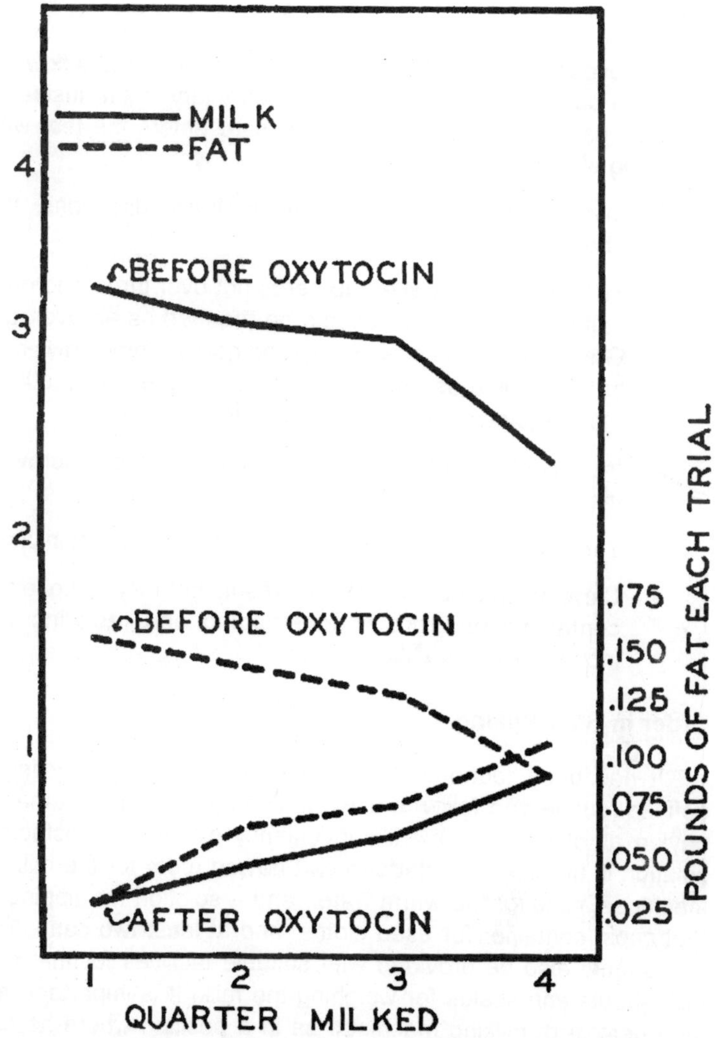

Fig. 22.5: Delayed milking results in incomplete evacuation of the milk. Each quarter was milked in succession. Note decreased amounts of milk and fat with each successive quarter milked and a corresponding increase following the administration of oxytocin.

milked out this way in less time than it takes for hand stripping. In hand milking, milk as rapidly as possible and avoid prolonged stripping.

Rule 5

Remove the milking machine as soon as the milk stops flowing. Failure to do this is responsible for much injury to the inside of the teats as at this point negative pressure enters the teat with damaging effect.

When cows are milked according to these directions, the following benefits are obtained:

1. Time is saved. In average herds not over three and one-half minutes per cow should be required as an average. Great variation in cows should be noted. Some cows milk out in as little as one and one-half minutes while others may require more than ten minutes.
2. Increased milk production will result mainly by improving the persistency.
3. There will be less mastitis because of reduced teat injuries.
4. Cleaner and better milk will result from avoiding extra contamination from hand stripping and reducing the incidence of mastitis.

Order in Stall Milking

It has been found that the best method is to establish a definite routine and follow it closely. The first essential is that of having all of the equipment conveniently placed. A satisfactory solution is the use of a platform cart having room for the milking machines, pails for the warm water, and a solution for dipping of teat cups, container for used cloths, and at least two cans. The cart should also be provided with suitable facilities for the daily milk sheets and scales for weighing the milk. It is important that the operator of milking machines be in a position where he can view the machines at all times and that his time is available for the attention to the milking job and not spent in carrying milk and going for various equipment to be used.

The following routine affords most efficient use of time and effort when a milker operates two units:

1. Wash, stimulate, and strip cup, No. 1 cow.

2. Wash, stimulate, and strip cup, No. 2 cow.
3. Attack milker unit to No. 1.
4. Attach milker unit to No. 2.
5. Wash, stimulate, and strip cup, No. 3.
6. Strip No. 1.
7. Attach unit to No. 3.
8. Wash, and stimulate, No. 4.
9. Strip No. 2.
10. Attach unit to No. 4, etc.

This routine requires a stall cock for each stall and a transfer pail be used. By use of a transfer pail the milking machine head is transferred to the empty pail while a cover is placed over the one containing the milk. The machine can thus be attached to the next cow without loss of time and the milk cared for later. Two units is the most that any operator can use efficiently. Many operators should use only one unit.

23

Efficiency and Cost of Milk Production

Determining the cost of producing milk is one of the important and at the same time one of the difficult problems connected with dairy farming. The interrelationship between the dairy and the other farm enterprises is such that it becomes difficult to separate the charges that should be made against the dairy from those that should be made against other farm operations. The customary method of expressing as profit the income from the sales of milk and butterfat less the cost of feed consumed, is inaccurate; and it frequently distorts the picture of profits from the dairy cow. Under certain conditions cows with a relatively low income above feed costs may have a lower cost of milk produced than cows with larger returns over feed costs.

The cost of producing milk or butterfat varies greatly from time to time with different farm conditions. Average figures have been worked out and will be presented later in this discussion. Such figures serve only as a guide and cannot be used indiscriminately in arriving at milk production costs. The general factors entering into the cost of producing milk hold true almost everywhere. A consideration of these factors is important in the proper approach to the problem of calculating the cost of production. The costs may be distributed under the following heads:

1. Cost of feed
2. Cost of labour
3. Cost of herd sire
4. Investment
5. Depreciation
6. Miscellaneous costs

In order to get at the net cost of producing milk, all the costs must be considered, and credit must be given for the calf and the manure.

Feed cost

Feed constitutes, in the main, the largest single item of expense in producing milk. It is also one of the most variable items in cost, depending upon the kinds of feed used, the market condition, and the utilization by the cow. The feed cost varies from as low as 50 per cent to as high as 75 per cent of the total cost of producing milk.

Coefficient of Efficiency, and fat-corrected milk

One of the most important factors in lowering the cost of milk production is the efficiency of the cow in returning nutrients of the feed consumed in the milk she produces. The percentage of the digestible nutrients of the feed returned in the milk is known as the Coefficient of Efficiency. A formula for calculating the Coefficient of Efficiency has been devised by researchers. The milk first is converted into an equivalent of 4 per cent milk, known as fat-corrected milk (F.C.M.). The formula is:

$$\text{F.C.M.} = .4 \times \text{yearly milk production} + 15 \times \text{yearly fat production}$$

One pound of fat-corrected milk contains .172 pounds of digestible nutrients and requires, according to the Haecker Standard, .327 pounds of the total digestible nutrients in the feed. One pound of animal live weight requires 2.893 pounds of total digestible nutrients for maintenance for one year. The formula for the Coefficient of Efficiency (C.E.) is developed as follows:

$$100\frac{.172\times(F.C.M.)}{2.893W+.327\times(F.C.M.)}$$

Dividing by .327 and transposing:

$$(C.E.) = 52.6\frac{(F.C.M.)}{(F.C.M.)+8.847W}$$

It is evident that increase in production enlarges and increase in weight decreases the Coefficient of Efficiency. A cow weighing 913 pounds and producing 6,657 pounds of F.C.M. has the same C.E. as a 1,021 pound cow producing 7,458 pounds F.C.M. Each one has a C.E. of 23.8. A 1,200 pound cow producing 6,657 pounds of F.C.M. has a C.E. of 20.3, as compared to a C.E. of 23.8 for a 913 pound cow producing the same amount of milk. When the 1,200 pound cow produces 15,000 pounds of F.C.M. her C.E. becomes 30.8, or the milk produced contains 30.8 per cent of the total digestible nutrients in the feed consumed.

It is evident that the feed cost per unit of milk decreases with the increased production of the cows, provided that the additional feed required to produce the larger amounts of milk is not too expensive. When roughages are much lower in price than concentrates, a condition may exist where lower milk production secured on roughage alone costs less than higher production on rations where a larger proportion of the ration consists of concentrates. The United States Department of Agriculture observed that for conditions existing in Montana, alfalfa, as the sole ration for dairy cows, produced only 70 per cent as much milk as was produced with a liberal grain allowance, but at a lower cost. The addition of a limited amount of grain made the most economical production of milk and butterfat. The large number of studies of the relationship between costs and levels of production will be used to further illustrate this relationship. Results of studies in Illinois showing a steady decrease in the nutrients required to produce one pound of butterfat with increases in annual production are reproduced in Fig 23.1. Cows producing 100 pounds of butterfat annually required approximately 23 pounds of digestible nutrients per pound of butterfat, while cows producing 500 pounds of fat annually required but ten pounds of digestible nutrients per pound of fat.

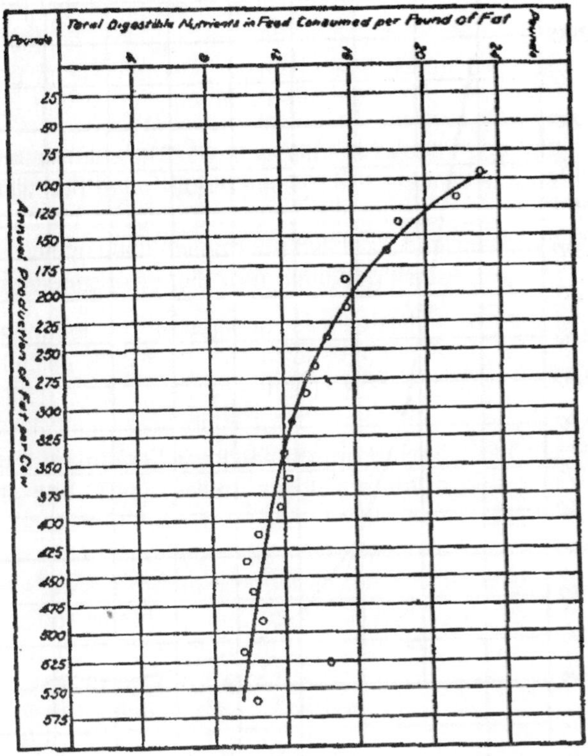

Fig. 23.1: Showing the decrease in pounds of digestible nutrients required per pound of butterfat with increasing annual milk production.

The extensive studies of Dairy Herd Testing Association reports made by McDowell furnish further evidence of lowered feed cost per unit of milk or butterfat with increasing production. The relationship between the annual milk production and the feed cost per 100 pounds of milk is shown in Fig. 23.2. It is to be noted that in the lower production range each increment in milk production is accompanied by a large decrease in feed cost per 100 pounds of milk. The advantages from each increment in production become less until 9,000 pounds is reached, when further increases in production do not decrease costs per unit of milk.

When very high producing cows are fed heavily upon high priced concentrates, milk production is usually made at increased

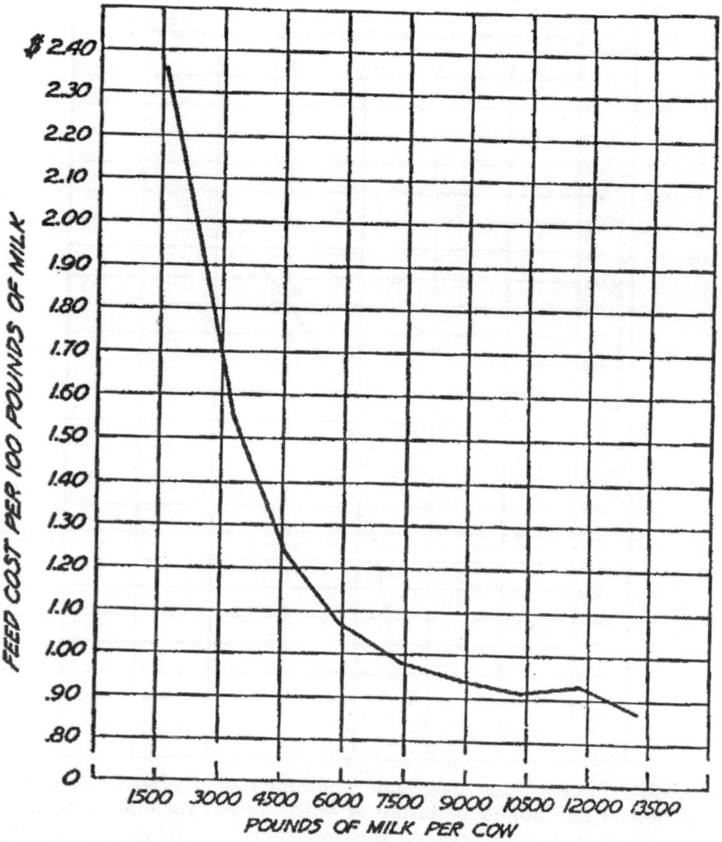

Fig. 23.2: Showing the decrease in the cost of 100 pounds of milk with increasing annual milk yields.

feed costs. Besides the high cost of the concentrates used under these conditions an excess of nutrients are fed beyond those required for maintenance and production.

It is apparent that when each additional unit is produced at increasing cost, the law of diminishing returns functions in the production of milk. At exactly what point this starts is not known as it varies for different conditions. In Fig. 23.2 it is apparent that feed costs per 100 pounds of milk are not materially reduced after a yearly production of 8,000 pounds of milk is reached. Other than feed costs also increase for higher production.

Amount of Feed Required to Produce Milk

The amount of feed required to produce 100 pounds of milk varies widely with the size of the cow, the amount of milk she produces, and the kind of feed she is given. A 1,000 pound cow needs at least 2,600 pounds of total digestible nutrients annually for maintenance. This is equivalent to approximately 5,200 pounds of hay. For each 1,000 pounds produced, an additional 335 pounds of total digestible nutrients are required. This amount represents about 670 pounds of hay or 450 pounds of good concentrate mixture. Table 23.1 shows the amount of hay and the concentrates required for varying production levels of a 1,000 pound cow producing 4 per cent fat milk.

Table 23.1: Amounts of hay and concentrates required to produce 100 pounds of milk at various levels of production

Annual milk production	Feed required per year		Feed per 100 pounds of milk	
	Hay	Concentrates	Hay	Concentrates
Pounds	Pounds	Pounds	Pounds	Pounds
1,000	5,870	-	587	-
3,000	7,210	-	260	-
5,000	7,210	900	144	12.0
7,000	7,210	1,800	103	25.7
10,000	7,210	3,150	72	31.5
15,000	5,870	6,300	39	42.0

These figures are calculated from the requirements according to the revised Haecker Feeding Standard. Silage may replace varying amounts of hay provided that three pounds of silage are supplied for each pound of hay replaced. If good pasture is supplied, it may replace as much as 40 per cent of the feed in the North and up to 75 per cent in the South.

Labour costs

Labour represents the next largest single item of expense in producing milk. Labour costs vary greatly, depending upon the production level of the cows, the cost of the efficiency of the labour, and the conveniences for work. On an average, labour represents about 20 per cent of the total cost of producing milk. The largest single item of labour is represented by milking. Researcher reports that milking requires 53.6 per cent of all labour incident to producing milk. This item can be reduced 50 per cent or more by the use of milking machines, although it is partially compensated for by increased investment and depreciation of the milking machine; and one must remember that increased power costs more for operation.

Another researcher found that 133.9 hours of labour are required per cow a year when the milking is done by hand, and 81.5 hours when the milking is done by machine. In a study of cost of milk production in Maine, he found that with larger herds labour is more efficient. He found that 209 hours of labour were required for each cow per year in smaller herds, and 163 hours per cow in larger herds. He also reports an increase in the amount of labour required for high producing cows over poorer cows, but smaller labour costs are required per 100 pounds of milk for the former. The annual cost of labour per cow producing 5,000 to 6,000 pounds of milk was $40.00, while the cost per cow producing over 9,000 pounds of milk was $53.00. The labour cost per 100 pounds of milk was $.71 for the former and $.50 for the latter.

The returns from the dairy may be expressed in returns per hour for labour. Researcher, studying costs for producing butterfat in Minnesota, found a good correlation between the return per hour of labour and the production level of the cows milked. After deducting all expenses and crediting all income, he found the returns for labour varied from 7 cents to 77 cents per hour.

Attention is called to the fact that more labour is required to produce milk for the market than to produce butterfat as cream. More time is required for the care of milk than for the separation; the extra precautions that must be taken in producing high quality market milk requires more labour than does the production of cream to be sold as butterfat.

Cost of the Herd Sire

The cost of keeping the herd sire is a considerable item of expense. The cost of keeping the herd sire is subject to the same variations due to the same causes as the cost of maintaining milking cows. It is obvious that the sire cost per cow or per 100 pounds of milk decreases with increased herd size.

Interest on Investment and Depreciation

Two charges that must be made if actual costs of milk production are to be determined are interest on the investment and depreciation. Dairy farming requires rather large investments in building, yards, equipment, and cattle, for which the going rate of interest and a fair depreciation should be charged. The charges to be made for these items per cow or per unit of milk depend upon the amount of the investment for the interest charge, and the type of buildings, equipment, and cattle for depreciation charges.

Buildings and Yards

The annual charges against the dairy for buildings include interest, depreciation and repairs, and insurance and taxes. The annual charge per cow for these items vary from as low as $1.00 when cheap sheds are used, up to more than $50.00 per cow, when expensive barns are used. A fair average investment in buildings is between $60.00 and $100.00 per cow in market milk-producing areas of the North, and from $40.00 to $75.00 in butter-producing areas. The interest amounts to about one-half of the total annual building charges.

Equipment

Equipment, which consists of such items as drinking cups, salt cups, litter carriers, milking machines, cans, pails, milk cooling equipment, washing equipment, etc., carries the same interest charges as buildings do, but the depreciation and repair charges are greater; they usually average about 10 per cent annually. The charges per cow for these items vary with the size of the herd and the amount of equipment used. In Maine where cows were milked by hand the annual charge was 68 cents per cow; when milking machines were used, the charge per cow was $2.63.

The Cows

Since cows are introduced into the milking herd either when they are purchased or when they are raised on the farm, they should be inventoried at cost. Annual interest charges should be based upon the inventory values. Cows are sold from the herd as beef when their usefulness is over, and as surplus stock for milk production in some other herd. In addition, 1 to 2 per cent of the cows die while in the herd. Cows sold for beef as a rule bring less than costs; this, together with losses from death, constitutes depreciation. It is difficult to establish actual depreciation for any one year as market values of animals sold for beef vary greatly from year to year.

While the interest charges vary proportionately with the inventory value of cows, the depreciation charges increase more rapidly with increases in the original cost of cows. There is but little relationship between the original cost of a diary cow and the sales value for beef. This is particularly true of purebred cows, where the original price bears no relationship to the beef values.

The most recent reports show an annual depreciation per cow in one area of $9.75, or 13 per cent of the average value per cow. In another area the average depreciation was $2.81, or 5 per cent of the average value per cow. In another comparison of grades and purebreds the depreciations were $5.00 and $11.00 respectively. The annual depreciation for purebred cows may be very high. A cow costing $500 may be sold for $50, after being in the herd for five years; since five years is the average productive life of a cow, this cow would carry an annual depreciation of $90.

Miscellaneous Costs

In addition to the cost items previously discussed there are a number of miscellaneous expenses, such as the costs of water, light, power, bedding, insurance, taxes on the cattle, testing, veterinary services, and various supplies. The cost of these items vary from a few dollars to $15 per cow. Representative figures would run from $5 to $10 per cow.

Credits other than Milk and Butterfat

After deducting all the items of expense that have been mentioned, there are certain credits that must be made before the cost of either milk or butterfat can be ascertained. Manure, calves, hides from cows that die, and, when butterfat is sold, skim milk are items that have values. From eight to twelve tons of manure and about .9 calf can be expected from each cow annually. Under normal price conditions these will have values of from $20 to $25. When butterfat is sold, the skim milk has feed value ranging from 15 cents to 30 cents per 100 pounds.

Cost of Milk Production Formulas

A number of formulas have been advanced that express the requirements for producing 100 pounds of milk in terms of feed and labour, together with a correction factor in some cases. The requirements of these formulas were arrived at from survey studies of the cost of producing milk and represent average figures. They do not, therefore, apply necessarily to any one herd. Low producing herds will find larger and high producing herds smaller requirements than those expressed in these formulas. The proportion of concentrates to roughages is also subject to great variation. In some cases hay only is fed; in others most of the nutrients come from concentrates.

The two most commonly used formulas are Warren's and Pearson's. Warren's formula for the requirements to produce 100 pounds of milk is as follows:

Concentrates	33.8 pounds
Hay	43.3 pounds
Other roughage	10.8 pounds
Silage	100.5 pounds
Labour	3.0 hours

Add 25 per cent for overhead.

By applying the prevailing prices for the various items the cost of producing 100 pounds of milk may be ascertained by this formula.

Pearson's formula is as follows:

Concentrates	44.0 pounds
Hay	50.0 pounds
Other roughage	39.0 pounds
Silage	188.0 pounds
Labour	2.42 hours

Attention is called to the wide differences in the requirements of these two formulas. The Pearson formula requires more of each of the feeds and less labour. To compensate for the higher feed requirements of the Pearson formula no correction factor for overhead is used.

Seasonal Variation in Cost of Milk Production

The cost of producing milk varies with the use of pasture. The variations in the cost of producing 100 pounds of milk are illustrated in the table above, taken from studies in Illinois.3 For June the cost of milk production is only 55.3 per cent as high as for December. With the decline in the amount of pasture the cost increases because of lowered milk production and increased use of pasture supplements.

The chief reason for low cost of milk production during the spring, summer, and early fall is the much lower cost of feed when secured from pasture. Other costs are essentially the same for all months of the year except labour. Indiana studies revealed labour requirements for the summer as being about 20 per cent less than for the winter.

Seasonal variation in the cost of producing 100 pounds of milk

Month	Cost	Per cent of high month
November	$2.01	96.6
December	2.08	100.0
January	2.00	96.1
February	2.08	100.0
March	1.93	92.8
April	1.76	84.2
May	1.26	60.6
June	1.15	55.3
July	1.36	65.4
August	1.66	79.8
September	1.66	79.8
October	1.54	74.0
Average	1.73	83.2

Other Considerations

While it is important to ascertain the cost of producing milk (and every effort should be put forth or reduce costs) a low margin of income over cost does not necessarily mean that the dairy enterprise is undesirable. When family labour is available and would not otherwise be used, the dairy permits additional farm income even though it be at low wages.

Dairy cattle also make use of crops that are not marketable or would be marketed at lower prices than can be realized if fed. Careful thought should be given to growing the highest yielding crops that can be utilized by the dairy cattle and the formulation of the most economical rations based upon the use of homegrown feeds.

24

Common Feeds: Characteristics and Treatment

Classification of feeds. Feeds are divided into three general groups:

(1) roughages,

(2) concentrates, and

(3) roots.

The roughages are divided into hays, of which there are the subgroups legumes and non-legumes, silage, fodders, and straws. The concentrates are classified in three different ways. On the basis of protein content they are:

(1) high,

(2) medium, and

(3) low protein concentrates.

On the basis of origin they are the cereals and by-products. On the basis of fiber content they are light, heavy, and medium concentrates.

A knowledge of the characteristics and values of the common feedstuffs, together with what constitutes quality in each of them, is essential for intelligent feeding.

ROUGHAGES

Roughage constitutes the basis of the ration for dairy cattle. Without good roughage it becomes difficult to make a satisfactory ration. The proportion of roughage that can be used in the production of milk is largely dependent upon the kind and quality. The quality of roughage is dependent upon the rankness of growth, per cent of the total that is leaves, the way it is cured and stored, and the stage of maturity when it is cut. The highest quality roughage is that which has the finest stems, the greenest colour, the highest proportion of leaves, and is cut in the earliest stages of maturity.

Legume Hays

Legume hays are the most valuable roughages for the dairy herd. Legumes are characterized by a high protein content, which is so essential in the dairy ration; and they are also more palatable than other roughages. Legumes are also high in calcium content; this insures adequate calcium in the ration when they are fed. The effect of the stage of maturity upon the protein content of alfalfa is characteristic for the groups. The average alfalfa hay contains 10.6 per cent digestible protein; if it is cut before bloom, the digestible protein increases to more than 14 per cent - almost a 40 per cent increase. At one-tenth to one-half bloom the protein content is intermediate. When it is in full bloom, the digestible protein drops to below 9 per cent. Crude fiber changes inversely with the protein in the various stages of maturity. Average alfalfa contains 29 per cent crude fiber, while that cut in the prebloom stage contains about 22 per cent. Palatability of the legume hays varies about proportionately with the earliness of cutting.

Of the legumes alfalfa ranks first because of its higher protein content and greater palatability. Next comes lespedeza with about 90 per cent as much protein as alfalfa for comparable qualities, then alsike clover and red clover with 70 to 75 per cent as much. Sweet clover yields more tonnage than other hay crops but makes a rather inferior hay because it is coarse and stemmy. If it is not properly cured sweet clover hay may produce sweet clover disease, which has been discussed previously.

Soybeans, cowpeas, ordinary field peas, and vetch are leguminous plants frequently grown for hay. These rank somewhat lower than alfalfa and clovers for dairy cattle and are mainly to be recommended for hay when other hay crops have failed. The vetchs and field peas may be grown for hay together with oats.

Non-leguminous Hays

Nonleguminous hays are characterized by much lower protein and calcium contents and are less palatable than the legumes. Early cut nonleguminous hays have the same comparative advantages over latter cut hays as have been shown for the legumes. The manner in which they are cured and stored affect their values in the same way as they affect the legumes. High protein supplements are necessary when any of these hays are fed to milking cows.

Timothy hay is the most common nonlegume hay. Average timothy hay contains about 3 per cent digestible protein and 47 per cent total digestible nutrients, and ranks ordinary from the standpoint of palatability. Early cut timothy hay is fairly palatable and somewhat higher in protein, but is still a low protein feed. It is frequently used as a mixture with the clovers and sometimes with alfalfa.

Kentucky bluegrass is very common in the Northern states. It yields less than timothy but is somewhat more palatable, and contains a little more total digestible nutrients and 50 per cent more protein. Bluegrass in the Northern states frequently establishes itself in alfalfa and other perennial hay crops, finally crowding them out.

Prairie or native hay is a variable product consisting of a number of different species of plants which vary with different localities. When cut in the early stages of maturity, it is on the average comparable to timothy hay.

Johnson grass, quack grass, Western wheat grass, Italian rye grass, brome grass, fescues, and other perennial grasses are used for hay. When cut early, they all have the same feeding values as timothy hay.

Reed canary grass or phalaris grass is frequently used for hay. If this is cut early, a hay of fair quality may be produced. Ordinary reed canary grass hay is coarse and lacks in palatability.

Apparently the protein content varies with the soil upon which it is grown, as well as the stage of growth in which it is cut.

A number of nonlegume annuals are used for hay, principally where the regular hay crops fail. All of these compare favourably with timothy hay in composition and palatability. The chief ones in this group are Sudan grass and the millets. Any of the cereal grains may be cut in the immature stage for hay. Oats are most commonly used for this purpose, and when they are cut in the milk or rough stage of the kernel they make a fairly palatable hay with about 5 per cent of digestible protein. Awned cereals should not be used for hay unless cut when very immature, as the awns may penetrate the lining of the mouth and throat and cause festering.

In years of great scarcity of normal roughages, Russian thistles, marsh grass, cattails, and other like plants have been used for feed. All of these are of very low feeding value and unpalatable. They should be used only in emergencies, as profitable cannot be expected from these low-grade roughages.

Fodders

Corn and sorghums grown and cut for forage are known as fodders. They may be cut before ears or heads have developed or after considerable seed development has taken place. If seeds have developed, they must be left on the stalks in order to qualify as fodders. Increase in maturity does not detract from the total feed value of fodders as has been noted with the hays. With maturity the fiber of the stalks increases, but this is compensated for by the transfer of nutrients from the stalks into the seeds. The palatability of the stalks, however, decreases with increased maturity.

The fodders, even when apparently dry, contain two or, more times the moisture found in cured hay. Largely because of this large moisture content, they deteriorate with age and offer problems in storage.

The fodders are not desirable feeds for milking cows; they rank with the nonleugme hays in this respect. When it becomes necessary to feed fodders, high protein concentrates must be added, and more concentrate must be fed than when good quality legumes furnish the roughage portion of the ration. The wastage, when fodders are fed, is much higher than when good hays are fed. The animals pick out the leaves and the more tender part of the stalk and leave the coarser portions.

Stovers

The portion of the plant that remains after the heads of sorghums or the ears of corn have been removed, is known as stover. Stovers are of low feeding value as most of the nutrients of the stalks have passed into the seeds that have been removed. They also rank very low in palatability. A large proportion of the stovers will be refused unless they are ground, finely cut, or shredded. Except under emergency feed conditions, stovers should not be used in the ration of milking cows.

Straws

As the seeds mature the fiber content of the stems is increased, and the protein, carbohydrate, and fat content are decreased, largely because of a transfer of the latter three to the seed. Since the plant has also been exposed to the weather after growth has ceased, leaching has taken place; this, together with the exposure to sunlight, causes a loss in the soluble material and destruction of the vitamins. The straws coming from mature plants from which the seeds have been removed are characterized by high fiber content and low contents of protein, digestible nutrients, vitamins, and minerals. While there are variations in the feeding values of the different straws, as a whole they are of low value and should not be included in the rations of milking cows. The feed value of straws is much less than indicated by the total digestible nutrient content as a large amount of energy is required to masticate and digest them. Wheat straw with 35.7 pounds of total digestible nutrients yields only 10 therms net energy, while timothy hay with 47 pounds of total digestible nutrients yields 43 therms of net energy per 100 pounds of hay.

The straws may be considered in groups according to the plants from which they originate, as follows: cereal, legumes, grass hays, flax, and buckwheat.

Oats, barley, wheat, and rye are the common cereal straws. They rank in feeding value in the order named. Oat straw has the softest and most pliable stem and is more leafy than the others. Sometimes oat straw may have a fairly high feeding value, since a portion of it may be immature second growth. Such straw has increased feed value in direct proportion to the amounts of immature plants present. Barley straw ranks next to oat straw, but the awned varieties may cause injury to the mouth and throat. Wheat and rye straws are so woody and of such low feed values that they should never be fed.

Legume straws contain more protein than the cereal straws, but otherwise are no better. Alfalfa, clover, and lespedeza straws are slightly more nutritive than those from beans, peas, and soybeans. Sweet clover straw is usually coarse and unpalatable but may sometimes be of fair quality.

Grass hay straws, such as timothy, bluegrass, red top, the millets, and phalaris, are of slightly higher values than the cereal straws. They have the same value as hay cut when the plant is mature, as but little nutrient material is removed with the seed except in the case of the millets.

Flax straw has a feed value equal to oat straw. There is some danger of prussic acid poisoning from flax straw containing immature flax seeds.

Buckwheat straw has practically no feed value and may cause digestive trouble.

CONCENTRATES

To no other class of livestock are concentrates so important as to high producing cows. Because of the high energy requirements of the heavy milking cow, it is necessary that a large portion of the ration consist of concentrates. As the capacity for feed intake is limited by the amount of dry matter, it is obvious that concentrates containing more than 50 per cent more digestible nutrients than do roughages make possible much greater nutrient intake. Since the protein requirement of the milking cow is higher than that of any other farm animal, in order to supply the protein needs it becomes necessary to add high protein concentrates to the ration, especially when nonleguminous roughage is fed. The kind of concentrate to select depends upon the needs for completing the requirement of the ration, and also upon the availability of the concentrate. Concentrates may be divided into two groups- those consisting of the whole or ground seeds of plants, and those that are the by-products of various plant and animal products. There are large numbers in each one of the two groups, but only the more common ones will be considered here.

SEEDS OF PLANTS

Corn

Corn is the most commonly used concentrate for dairy cattle. In the corn belt it is the cheapest source of energy, being a heavy yielding crop. Corn ranks first among the grains as a source of energy, having more than 80 per cent total digestible nutrients; and it is also the lowest in protein, with 7.0 per cent digestible protein. In addition to being the most palatable of all feeds, it is also one of the heaviest, and if fed in quantities larger than 5 or 6 pounds daily, it should be mixed with lighter feeds, such as oats or bran. For average milking cows corn may be used satisfactorily as the only concentrate with a good quality of alfalfa hay.

Corn and Cob Meal

When the entire ear of corn is ground, the meal is known as corn and cob meal. The ground cob has no food value; therefore the feed value of corn and cob meal is as much less than that of corn as there is cob in the meal. Because the cob lightens the mixture, corn and cob meal is preferred to ground corn where large amounts are fed. It is also sometimes more convenient to grind the entire ear than to shell the corn before grinding.

Barley

Barley is slightly lower in total digestible nutrients than corn, but it is higher in protein. Feeding trials have shown barley to be about equal to corn for milking cows. Barley is very palatable, although it is not quite so palatable as corn. Like corn, barley is heavy, and when fed in large quantities should be mixed with lighter feeds.

Oats

Oats are excellent for dairy cows but are frequently overrated as a source of energy. On account of the hulls, they contain about 12 per cent less total digestible nutrients than corn. Oats are extremely variable; light weights may be as much as 30 per cent less valuable than normal oats. Oats are highly palatable and may be fed alone in any amount because of their lightness. For the same reason they serve a very useful purpose in lightening the concentrate mixture. Oats may be used as the only concentrate with legume hay for average producing cows.

Wheat

Wheat is used for feed in years of low prices, and frosted and shriveled wheat unsuited for milling purposes is used constantly. Wheat is equal to corn as a feed for cows, but it is less palatable and heavier. It should always be mixed with some lighter feed. The food value is apparently not affected by frost or shriveling.

Rye

Rye has practically the same composition and consequently the same nutritive value as wheat; it contains all the other characteristics, except that it is unpalatable. It is also quite frequently contaminated with ergot, which adds to the lack of palatability, and if present in large quantities may "dry-off" cows.

Sorghums

The sorghums- kaffir, feterita, milo, and others, except the sweet sorghums- rank with corn in composition and feeding value. They are slightly less palatable than corn.

Emmer and Spelt

Emmer and spelt resemble oats in composition, palatability, lightness, and in feed value.

Buckwheat

Buckwheat has a lower nutritive value than oats; it is quite unpalatable, and will cause eruptions on the skin of animals.

Flax Seed

Flax seed, because of its high oil content, contains nearly 100 pounds of total digestible nutrients per 100 pounds, the highest energy value of any natural seed. It is also high in protein. Flax seed is usually too high priced to be used as a feed, but when it is used it is found to be palatable. Flax seed is very laxative, and it is sometimes used for that purpose. It produces a soft butter when fed to milking cows.

Soybeans

Soybeans are increasing in importance as a feed for dairy cows. They have the highest protein content (33 per cent digestible protein) of any natural seeds. While soybeans are fed principally as a source of protein, they are high in total digestible nutrients (86 per cent), exceeding corn in this respect. They are palatable and also heavy in character. The ground beans are likely to turn rancid if kept for any length of time in warm weather.

Cowpeas, Peas, Velvet Beans, and other Leguminous Seeds

Cowpeas, peas, velvet beans, and other leguminous seeds are sometimes fed dairy cattle. They are excellent sources of protein and are quite palatable.

PLANT BY-PRODUCTS

By-products of Corn

Corn is used extensively in the manufacture of corn meal and starch, which gives rise to a number of by-products used for feeding. From the manufacture of starch, corn gluten meal, corn gluten feed, and corn oil meal are secured. From the manufacture of corn meal hominy feed is a by-product.

Corn Gluten Meal

Corn gluten meal, which consists chiefly of corn gluten, contains about 43 per cent of protein and is, therefore, one of the high protein concentrates. It is palatable, but a heavy feed.

Corn Gluten Feed

Corn gluten feed differs from gluten meal in that besides the corn gluten, it also contains the corn barn plus some other portions of the corn kernel. It contains only about 26 per cent of protein. Like corn gluten meal it is an excellent source of protein.

Corn Germ Oil Meal

Corn germ oil meal is the residue of the corn germ after the oil has been expressed. It differs from other oil meals in having a much lower protein content.

Hominy Feed

Hominy feed is equal to corn in feed value; it has about the same composition, and it is somewhat lighter than corn.

By-products of Wheat

In the milling of wheat for flour more than 25 per cent of the total weight of the wheat goes into by-products.

Wheat Bran

Wheat bran, from the outer coatings of the wheat kernel, is one of the most commonly used dairy feeds. Wheat bran contains about 12 pounds of digestible protein and 70 pounds of total digestible nutrients per 100 pounds. It is fairly palatable, mildly laxative, and bulky. The latter makes it a valuable feed in lightening up heavy concentrate mixtures. Wheat bran is also one of the best sources of phosphorus. Wheat bran comes in two forms: pure wheat bran, and standard wheat bran. The standard wheat bran contains the finely ground screenings of the wheat. The feed value of the two is equal.

Standard Wheat Middlings

Standard wheat middlings, or shorts, consist of finer particles than bran and include the wheat germs. Standard wheat middlings are slightly higher in both protein and total digestible nutrient content than bran but are not so desirable as barn for feeding dairy cattle. Because of the finer particles and some flour, they are heavy and have a tendency to form into a sticky mass when wetted.

Wheat Germ Meal

Wheat germ meal has recently assumed some importance as a feed. Besides being a good source of protein, wheat germ meal is a good source of vitamin E.

By-products of barley

The chief by-products of barley are brewers' grains and malt sprouts.

Brewers' Grains

Brewers' grains are fed both wet and dried. Dried brewers' grains contain about 23 per cent of digestible protein and 65 per cent of total digestible nutrients. They lack somewhat in palatability and should be mixed with more palatable feeds. Because of their bulkiness, they may be used in place of oats or bran in the ration.

Wet Brewers' Grains

Wet brewers' grains vary greatly in water content; the dry matter is the same as for dried brewers' grains. Care must be taken in warm weather that wet brewers' grains are not permitted to decompose in the mangers as odors are produced that may affect the milk. Up to 30 to 35 pounds of wet brewers' grains may be fed to milking cows daily.

By-products of oats

In the manufacture of oatmeal the hulls and the oats shorts are removed, and these form what is called oat feed. This material has approximately the feed value of timothy hay.

Cottonseed by-products

The two chief by-products of the cottonseed are the meals and the hulls. After the cottonseed oil is expressed, the cottonseed residue is graded upon the basis of the protein content, which varies from 25 to 43 or more per cent. The difference in protein content is largely due to variations in the amount of hulls present, as the hulls contain only about 2 per cent of protein. When the total protein is below 36 per cent, the product is known as cottonseed feed. When all the hulls are included, the protein content is 25 to 30 per cent and the product is known as whole pressed cottonseed. The hulls have but little feed value.

Cottonseed meal is one of the cheapest and most widely used sources of protein supplement in the ration. Outside of the cotton territory the higher protein grades are usually the cheaper sources of protein. Cottonseed meal has gained the reputation of being poisonous to cattle. This has been shown not to be the case. Animals restricted to cottonseed meal and hulls have suffered from deficiency diseases due to insufficient vitamin A, but when good roughage is fed in connection with cottonseed meal, there is no danger from injury even where ten or more pounds are fed daily. Cottonseed meal likewise has been shown not to be constipating, as some people have claimed.

Flax seed by-products

Linseed oil meal, the residue left when oil is extracted from the flax seed, varies from below 30 per cent to over 37 per cent of protein; it should always be purchased upon the basis of its protein content. In the making of the new process oil meal the oil is extracted with solvents, and therefore the meal contains less oil and more protein than in the "old process," where the oil is expressed by pressure. Linseed oil meals, particularly the old process meals, are laxative, and are especially valuable where nonlaxative feeds are fed. Because of its popularity, protein is usually higher priced in linseed oil meal than in cottonseed meal.

Soybean and peanut oil meal

Soybean oil meal is the residue left when oil is extracted from the soybean. Soybean oil meal contains from 40 to 48 per cent protein, and is the highest protein plant product. The meal is palatable and the protein is of high quality.

Peanut oil meal is of about the same composition as soybean oil meal.

Screenings

Screenings are so variable in composition and values that only the most general statements can be made. Screenings should always be bought on the basis of the chemical composition, and should never be bought if they contain noxious weed seeds or seeds that produce off flavours in the milk. Flax screenings or other cereal screenings may contain a large proportion of broken seeds together with some weed seeds of high feed value.

Roots, Tubers, Pumpkins, and Molasses

Roots, tubers, and pumpkins may be considered as watered concentrates on a dry matter basis. They analyze about the same as low protein concentrates. Mangles, rutabagas, stock carrots, beets, and pumpkins contain only about 10 per cent dry matter. Ten pounds of these may, therefore, take the place of one pound of grain. These very succulent feeds are greatly valued by feeders for high producing cows. Potatoes contain about twice the amount of dry matter as roots and pumpkins. They are not relished by cattle as well as are roots. Roots may be fed up to 60 or more pounds per day and potatoes up to 40 or 50 pounds. Turnips and rutabagas should be fed immediately after milking to avoid tainting the milk.

Beet Pulp

Beet pulp, the dried residue of the sugar beet after extraction of the sugar, is valued highly by feeders of milking cows. It has about 10 per cent less total digestible nutrients than corn. Most people prefer to feed the dried beet pulp after it has been resoaked, with about four pounds of water to one pound of the dried pulp. Dried beet pulp may, however, be mixed with the concentrate mixture without soaking to give equally good results. Beet pulp with molasses has slightly higher feeding value than without molasses.

Molasses

There are two kinds of molasses used in the feeding of livestock: cane molasses, a by-product from the making of cane sugar; and beet molasses, a by-product from the making of beet sugar. Both of these have essentially the same feed value, about 70 per cent of that for corn. The chief difference between the two is that beet molasses is much more laxative because of its salt content and must be fed more carefully than cane molasses. Cows should be gradually accustomed to beet molasses, and should never be fed more than three pounds per day.

The greatest value of molasses is in its appetizing effect. It is probably the most palatable feed for cattle; and because of its liquid nature, it may be used in improving the palatability of many otherwise unpalatable feeds. Mixed with two or three parts of water to improve the palatability and increase its consumption, it may be sprinkled over roughage in the manger.

ANIMAL BY-PRODUCTS

Tankage and meat scraps

Tankage and meat scraps may be fed as a source of protein. However, these are not palatable and many cows will refuse mixtures containing but small amounts of these two high protein concentrates.

Fishmeal

Fishmeal has been used as a protein supplement in dairy cattle rations with fair success. Like tankage and meat scraps, it is not palatable, and in some cases, may reduce the fat content of the milk. It is an excellent source of both calcium and phosphorus.

Skim milk

Skim milk is an excellent source of protein, and some energy, although not very much. On a dry matter basis skim milk contains 35 per cent of digestible protein and 86 per cent of total digestible nutrients. Ten pounds of skim milk equals one pound of dry matter. One gallon of skim milk has been found equal to one pound of linseed oil meal for milk production. At first cows do not like skim milk. It may be fed by mixing it into the grain mixture to form a slop.

VARIOUS TREATMENTS OF FEEDS

Ensiling

One of the oldest treatments of feed to preserve and improve the feeding value is that of ensiling, or preserving green fodders in pits. In the United States the beginning of silage making goes back to 1875, when the first silo was constructed in Michigan. Since that time the interest in silos and silage has grown until about a million silos have been constructed.

Silage Fermentation

Silage is made from green material through natural fermentation or by acid preservation.

In natural fermentation bacteria, in the absence of air, break down the sugars of the green plant material principally into lactic and acetic acids, with traces of other acids and some alcohols. The acid so developed prevents putrefactive bacteria from acting and decomposing the material. In the fermentation process some of the dry matter is lost, being converted into carbon dioxide and water. The exact amounts lost by this action are not known, but probably the losses due to the silage processes do not exceed 10 per cent of the total dry matter.

Acid Preservation of Silage

Acid preservation of silage: the A.I.V. Process. Some plants, such as grasses and legumes, do not contain enough sugar for fermentation of the necessary amount of acid needed for preservation. As a result attempts a.. ensiling legumes and grasses frequently terminate in failure. Recently a method has been developed and patented by Virtanen of Finland in which a mixture of hydrochloric and sulphuric acid is added to the green material as it is put into the silo, to bring the acidity to that caused by normal fermentation. This process is known as the A.I.V. Process. The proponents for this method claim that in addition to enabling the making of silage with surety from low sugar plants, it reduces the losses from fermentation to practically nothing. Further, it has been shown that the acid preservation of the green material preserves the carotene much better than can be done through normal fermentation or dry curing of material.

The Minnesota Station has shown that the addition of phosphoric acid accomplishes the same result as the A.I.V. acids, and in addition adds phosphorus, which may be needed both as a nutrient and fertilizer. Special equipment for adding the acid must be used with both of these methods. Skilled attention is also needed, that the right amounts of acids are added.

Preservation by addition of molasses or sugar.

Several experiment stations have reported successes in preserving the material as silage by adding molasses or sugar solutions as the material is put into the silo. By artificially increasing the sugar content of the low sugar material enough acid is formed for preservation of the silage. From 40 to 60 pounds of molasses per ton of green legumes or grasses has been found adequate. Recent reports indicate that the addition of molasses preserves the carotene nearly as well as the A.I.V. Process. Molasses has the advantage over the inorganic acids in that it is easier to handle, and if too much is added, no harm is done; whereas if too much inorganic acid is added, the material may be ruined for feed.

The molasses may be diluted with one or two parts of water and the solution run into the silage cutter from an elevated barrel.

Advantages of Silage

While a dozen or more advantages may be listed for silage the most important ones are as follows:

1. The real advantage of a silo on a livestock farm is that it enables the saving of feed much of which would otherwise be wasted or would deteriorate in value. The silo enables the saving of feed in at least four different ways:

   a. While the loss of dry matter in the silo amounts to about 10 per cent, much greater losses are experienced in curing and storing such crops as corn, sorghums, and sunflowers. The Colorado Station reported 43 per cent losses in dry matter of corn left in small shocks. Eckles also found a loss of 43 per cent in dry matter for corn left in the field for 134 days.

b. The silo makes possible the saving of legume and other hay crops during rainy seasons, when attempts to make hay would result in a forage of decided inferior quality.

c. It makes possible the use of plants that would otherwise not be eaten, such as weeds. When weeds of the cornfield are put into the silo, the otherwise unpalatable weeds may be eaten, and the seeds are destroyed.

d. Wastes in refused feeds are reduced or eliminated. When, for example, dry corn fodder is fed, from 15 to 34 per cent of the total weights are refused by cattle, while practically nothing is refused when corn silage is fed.

In the corn belt corn yields the largest amount of total digestible nutrients, and in order to make efficient use of the crop, it must be ensiled. In mature corn 60 to 70 per cent of the nutrients are in the ears and from 30 to 40 per cent in the stalks. By ensiling the while crop 30 to 40 per cent more nutrients are made available for livestock than when only the corn grain is used.

2. Less storage space is needed for storing a given amount of dry matter in silage than in the dried form. Approximately 2.5 times as much dry matter can be stored in the same space in the form of silage as when stored in the dry form.

3. Silage furnishes the cheapest and most satisfactory source of succulent feed.

4. Silage may be kept indefinitely without any deterioration, while roughages stored in the dry form continue to deteriorate with the length of time stored.

5. By ensiling, the crop is removed from the soil immediately, leaving the soil free to be worked.

Disadvantages of Silage

While on most farms silage is an economical feed, there are conditions under which it becomes too expensive to warrant use. Recent work has shown that when a good quality of legume hay is fed, silage is not essential for optimum milk production. Therefore, where a greater yield of alfalfa can be secured than of corn or sorghums and where it is not necessary to grow the latter, silage is not to be advised except in so far as it may be advisable to place legumes in the silo. The large amount of expensive equipment needed, together with the large amount of labour required for filling the silo, frequently brings the cost of silage above that of an equal amount of dry matter in hay. In Iowa the cost on a dry matter basis is reported to be about the same for corn silage and alfalfa hay. In Wisconsin, Minnesota, and New York the costs of silage are reported as being considerably higher than for equal dry matter in alfalfa hay.

The belief that silage is an essential feed for high milk production has kept a number of dairymen in the Northern states growing corn for silage. In many places it is uneconomical because corn yields are too low in comparison with clovers or alfalfa.

Requirements for Good Silage

The first requirement for making good silage is good airtight silo. Air leaking through the walls or doors permits spoilage of silage by molds and bacteria. Before the silo if filled, all cracks in the walls should be stopped, to avoid extensive losses from spoilage. The next most important factor is the quality of the material with which the silo is filled. The silage process does not increase the digestibility of the material; it merely preserves the nutrients already present. It is, therefore, important that the materials to be ensiled contain the optimum amount of nutrients. For crops with large seed development the more nearly mature they are when ensiled, the greater will be the yield and the higher the digestible nutrients. When legumes and grasses are ensiled, the same stage of maturity that is best for hay making will produce the best silage.

Another important factor in the making of good silage is the water content of the material. If the silage is too dry, water must be added or the material will not pack sufficiently to prevent spoilage from molds and other microorganisms. If the silage is too watery, the material should be permitted to partially dry out before being ensiled or too sour silage is likely to be produced.

Another very important consideration is that the material to be ensiled must contain sufficient sugar for proper fermentation, or spoilage will result from putrefaction. Corn, sorghums, and sunflowers always have enough sugars, but many other crops require the addition of sugar in some form, such as molasses, or the addition of the proper amounts of some acid to insure perfect keeping.

Value of Silage in the Ration

The value of silage in the ration of milking cows has been somewhat overemphasized. The claims that succulence contributed materially to the economic production of milk and that silage has values in addition to its digestible nutrient content are not warranted by facts. The value of silage is limited to its digestible nutrient content, plus the benefits of a lightly laxative effect when fed with some rations. The Connecticut and Minnesota Stations have shown that silage fed in tests did not increase milk production, and increased costs per 100 pounds of milk.

Definite experimental evidence is lacking as to whether silage stimulates the appetite; it is also not known whether more nutrients are consumed in roughage when silage forms part of the ration than when only dry roughage is fed. When hays of low quality are fed, the addition of silage increases the amount of dry matter consumed because of its greater palatability. When the hays fed are of good quality, it is questionable whether the addition of silage will increase the consumption of dry matter in the total roughage.

Silages made from anything but legumes are low in their protein content, and more high protein concentrates must be fed cows receiving such silage as part of the ration than when a legume hay is the only roughage fed.

Silage may be fed as a supplement to pastures during the summer. Unless the silage is made from legumes, a protein concentrate must be supplemented, particularly when the pasture grasses are mature and dried up.

Corn Silage

By far the majority of silage used is made from corn. The feeding value of corn silage depends upon the stage of maturity when cut. Well matured corn will make a silage containing over 20 per cent of total digestible nutrients, whereas silage made from immature corn with no ear formation may contain as little as 12 per cent total digestible nutrients. Average corn silage contains about 17 per cent total digestible nutrients, or is about one-third the value of hay. Being low in protein, corn silage should be compared with the grass hays: three tons of average corn silage equal one ton of hay in feed value. Corn silage is the most palatable of the silages, cows having consumed over 90 pounds daily.

Dried corn fodder or stover may be ensiled. If adequate water is added, normal fermentation will take place and a fairly normal silage will result. Such silage is a little less palatable than that made from green material. The fodder silage has a feed value equal to normal corn silage. The stover silage has a much lower feed value.

Sorghum Silage

Next to corn, sorghums are the most important silage crops. The grain sorghums- kaffir, milo, feterita, etc.- are similar to corn in composition and produce silage equal in value to corn. The sweet sorghums will make silage of good quality if they are mature when ensiled. Such silage has about 90 per cent the value of good corn silage. If the sweet sorghums are immature when ensiled, a sour, less palatable silage results.

Silages from Grasses and Legumes

In the past it has been held that where weather conditions are favourable for the making of good hay, there is no advantage in putting up grasses and legumes in the form of silage. It was also generally believed that not as much dry matter would be consumed in silage as in the well-cured hay. Recent experiments with legumes cut at the same time, one part being ensiled and the other put up as hay, showed that more digestible protein and total nutrients were obtained from the silage than from the well-cured hay. Significantly more milk with a higher vitamin A and carotene content was also obtained from the silage. The silage was found to be at least as palatable as the hay and in some cases more palatable. There was no significant difference in the cost of the two methods. These results indicate that it may be well to put up more hay crops as silage, particularly where difficulty is experienced in proper curing. By ensiling the hay crops, cutting can be done irrespective of the weather and therefore before the plant becomes too mature; curing is difficult in many places when these crops are put up in the form of hay.

It has long been recognized that the best way to salvage legumes with coarse stems and plants that are too mature is to make them up as silage. Sweet clover and soybeans, because of woody stems, are most commonly ensiled.

Grasses and legumes have low sugar contents and, consequently, acid is formed slowly in the silage making. This gives rise to decompositions that produce stout, undesirable odors under most conditions. These odors do not detract from the palatability but are objectionable from the human point of view. By wilting the material so that not over 70 per cent and not less than 60 per cent of moisture is present, excellent grass and legume silage can be made without any preservatives being used. Soybeans and peas that have seed formed in the pod have enough sugar for normal fermentation.

When the fresh material is placed in the silo, the development of offensive odors may be prevented by the addition of either sugar or acid. The most common sugar used is molasses, of which 40 to 60 pounds diluted and mixed with the fresh cut material will develop the preserving acids in sufficient quantities to produce pleasantly smelling silage. About 25 pounds of powdered whey has proven satisfactory but more difficult to properly incorporate in the freshly cut material. Acids may be added directly to the material. Hydrochloric and sulfuric acid mixtures are commonly used in Northern Europe, where the technique is known as the A.I.V. process after A.I. Virtanen, its developer. Acids should be added to bring the pH value down to about 4.0. Different materials will require different amounts of the acid. A fair amount will be about 15 gallons of a 2-normal solution of equal parts of the two acids per ton of green material. Usually linae is added to the silage when fed to counteract the effects of the acid. These acids are detrimental to equipment and clothing. Phosphoric acid is used by some with satisfactory results. This acid not only preserves the silage but is also a good source of phosphorus in the ration and for the soil where additional amounts of this element is needed.

Legume silages will have similar T.D.N. values to corn silage with comparable amounts of moisture. The protein content, however, will be much higher. For grass silage, the T.D.N. values are similar to legumes but the protein values will vary with the stage of maturity when cut. Young immature grass silage may have up to 14 per cent protein on a dry matter basis while mature hays may be as low as 4 per cent.

Pea vine silage has about the same feeding value as alfalfa silage. The odor of this material is often offensive but not harmful to cattle nor will it flavour the milk from feeding. Sweet clover silage may produce the sweet clover disease from the same substances that are sometimes produced in the sweet clover hay and which prevents the blood from clotting.

Sunflower Silage

In cooler climates sunflowers yield much more nutrients than corn and are frequently used for silage. Sunflower silage has only about 70 per cent of the feeding value of good corn silage and is rather unpalatable. Where corn can be grown successfully, sunflowers should be used for silage.

Beet top silage

Beet tops may be preserved in piles, trench silos, or regular silos to form a fair silage with feeding values of approximately 65 per cent of that of corn silage. Beet tops are decidedly laxative and contain oxalic acid. Although they are palatable, because of these facts not more than 30 to 35 pounds should be fed daily.

Other fermenting or predigesting processes

At various times patented processes for fermenting or predigesting feeds have appeared upon the market. Claims are made by the promoters that these processes increase the digestibility of roughages. Some even claim that roughages are converted into concentrates. The process consists of placing the "ferment" with the chopped roughage into a tank, adding water, and allowing the mass to ferment.

Various experiments have shown that no value is added to the feed by any of these processes. In many cases there are actual losses of nutrients by the "process."

GRINDING, CUTTING, COOKING, SOAKING

Grinding Grain

It is well known that cattle do not masticate food thoroughly when eating. Hard seeds are therefore swallowed without being chewed, and since, unlike the roughages, they are not regurgitated and rechewed, they pass on through the digestive tract. On account of their hardness, seeds like corn, barley, and oats are not sufficiently acted upon by the digestive juices to be digested, and a large potion passes through undigested. The Purdue Station found that from 20 to 25 per cent of the oats and 30 to 35 per cent of the corn fed, were recovered in the feces when these grains were fed unground to dairy cows. Even larger portions of whole sorghum seeds pass through the digestive tract.

Grinding to medium fineness has been found to produce the best results. Cracked corn and crushed oats showed losses of 5 to 10 per cent and 1 to 2 per cent respectively. Finely pulverized feeds produced 5.4 per cent less milk than medium ground feeds, and in addition cost more to grind. Whole corn and oats produced 11.2 per cent less milk than these feeds did when ground to medium fineness, and cracked corn and crushed oats 5.8 per cent less.

For calves up to six or eight months of age it is not necessary to grind the grains fed; up to that age, calves masticate their food quite thoroughly.

Grinding Roughage

Grinding roughage for dairy cattle has been advocated by some who claim increased digestibility of the ground roughage. This claim is not borne out by a large number of experiments, where it has been found that grinding sometimes decreases the digestibility. In the few cases where increased digestibility has been reported, the difference was so slight as to be insignificant. Another claim for grinding the roughage is that animals cannot select one part o the roughage and refuse other parts. This is substantiated, but for heavy milking cows it is probably best that they not be forced to eat the coarse refused roughage.

Any advantages that may be gained by the reduction of the amounts of roughage wasted is more than offset by the cost of grinding. Grinding costs range from $1.75 to $3.50 per ton, depending upon the costs of labour and power.

The ground roughage has been found to be less palatable than the unground roughage.

Cutting, Chopping, and Shredding

Inasmuch as cutting roughage is a rather inexpensive process, many people find it advantageous in preventing wastage of coarse roughages. The cut roughage, too, is more palatable than when ground. Many people cut hay for storage in the barn by running it through a silage cutter to increase storage capacities.

When fodders are fed, chopping or shredding is advisable. The refused fodder stalks are hard to handle, while the refused portion of the cut or shredded material makes good bedding.

Cooking Feeds

From time to time equipment for cooking feeds has been offered on the market with claims that cooked feeds are both more palatable and more digestible. Numerous experiments have not only proved such claims false, but have shown that protein is made less digestible by heating. The labour and fuel used in cooking feeds are therefore wasted.

Soaking Feeds

Hard, unground grains are made more digestible by thorough soaking. If grinding facilities are available, grinding the grains and feeding them dry is to be preferred to soaking. Feeding concentrates as a slop has no advantages, but increases the labour requirement and dirties the mangers.

Digestion Processes

With the claim that the digestibility of feed stuffs, particularly roughages, can be increased, several different proprietary processes have been offered. For most of them the roughage is chopped, mixed with the concentrate, and a ferment (enzyme) is added. Warm water is then added at the rate of two pounds per pound of feed mixture, and the mass is put into a small silo-like container and permitted to ferment for several days. Experiments have shown that little if any improvement in digestibility can be expected from such processes.

ALL FOLLOWING PROJECT REPORTS ARE READILY AVAILABLE

- Steel Furnitures And Electrical Appliances
- Steel Furniture And Fire Fighting Equipments
- Steel Furniture And Room Cooler
- Steel Wire Drawing And Galvanizing
- Steel Wire/Rod
- Steel Wool
- Ston Scrusher And Screening Plant
- Submerged Arc Welded Pipes
- Submersible Pump Manufacturing
- Super Enamelled Copper Wire
- Super Enamelled Copper Wire (From Copper Cathode Rod)
- Three Wheelers
- Tie-Rod Ends
- Tin Containers
- Toolroom And Sheet Metal Products
- Trolley (Shopping) For Carrying Of Stores At Super Market And Ware Houses
- Tractor Trailers
- Transmission Power Fitting
- Tubular Poles
- Tyre Retreading By Cold Process
- Super Enamelled Copper Wires
- Trolley (Shopping) For Carrying Of Stores At Super Market & Ware Houses
- Tmt Bars
- Tubular Poles For Electrical Transmission (By Fabrication Process)
- Tubular Poles Of M.S. & High Tensile Steel
- V- Belt
- Vacuum Cleaners
- Vacuum Flask (Stainless Steel)
- Valves For Refrigeration And Air-Condition
- Vehicle Welding & Painting
- Venetion Blind
- Washing Machines (Automatic & Computerised)
- Water Controller (Automatic)
- Watch Straps/Chains/ Bracelets/Belt Brass & Stainless Steel
- Water Coolers
- Welded Wire Mesh
- Welding Electrodes
- Wheel Barrow
- Wick Stoves
- Wind Mill Window Frame (Ferrous & Non-Ferrous)
- Wrist Watch

CHEMICALS (ORGANIC & INORGANIC) WITH PETROLEUM PRODUCTS

- Acetic Anhydride
- Acetic Acid (Glacial)
- Acetic Acid From Ethanol
- Acetone
- Acetylene Black
- Acetyl Chloride
- Acetylene Gas
- Acetylene Gas & Oxygen Gas (Integrated Unit)
- Acid Black Dye
- Acid Slurry
- Activated Alumina
- Activated Bleaching Earth (Activated Fullers Earth)
- Activated Carbon From Cashewnut Shell
- Activated Carbon From Rice Husk
- Activated Carbon From Rice Husk, Coconut Shell & Coconut Powder
- Activated Carbon From Wood
- Activated Carbon Powder & Granules From Coconut Shell
- Activated Carbon & Sodium Silicate From Paddy & Rice Husk
- Alcohol From Broken Rice
- Alum For Water Treatment
- Adhesive (Fevicol Type)
- Aerosol Insecticides Spray (Baygon, Hit, Mortein Type)
- Agarbatti Synthetic Perfumery Compounds
- Alcohol From Potato
- Alcohol From Rice Grains
- Alcohol From Rice Husk
- Alcohol From Molasses
- Alcohol, Beer, Starch, Liquid Glucose, Dextrose, Sorbitol, Vitamin-C,
- Alcoholic Beverages And Vinegar From Coconut Water
- Germ Oil, Cattle Feed Etc. From Maize
- Alkyd Resin
- Alkylated Phenol Likenonyl Phenol, Dodecyl Phenol
- Alum (Non Ferric)
- Alum (Ferric)
- Aluminium Chloride From Aluminium Ore
- Alum Cake
- Alum From Aluminium Hydrate
- Aluminium Ingot By Bauxite
- Aluminium Phosphide
- Aluminium Phosphate
- Aluminium Sulphate (Non Ferric Alum) 17% - 18% Alumina Content In Granules (2 Mm To 4 Mm) And Flakes
- Amines & Allied Products
- Amino Acid
- Ammonia Gas
- Ammonia Gas Bottling
- Ammonia Liquor
- Ammonium Nitrate
- Ammonium Chloride (Pure & Technical)
- Ammonium Sulphate
- Annato Seed Extraction And Processing
- Anti Corrosion Chemicals
- Anthranilic Acid From Phthalic Anhydride
- Anesthesia (All Types) Used In Hospitals
- Aniline
- Argon Gas
- Ariel Type Detergent Powder
- Anthraquinone
- Antimony Trioxide
- Atenolol
- Auramine "O"
- Azodicarbonamide
- Baking Soda From Ash
- Barium Carbonate
- Barium Compounds
- Barium Nitrate
- Barium Peroxide
- Barium-Thio-Sulphate Banzene
- Baryte Powder
- Bar Soap (All Varieties) Using Soap Noodles
- Beer Plant
- Belt Paste
- Beneficiation Of Chromite Ore Processing Charge Chrome
- Benzyl Acetate, Benzyl Benzoate, Benzyl Alcohol
- Beta Naphthol
- Bentonite Powder
- Benzoic Acid
- Benzidine
- Biofertiliser From Mother Culture
- Bio Oil For Power Generation From Coffee Husk
- Bio Gas Plant
- Bio Gas Filling In Cylinder
- Bio Tech Unit
- Bi-Chromate Of Sodium, Potassium & Ammonium
- Bi-Functional Black Mfgr.Reactive Dye (Dye From Cotton Yarn Dyeing)
- Bio-Fuel (Jatropha Cultivation And Extraction)
- Bituminous Roademulsion
- Black Phenyl
- Black Sulphur
- Bleaching Powder (Stable)
- Blue Detergent Powder
- Bone Crushing Plant
- Bone Meal (Calcined) Enrichment With Calcium & Phosphorus
- Boric Acid
- B.O.N. Acid
- Bromine Gas Plant
- Brandy
- Butanol
- Butyl Rubber For The Manufacture Of Tubes For Truck And Car Tyres
- 1,4, Butanediol
- Butyl Acetate
- Caffein From Tea Waste
- Calcined Lime (Dead Burnt Dolomite)

Market Survey Cum Detailed Techno Economic Feasibility Report on all Projects are available Contact.
"ENGINEERS INDIA RESEARCH INSTITUTE", 4449, Nai Sarak (D), Main Road, Delhi-110006 (India)
Ph. : 09811437895, 9811151047, 91-11-23918117, 23916431, 23947058, 64727385, 45120361
E-mail : eiriprojects@gmail.com, eiribooks@yahoo.com • website: www.eiri.in, www.eiriindia.org • www.eiribooksandprojectreports.com

ALL FOLLOWING PROJECT REPORTS ARE READILY AVAILABLE

LEATHER & LEATHER PRODUCTS

- Handmade Leather
- Leather Auxillaries & Chemicals
- Leather Dyes
- Leather Washers
- Leather Board From Leather Waste
- Leather For Upholstry(Sofa)
- Leather Finishing Lacquer (Nitrocellulose Lacquer For Leather)
- Leather Garments
- Leather Goods
- Leather Shoes
- Leather Shoe & Chappal
- Leather Suitcases, Briefcases & Travelling Bags
- Leather Goods And Garments
- Leather Garments, Shoe & Chappal
- Leather Pigment Used For Colouring Of Leather
- Leather Tanning
- Leather Tanning & Garments (Eou)
- Sheep Skin Pickling Plant
- Shoe Upper
- Sport Shoes (Plastic)

MISCELLANEOUS PRODUCTS

- Agarbatti (Insence Stick)
- Abrasive Paper
- Agarbatti (Mosquito Repellent)
- Agarbati Bamboo Stick
- Agarbatti Synthetic Perfumery Compound
- Air Freshner(Odonil Type)
- Air Taxi
- Amusement Park
- Anodic Aluminium Label
- Aquaculture Prawn Farming (100% Eou)
- Aqua Culture Shrimp Farming (100% Eou)
- Artificial Flowers
- Artificial Jewellery
- Asbestos Yarn
- Ash Trays For Maruti Vehicle
- Air Bubble Packaging
- Asphaltic Roofing Sheet (Metal Components)
- Automatic Book Binding
- Alkyd Resin
- Apple Juice Concentrate
- Ball Point Pen Fefills (Jotter Type)
- Bank Branch Building
- Banquet Hall
- Bio-Coal Briquettes From Agriculturalcellulose Waste
- Boot Cream/Polish
- Buffing & Polishing Compound
- Brass Badges By Etching
- Briquetted Fuel From Agro Waste
- Briquetting Of Lignite Coal
- Buffalo Horn Tip, Hoof
- Banquet Hall
- Button
- Calcined Petroleum (C.P) Coke
- Canvas Shoes
- Canvas Shoes, Jungle Boots
- Carbon Brush, Brush Holder & Slip Ring
- Cement Sheets With Coir Fibre & Other Segments
- Ceramic Tiles (Glazed) By Double Firing/Heating
- Children Recreation Centre
- Coal Briquettes
- Cold Storage & Ice
- Cold Storage For Fruits And Vegetables
- Compressor (Hermetic) For Air Conditioner
- Costume Jewellery/Imitation Jewellery
- Decorative Laminated Sheet (Sunmica)
- Dental Colleges
- Diamond Cutting & Exports
- Drinking Straw From Propylene
- Engineering College
- Engineering College, Management Institute, Cbse School, Hostel (Boys And Girls), Medical College With Hospital And Research Institute
- Electropolishing On Gold Jewellery (Gold Ornaments)
- Entertainment Club
- Fashion Technology Institute
- Fast Food Parlour
- Fast Food (Instant Food & Fast Food Parlour)
- Fire Extinguishers (Soda Acid Type)
- Fish Net
- Floriculture (Cut Flower Rose) With Green House
- Floor Covering Sheet
- Film Studio (Video)
- Flush Door, Chip Board, Wood Wool & Other Insulating Boards
- Gas Detectors Of L.P.G
- Gems Manufacturing
- Glass Bottle By Scrap
- Glass Jars Manufacturing Plant For Packaging Of 50, 100, 150, 200 Grams Coffee Packaging
- Goat & Sheep Farming
- Gold Electroplating
- Gold Jewellery (E.O.U)
- Gold Plated Silver Jewellery & Cutlery
- Granite Slab And Tiles
- Granite Mining
- Green House
- Hard Chromium Plating
- Health Club And Beauty Parlour Cum Hair
- Saloon With Sona Bath
- Health Club Cum Beauty Parlour Training Institute
- Horn Tip,Hoove Button
- Hospital

EIRI is fully capable to prepare any Project Report of your Choice

- Hospital (100 Beds)
- Hospital (200 Beds)
- Ice Making Plant
- Imitation And Costume
- Jewellery (Necklace, Earrings Ear Top Etc.)
- Initmate Scent Chemicals From All Types Of Flavour
- Investment Casting
- Jute, Coir, Glass Rope/ Sutli
- Jute Twine
- Jute Bags From Yarn Without Spinning Process
- L.P.G Bottling Plant
- L.P.G Regulator (Domestic Purpose)
- Laminated Particle Board & Hard Board
- Laminated Safety & Toughened Glass
- Leasing & Hire Purchase
- Lichen (Charila)
- Manila Ropes
- Medical College
- Medical University
- Metal Pretreatment Chemicals Powder, Coating Chemicals
- Match Unit From Waxed Paper
- Medium Density Fibre Board
- Melamine Crockery
- Mineral Water
- Mini Cement Plant
- Mirror Silver, Golden, Pink, Black & Smokes
- Modern Advt. Agency With Dtp & Film Studio
- Motel/Small Hotel
- Multi Colour Printing
- Multi Purpose Cold Storage And Dehydration And Canning Of Fruits And Vegetables
- Multi Storey Commercial Complex Alongwith Residential And Delux Flats For Foreign Tourists & Revolving Restaurent At The Top
- Multiple Lamination Industry
- Mushroom Growing And Processing (By Deep Freezing Method)
- News Paper Printing
- Nickel Lined Industrial Screen
- Non Coking Coal To Coking Coal
- Nursing Home
- Offset Colour Printing Press (Six Colour)

Market Survey Cum Detailed Techno Economic Feasibility Report on all Projects are available Contact.
"ENGINEERS INDIA RESEARCH INSTITUTE". 4449, Nai Sarak (D), Main Road, Delhi-110006 (India)
Ph. : 09811437895, 9811151047, 91-11-23918117, 23916431, 23947058, 64727385, 45120361
E-mail : eiriprojects@gmail.com, eiribooks@yahoo.com • website: www.eiri.in, www.eiriindia.org • www.eiribooksandprojectreports.com

ALL FOLLOWING PROJECT REPORTS ARE READILY AVAILABLE

- Offset Printing Press
- Old Age Home
- P.C.C Electric Poles
- Photographic Developer & Fixer
- Pvc Extrusion Profile (Door & Windows)
- Pop-Corn
- Photo Etching Of S.S.
- Pre Stressed Cement Concrete Pipes
- Pilfer Proof Caps
- Pilfer Proof Caps And Crown Cap
- Pouch Making & Gravure Printing (Roto Printing)
- Poultry & Fish Farming (Integerated Unit)
- Printing Of Tin Sheets
- Radio Station
- Radio Taxi
- Readymade Garments
- Refractories With Ceramics
- Restaurant
- Rose Plantation And Rose Oil Extraction
- Rotogravure Printing
- Safety Belts
- Safety Matches
- School
- School With Hostel
- Shoe Laces
- Silk Cocoon Cultivation (Growing Of Silk Cocoon Warm)
- Silk Screen Printing Formulations For Plastic, Paper & Cloth
- Spikenard (Jatamansi)
- Stencil Coating Solution
- Sugar Candy (Misri)
- Sugar Cane Plantation
- Sugar Cane Juice Preservation
- Super Speciality Diagnosis Centre
- Surat Zari
- Synthetic Shoes & Soles
- T.V. News Channel
- Tea Packaging Industry
- Toughened Glass
- Tennis Balls
- Three Star Hotel
- Travelling Agency
- Trays, Trolleys For Hospital With Scratchless Coating
- Wax Extracts (Tanning Powder)
- Wire Rope Slings
- Wood Wool Slab
- Wooden Cane Furniture With Export Potential
- Wooden Door And Windows
- Wooden Furniture
- Wooden Panel Including Kiln Seasoning
- Wooden Furniture
- Watch Case Buffing
- Watch Dial
- Wrist Watches
- Watches (Electronic)
- Zedoary (Kachur)

Contact
EiRi
for required Project report apart from this list.

EDIBLE OILS, ESSENTIAL OILS LURICATING OILS, GREASES, VEGETABLE OILS, WAXES, CAMPHOR, PERFUMES & PERFUMERY COMPOUNDS AND REFINED OILS ETC.

EDIBLE OILS, ESSENTIAL OILS, LURICATIING OILS, GREASES, VEGETABLE OILS, WAXES, CAMPHOR, PERFUMES & PERFUMERY COMPOUNDS AND REFINED OILS ETC.

- Aromatic Perfumery Compound
- Aerosol
- Agarbatti Perfumery Compound
- Bees Wax Manufacture
- Camphor
- Cardanol From Cashew Nut Shell Liquid
- Castor Oil
- Castor Oil Derivative Oleoresins
- Chilli Oil
- Citronella Oils
- Clove Oil
- Concentrate Of Rose Jasmine & Lily Etc.
- Coloured Flame Candle
- Candles (Semi-Automatic)
- Corn Oil (Maize Oil)
- Dehydrated Castor Oil
- Eugenol From Cinnamon Leaf Oil
- Extraction Of Essential Oil (Cardamon, Jeera, Ajowan, Ginger Oils Etc. & Packaging Of Ground Spices)
- Extraction Of Jasmine Essence
- Extraction Of Essential Oils By Super Critical Fluid Method From Flowers, Herbs & Spices
- Eucalyptus Oil
- Extraction Of Oil From Oil Seed Expander Extrusion Technology)
- Fat Liquor Sulphated Oil
- Flavours For Food
- Fish Oil
- Garlic Oil & Powder
- Ginger Oil, Sandalwood Oil And Nagarmotha Oil
- Ginger Oil
- Ginger Oil & Ginger Dust
- Ground Nut Oil
- Integerated Wax Complex
- Ionone From Lemon Grass Oil
- Jasmine & Lilly Flower Oil
- Lemon Grass Oil
- Liquid Paraffin
- Lube Oil & Grease
- Lubricating Oil
- Menthol Crystals
- Menthol Oil & Crystal
- Micro Crystalline Wax
- Mustard Oil (Edible Oil)
- Oleoresin From Spices
- Oil From Artemisia Herbs
- Palm Oil Crushing Unit
- Pan Masala
- Paraffin Wax
- Paraffin Wax From Slack Wax
- Perfume For Food Industries With Pan Masala Perfume
- Pouch For Oil And Ghee Packaging
- Refined Oil-Sun Flower Oil, Groundnut Oil, Staff Flower Oil & Cotton Seed Oil
- Refined Vegetable Oil
- Reclamation Of Used Engine Oil
- Rice Bran Oil (R.B.O)
- Rose Oil Extraction
- Smoke Less Candle
- Spice Oil & Oleoresins
- Solvent Extraction Plant (Oil Cake Based)
- Synthetic Almond Oil
- Synthetic Wax
- Synthetic Tallow
- Synthetic Ghee
- Synthetic Musk
- Turmeric Oil Oleoresin
- Vanilla Cultivation And Extraction/Processing
- Vegetable Oil Extraction & Refining
- Wadding Oil (100%) For Wadding Of Cotton Hosiery Cloth In Dyeing Process
- Wax Emulsion For Textile
- Wax Floor Polish

ELECTROPLATING, ANODIZING & ALLIED PROJECTS

- Nickel Plating Brightener
- Pcb With Garphite & Silver Coating
- Rainbow Colours On Metal
- Silver Refining By Electrolysis & By Acid
- Silver Extraction
- Silver Extraction From Waste Hypo Solution
- Silver & Gold Plating On Pvc & Nylon-6
- Tin Printing
- Titanium Jewellery Plating
- Vacuum Metallizing
- Zinc Electroplating Brightner
- Zinc Electroplating On Nut, Bolts,